Lifetime Contributions in Physical Education:

Celebrating the lives and work of
Len Almond *(1938 - 2017)* and
Joy Butler *(1957-2019)*

First published in 2021 by Scholary
Suite 7, The Oval Office, Cobbler's Way, Radstock, BA3 3BX, United Kingdom

Scholary is an imprint of Scholary Ltd

© 2021 selection and editorial material, Dr Stephen A. Michell and Dr Linda L. Griffin; individual chapters, the contributors

Typeset in Avenir

All rights reserved. No part of this book may be reprinted or reproduced or utilised in any form or by electronic, mechanical, or other means, now known or hereafter invented, including photocopying and recording, or in any information storage or retrieval system, without permission in writing from the publishers.

British Library Cataloguing in Publication Data
A catalogue record for this book is available from the British Library

ISBN: 978-1-9999-0921-5 (pbk)
ISBN: 978-1-9999-0922-2 (ebk)

Table of Contents

Lifetime Contributions in Physical Education:
Celebrating the lives and work of Len Almond (1938-2017)
and Joy Butler (1957-2019)

Forward. Val Almond and Claire Robson 006

Introduction 011
Steve Mitchell, Kent State University, and Linda Griffin, University of Massachusetts, Editors

Chapter 1 014
Asking Teachers to Research
Len Almond (1986). In R. Thorpe, D. Bunker, & L. Almond (Eds.)
Rethinking games education, (pp.35-44). Department of Physical Education and
Sports Science, University of Technology, Loughborough, Leicestershire.

Chapter 2 028
Games Classification Systems as a foundation for Curriculum
Steve Mitchell, Kent State University.

Chapter 3 040
Physical Literacy and Human Flourishing
Elizabeth Durden-Myers, University of Gloucestershire & Bath Spa University
& Margaret Whitehead, University of Bedfordshire.

Chapter 4 054
Physical Literacy and the Primacy of Movement
Margaret Whitehead, University of Bedfordshire & Elizabeth Durden-Myers,
University of Gloucestershire & Bath Spa University.

Chapter 5 072
Fundamental Movement Skills

Kathryn Ezzeldin & Kim Lambden, St Mary's University.

Chapter 6 079
Purposeful Physical Play in the Early Years:
The missing ingredient

Kim Lambden & Kathryn Ezzeldin, St Mary's University.

Chapter 7 086
Health-Based Physical Education:
The Journey from Early Rationale to Established Practice

Lorraine Cale, Sonia McGeorge & Jo Harris, Loughborough University.

Chapter 8 104
Teaching Games for Understanding:
From conception to Special Interest Group

David Guttierez, Universidad de Castilla-La Mancha & Alan Ovens, University of Auckland.

Chapter 9 120
Top 10 Research Questions Related to Teaching Games for Understanding

Daniel Memmert, Len Almond, David Bunker, Joy Butler, Frowin Fasold, Linda Griffin, Wolfgang Hillmann, Stefanie Hüttermann, Timo Klein-Soetebier, Stefan König, Stephan Nopp, Marco Rathschlag, Karsten Schul, Sebastian Schwab, Rod Thorpe & Philip Furley (2015).
Research Quarterly for Exercise and Sport, 86:4, 347-359.

Chapter 10 148
The Way Forward for TGfU: Filling the Chasm between Theory and Practice

Joy Butler, Judy Oslin, Stephen Mitchell & Linda Griffin (2008).
Physical and Health Education Journal, 74(2), 6-12.

CONTENTS

Chapter 11 160
Stages for Children Inventing Games
Joy Butler (2013).
Journal of Physical Education, Recreation & Dance, 84:4, 48-53.

Chapter 12 174
Teaching and Learning Social Justice Through Inventing Games.
Joy Butler (2016). In Butler, J (Eds.)
Playing Fair: Using student-invented games to prevent bullying, teach democracy, and promote social justice. Champaign, IL, Human Kinetics.

Chapter 13 190
TGfU pet-agogy: old dogs, new tricks and puppy school
Joy Butler (2005).
Physical Education and Sport Pedagogy Vol. 10, 3, pp. 225-240.

Chapter 14 208
A personal journey: TGfU teacher development in Australia and the USA.
Richard Light & Joy Butler (2005).
Physical Education and Sport Pedagogy Vol. 10, No. 3, November 2005, pp. 241–254.

Chapter 15 226
Final Reflections
Linda Griffin & Steve Mitchell

Foreword

Val Almond & Claire Robson

We are honoured to write the foreword for this book focusing on Len's and Joy's work.

A gifted PE teacher, Len was studying for an M.Ed in Curriculum Development and Philosophy at Manchester University when I (Val) met him in 1971. It was this interest in and commitment to pedagogy that led Len to become a research fellow at Loughborough University of Technology (as it was called then) in 1975 and spend an academic year at the University of Otago in Dunedin, New Zealand, before becoming a member of the PE and Sports Science department in Loughborough in the autumn of 1979. At Loughborough in the 1980s Len met and persuaded David Bunker and Rod Thorpe to publish their ideas on rethinking games teaching that gave rise to *Teaching Games for Understanding*. These were ideas that transformed thinking in physical education not only in the UK but also around the world and continue to do so.

Passionate about health-related exercise, Len promoted 'the healthy school' initiative and managed the Health Education Authority project at Loughborough. He was instrumental in developing the *Jump Rope for Heart* Fund, which is still active today and has raised millions of pounds for heart research. In 1999 he was responsible for the establishment of the British Heart Foundation National Centre for Activity and Health at Loughborough and became its first Director. This led him into the realm of public health and his promotion of physical activity for life: "one of the worst things older people can do is to buy a bungalow and forego the stairs!" he said. This also influenced the establishment of the National Coalition for Active Ageing in England.

It was this concern with health and the link with physical activity that led Len into his work with Physical Literacy and the Early Years. He was a founding member of the new AIESEP SIG for the promotion of Purposeful Physical Play in Early Years settings and significantly this subject was to be the focus of the last book he wrote.

Len's over-riding belief was that theory was sterile unless translated into practice and it was for this reason that he would go to the grass roots to talk to people on the 'factory floor' who were able tell him if his ideas would work. He went into schools and talked to the relevant staff and pupils; he went into nurseries and Early Years settings as far away as Japan as well as in England and listened to what they had to say and worked with practitioners to determine what would work. It was from discussions and interactions like these that Len formulated the 'pedagogy of engagement' that became central to his thinking: to reach out, connect, engage and ultimately draw out and stretch as many people as possible: students, practitioners, academics.

Len invited controversy and challenge and an example is the so-called 'graveyard' slot lecture on Friday afternoons! This regularly became a hot bed of debate and discussion because Len would deliberately put forward an opinion contrary to accepted belief and encourage students to challenge it because 'everyone has feet of clay'. Len was able to inspire and instil self-belief in people and give them the confidence to think critically and to challenge.

Above all, Len was a 'people person', kind, patient and generous especially with his time and had a facility of putting people at their ease. I met Len at a Christening and I observed then how much time he spent with the children and how good he was at interacting with them. This was translated into practice with his own children: Matthew was two when he went to the nursery on the university campus and Len used to take him there in the morning and have his lunch with him as many times as he could. After the girls were born, Len encouraged me to continue with my teaching career and drew the short straw in that it was he who took the girls to school in the morning, sorted them out and checked if they had everything with them they needed. I am sure they played him up but he had endless patience!

Activity was key for Len and he encouraged all three children to engage in all kinds of sport and physical activity and took them to endless cross country venues, basket ball matches, football games and swimming sessions. The children taught him salutary lessons though! Matthew was doing well in the junior school cross country race and Len waited at the finishing line expecting to see him come in the first three at least. There was no sign of Matthew for ages and when he did eventually make it to the line and Len asked him what had happened, Matthew replied that he had seen some conkers and had stopped to pick them! Similarly Len used to run with Hannah and Charlotte when they were children until they told him at the age of 14 that they didn't want to run any more! However, he had sowed the seeds because all three are physically active today: Matthew plays hockey and keeps fit, Hannah teaches yoga and both girls run.

They ran a half marathon in Sweden in 2018 and raised over £1000 for the hospice that had looked after Len.

It is a tribute to Len the person that so many of his colleagues have found the time to write articles for this book. In addition to the qualities I have already mentioned he was self effacing and never made people feel 'less than': this is so important because many people are afraid of saying what they think and as a result valuable insights and observations can be lost. Len wanted people to be active and to flourish, to be the best they could be: he wanted people to run with his ideas and to develop them further. In writing this book, his colleagues are taking Len's legacy forward and doing just that. My heart-felt thanks goes to them and all the people who have known Len and helped to inform his theory and practice.

Joy Butler was born into a working-class family where everyone was expected to contribute to the family income. If you were a girl, then of course you were expected to give up work after marriage and the first kid and become a stay-at-home mom. Significantly, Joy's mother was deaf, and she and her brother Laurie were CODA children (Children of Deaf Adults). Today, Joy would have received extra help with language skills, since her mother's first language is British Sign Language (BSL). No such support was available in the 50s and 60s. Sick with worry the night before the 11+ exams, Joy performed poorly and was placed in a vocational track in a secondary modern school.

I (Claire) think Joy's great strength of spirit and determination was forged in those early years. Though she received no encouragement to go on to further education, and indeed, some pretty active opposition, she decided that she wanted to be a teacher. Even her teachers thought that this was a bit of a stretch, but Joy made it happen. She worked after school jobs from the age of 14, to fulfil her financial obligations to her family, and hard scrabbled her way to achieve the necessary A-levels for college entry – no mean feat for a secondary modern student, barred from studying sciences or languages, and unused to academic writing.

Joy threw herself into her studies at Nonnington College, and went on to become a teacher, but more than that – a teacher with a finely tuned ear for justice, fair play, and equal access. She became an advocate for the underdog and began to think about the ways her teaching and coaching impacted her students. As a teacher in Inner London, she took over coaching the school's prestigious basketball team, already national champions. She coached the team her way, rotating her bench frequently to bring along all players, refusing zero sum approaches to winning and losing, and having skilled students coach less skilled students. Despite raised eyebrows and a lecture from the principal, she stuck to her guns and her team won two national championships.

Shortly afterwards, Joy moved to Kent as Head of Physical Education in a social priority school. She revised the curriculum, away from the predictable grind of seasonal sports and toward curricular modules based on the TGfU categories. She loved this work, but there was something she didn't understand. Why did the male teachers in her department resist holistic approaches that were demonstrably more effective and more engaging?

This wasn't just a theoretical question for Joy. It was a question that fueled our move to the US, formed the basis of her doctoral dissertation at Boston University and her first major paper, still the most cited, How would Socrates teach games?

That paper explored the spaces and connections between teachers' beliefs, intentions and actions, and this became a thread that can be followed through the publications offered here, her SSHRCC projects, and her book, *Playing Fair – a practitioner's guide to teaching social justice through games*. Joy was both a constructivist, in terms of her beliefs about how knowledge is assembled, and a deconstructivist, in that she liked to follow pedagogical practices back to their philosophical origins, both tacit and explicit. In the last few years, she thought a lot about the ways in which our worldviews are affected by cultural influences, particularly gender. For instance, her 2016 Plenary Opening Lecture at the Teaching Games for Understanding conference in Cologne explicitly called on the physical education community to step up in terms of gender equity.

In June 2019, Joy presented a conference paper about dodgeball that generated a great deal of media attention. She dared to question the educational purpose of dodgeball - a game that many athletic students adore, and many less athletic students fear and detest. Joy gave over twenty interviews in the three months before her death, including CBC, the Washington Post, the BBC, and Fox News. She actually got quite a bit of hate mail - someone suggested that she might benefit from spending time in a Siberian work camp, but she wouldn't back off the debate, despite her declining health.

Joy never did what people told her to do unless she was presented her with a sound rationale. This could be frustrating if you were in a hurry (and believe me, we were often late for dinner parties), but it also meant that whatever Joy undertook, she carried through according to sound principles, great clarity of vision, and meticulous preparation.

My thanks to Steve, Linda, and all the teachers, students, and colleagues who have preserved her remarkable legacy and that of her valued colleague, Len, in this collection of their work.

Introduction

Contributions to Celebrate

Steve Mitchell, Kent State University
and Linda Griffin, University of Massachusetts
Editors

This book is dedicated to the memory of our dear friends and colleagues Len Almond and Joy Butler. Len passed away in 2017 and Joy in 2019, both after prolonged cancer treatments. Both contributed immensely, both separately and together, to the development of innovative and long-lasting approaches to teaching and through this book we honor and celebrate their work.

Len Almond (1938-2017) spent three decades as a faculty member in the Department of Sport, Exercise and Health Sciences at Loughborough University, and latterly in his career at St Mary's University. During this time period, through both personal and professional interactions, he influenced many emerging and established scholars by contributing ground-breaking thinking in areas of physical education, physical literacy, early childhood and health-based physical activity, and coaching. In this book, some of Len's colleagues celebrate and commemorate his work by revisiting and commenting on some of his seminal works from the past 40 years. In some cases, contributing authors have selected a specific piece of Len's work and commented on the contribution it made to the literature and to their own professional work. In other instances, authors have taken an area in which Len contributed and have summarized his influence with reference to both published and unpublished work. We hope this book will keep alive the legacy of Len's work and his commitment to the health and physical literacy of people across the lifespan.

Len made valuable contributions in several areas, and the book begins with a reprint of one of his seminal works in which he, Rod Thorpe and David Bunker ask teachers to become researchers on their own practice. Then, in chapters 2-7, colleagues remember his work in Teaching Games for Understanding (TGfU); the Physical Literacy movement which changed the way the discipline of Physical Education viewed itself;

teaching Fundamental Movement Skills; Purposeful Physical Play in the Early Years, and Health-based Physical Education. All were curriculum areas about which Len was passionate.

Joy Butler (1957-2019) passed away in the summer of 2019 but her memory and work will live on through those she inspired. Joy was a visionary – an individual who thought about the future with imagination and wisdom. Through her tenacity Joy was able to lead, shape and support an international movement around sport and physical education, with a specific focus on Teaching Games for Understanding (TGfU).

Joy was the founder and organizer of a seminal international conference series on TGfU, the first of which was held at Waterville Valley, NH, USA, 2001. Subsequent conferences were held in Melbourne, Australia (2003), Hong Kong (2005), Vancouver, Canada (2008), Loughborough, England (2012), Cologne, Germany (2016), and Worcester, England (2022). Joy has been a keynote speaker at six of these conferences focusing on various research, topics and issues related to TGfU.

Joy's impact on the international scholarly community has been demonstrated by a marked increase in scholarly presentations, articles and books related to TGfU. For example, prior to the first conference there were 37 articles over 11 years. Substantial increases can be seen since the 2012 conference yielding a three-year total of 507 articles, an average of 169 per year, in addition to five books. Joy's final book publication (2016) entitled *Playing Fair: Using Student-Invented Games to Prevent Bullying, Teach Democracy, and Promote Social Justice* is both innovative and timely, particularly in today's world. Though inventing games is not new, what makes this book innovative and timely is that the book was written to help teachers and coaches teach not only the principles of game play but those of democracy and citizenship in thoughtful, concrete ways that contribute to a dynamic shift in the school culture. Joy's dedication in this book sums up her spirit. "To all teachers who love to watch students learning through play and who are willing to risk new ideas, and to their students, who were born to play well with others"

So we also honor Joy's legacy in this book. After an initial chapter by David Guttierez and Alan Ovens summarizing her contributions, Joy's work is celebrated with a selection of her published work being reprinted with the publisher's permission. Our thanks to Human Kinetics publishing, Taylor and Francis publishing, PHE Canada, and the Association for Physical Education for these permissions.

INTRODUCTION

Len and Joy, thank you. You will be remembered, and your commitment and work will live on. Rest in peace with our love and admiration.

Len Almond
(1938 - 2017)

Joy Butler
(1957 - 2019)

1

Asking Teachers to Research

Len Almond

Editors note: This chapter appeared in the seminal 1986 book Rethinking Games Teaching, which itself was a compilation of the early published work of Teaching Games for Understanding (TGfU) advocates. At the time of publication, TGfU had been present in the Physical Education literature for several years but was still in its infancy as an established teaching approach. Len long believed that teachers should be researchers into their own practice in order that they might reflect on, adapt, and improve their teaching. This chapter was his call to action.

It should be said that a major reason for writing the articles was to ensure that the teacher was shaken out of a complacency about games teaching. Gymnastics, dance, outdoor education, etc., has been scrutinised over the last 20 years, but somehow teachers seemed to think that 'Games' could look after themselves. As a result of the many practical demonstrations, lectures and articles we discovered that teachers were responsive to the ideas we suggested - but did they change their teaching as a result? What was needed was a method of helping teachers to reflect in their teaching. This chapter explains a particular approach to this.

At the same time that the work on 'teaching for understanding in games' was underway I was concerned that there was a lack of teacher involvement in educational research and particularly in physical education. The late Lawrence Stenhouse (1975) had introduced the idea of the teacher as researcher and the notion of 'the self-monitoring teacher in the Ford Teaching Project had influenced my thinking about teacher involvement in the development of ideas. Thus, as the teachers began to express interest in trying out ideas in their games teaching I encouraged them to monitor their own practice and I monitored their engagement in this work.

This work was attempted in a number of local education authorities supported ably by the Physical Education Advisor whose encouragement was invaluable. In order to find out what happens when teachers engage in their own research the support for teachers was minimal, except for the following:

1. Induction course on 'teaching for understanding'
2. Documentation on games teaching
3. A short manual on how to monitor one's practice
4. Meetings arranged by the local advisor.

In addition to this work all involvements with teachers on courses, discussions, and practical demonstrations were recorded on video and audio tape and case notes were written up by at least two people. This enabled us to build up a picture of teachers' involvement in research based teaching and also their reactions to teaching for understanding as an innovation.

An Action Research Perspective

As an alternative to monitoring the teachers' practice by outsiders, an action research perspective was selected because it involves the teachers in systematic reflection and critical scrutiny of their own actions. As no two classrooms are alike, the only person who is able to express an idea in practice with students is the teacher. Thus, if teachers are to be intelligent in what they are doing they need to submit their practices to systematic observation and careful scrutiny. In this way the teacher is adopting a research stance with a view to improving the quality of the action within it, which is concerned with strengthening and informing the professional judgments of the teacher. This should enable the teacher to establish greater control over translating ideas into practice and help to achieve greater understanding of the variables involved in teaching and encouraging learning. Thus, research by teachers into their own practice provides the potential and capability for the development of practices, because it is grounded in a systematic and critical appraisal of the consequences of actions and the decisions which are made in teaching. It enables teachers to act intelligently because they can take steps to overcome the barriers that create unconscious behaviour patterns and perpetuate untested assumptions. By taking steps to overcome the arbitrariness, impressionistic or whimsical way in which practical decisions and judgments are made, one is attempting to develop a sensitive and self-critical subjective perspective on one's teaching.

However, there is a limit to individual reflection upon practice and the opportunity to develop it. Adopting a research stance to one's teaching needs a support structure in which teachers can communicate with one another and report their investigations. This reporting involves rendering an account of one's investigations and deliberations - in written, spoken, or visual form for the purpose of discussion and critique. This makes the work of teachers a democratic process because it makes the basis of one's practical judgments open to public scrutiny in order that contrary and alternative perspectives can be considered.

Discussion Of Results

First Order Research by teachers

Even though the games project emphasised the tactical aspects of games, teachers had difficulty in breaking out of the entrenched position which places the technical requirements of games as the central focus for learning a game. The domination of the lesson plan which moves from:

1. Introductory activity
2. Technique practice
3. Small-sided game
4. Full game

was difficult to break and teachers experienced some difficulty in considering alternatives. This was particularly the case in invasion games which proved to be more complex for teachers to think of ways of representing game forms or devising enabling games to illustrate certain principles. For the teachers, net games, e.g. badminton, appeared to be easier to work with. This may be because they are more simple and straightforward tactically but it could be also that the teachers received more support in conceptualising this game during the induction courses. However, all the teachers consistently reported difficulty with invasion games and this group of games does appear to be the most difficult to teach. During the project, no teachers undertook any case studies of fielding games, e.g. softball or cricket, therefore no feedback has been obtained.

A further problem with the technical requirements of a game arises because teachers can acquire the impression that 'teaching for understanding' is not concerned with the teaching of techniques. As Thorpe and Bunker (1983) rightly point out this is not the case, but teachers need to be reassured. In 'teaching for understanding' the principal focus is on those features which make a game a 'game'; these are essentially tactical and decision-making: however, if a game consistently breaks down, one of the causes may lie in the lack of technical ability and intervention may be required.

After about seven lessons, the teachers reported problems in knowing what kind of game forms were appropriate to develop their work. They had exhausted ideas which they had learned during the induction courses and from resource documents. At this point they felt isolated and unsure of what lay ahead. Teachers who are working alone are likely to stop and seek more help: if it is not readily available they will not proceed any further. Where teachers work in a group, this stage can be overcome because ideas can be generated by sharing and discussing possibilities. However, teachers with little experience or knowledge of games will not make further progress, they will simply revert back to traditional practices where the emphasis is on technique. This problem clearly reveals one of the shortcomings of the innovation - the lack of support. There is a shortage of resource documents which identify game forms and enabling games to illustrate the tactical features of games. At present only net games have been documented in detail.

The previous points illustrate also a critical element within the teaching profession. This project reveals some evidence that teachers of physical education feel more confident when they are repeating or copying ideas presented to them rather than developing ideas which can be translated into practical suggestions in their teaching. Whether this is due to the lack of a support structure to encourage teachers to work together to develop practical ideas, or that their training has encouraged them to be passive recipients of ideas and not creators of ideas is difficult to determine. This point also relates to the need for teachers to be more thoroughly knowledgeable about games and have had practical experience of what games have to offer.

During the project the teachers explored the idea of allowing pupils to devise their own games, and this proved to be very successful. All the teachers reported that they had not tried this approach before, but they were very pleased with the results and surprised how well the pupils were able to devise their own games. The teachers reported also that technically less able pupils responded better to this approach than their more able peers. This result is most interesting and deserves a great deal more investigation because it was impossible to determine why this was the case.

A number of issues arose during meetings where teachers discussed freely their teaching of games. Some teachers expressed the view that young children in primary schools and in the early years of secondary school are convinced that they are incompetent at games because they have not been chosen to represent the school team against other schools.

The teachers in the project believe that this barrier is created by the emphasis in English schools of playing competitive inter-school fixtures from an early age. For some teachers, coaching the élite may be more important than teaching all young children to play games. The main emphasis in inter-school fixtures is 'winning', whereas in games taught in curriculum time the main emphasis is 'learning a game' (or 'understanding' what games have to offer). This distinction can often be forgotten by teachers and the philosophy of inter-school games may encroach into games taught during curriculum time.

From the observation of practical induction courses where teachers explored game problems and in discussions about games, it became obvious that the teachers in the project displayed a wide range of knowledge about what games can offer. Some teachers did not understand or appreciate the tactical and strategic features of the games they played, it is little wonder, therefore, that for some teachers, a list of techniques to be taught offers a strong framework for thinking about games teaching.

During games where specific problems have been posed, some teachers play without thinking and do not attempt to examine how the problems can be resolved – they play to win. Some technically able teachers also play without thinking about the problems posed, but, because they have been drilled in the tactical aspects of games, they are able to resolve the problems. When the teachers discuss the tactical aspects of games, they have some difficulty in grasping their significance and the role they play in making a game a 'game'. This observation surprised the project team and requires more detailed study because it may explain why teachers have difficulty in representing games after they have exhausted their store of 'received' ideas. There is a further implication for those involved in teacher training, because if teachers have difficulty in understanding games, there is a need to reappraise the form in which prospective teachers are trained, or more appropriately the way they are initiated into a games education.

Presentation of an Innovation

During induction courses and meetings with the teachers it was apparent that a new terminology was emerging. Teachers who came to the project without any prior reading requested guidance about the use of certain words. From their inquiries and field notes of meetings the following phrases are considered to be part of a new terminology:

- invasion games
- net/wall games
- fielding/run scoring games
- game form
- enabling games
- principles of play
- games making/creating games
- representing games

The idea of a common shared language is important for teachers, but new terminology may create a barrier that separates those involved in the project and other interested teachers. In this project, the new terminology was not part of a common shared language and it created an unnecessary barrier that was hard to remove.

Besides misunderstandings, teachers also misinterpret the messages that come from practical induction courses. A number of teachers see 'teaching for understanding' in terms of small-sided games and mini-games and then they argue that they are doing this work already. These teachers see only games with small sides or mini-games and fail to recognise that the focus has shifted from practising techniques within a game to game forms which represent certain principles of play and have been designed with these in mind. This misinterpretation means that a number of teachers will switch off their thinking and not explore the implications of the changing focus. As a result, they go away and the substance of what they are teaching does not change, yet they will still claim that they are 'teaching for understanding'.

The teachers' reactions to an innovation are interesting because the needs of teachers as perceived by the project team and the actual needs of the teachers differ in a very significant way. The teachers want ideas they can go away with and teach, consequently they compare the practical induction courses with their own classes and they question whether they will be able to teach in exactly the same way as the tutor taking the course. The tutors in the project see the needs of teachers in terms of 'what is this idea all about', and as a result the induction courses attempt to illustrate this.

The teachers want class organisation tips to deal with small-group teaching and situations where different equipment may be used by different groups. They ask also for proof that this new approach they are considering is better than the existing form. In the project, we attempted to answer these questions by proposing that ideas need to be disciplined by the problems of practice, consequently the only way to answer their queries was for them to attempt to teach using this approach and monitor their own understandings. While this idea was central to the whole project, the project team were still not satisfying the perceived needs of the teachers and not addressing themselves to the issues that the teachers saw as important. These considerations have been identified, and now induction courses attempt to remedy these issues.

Second Order Research

In previous studies (Boyall, 1983), teachers had experienced difficulty in using monitoring procedures in their teaching, consequently access to a booklet which outlined a range of techniques to monitor one's teaching proved to be an important asset. Nevertheless, teachers did report difficulty in using some techniques. They found that writing field notes or any kind of report was difficult to fit into a teaching day - finding time was a problem. However, the teachers expressed the view that writing notes after their teaching is more complex than they imagined and it took time to acquire both the habit and the facility. After a while the exercise became easier with practice, but finding time to sit and reflect proved to be a major barrier.

Short questionnaires for pupils were found to be more suitable than other techniques for monitoring progress and some of the teachers explored using questionnaires in a variety of ways. Interviews proved to be difficult and the teachers felt uncomfortable in using them. Using tape recorders and video equipment created a number of problems. Unless one used sophisticated equipment, which was often unavailable, the teachers had difficulty in recording dialogue in small groups on playing fields. The results were often spoiled by interference and difficult in distinguishing who was speaking with all the background noise. Making video recordings outside on playing fields was also difficult. Unless there is very strong support from some outside agency, like a University or College, the use of sophisticated audio-visual techniques may be inappropriate for teachers investigating their own practice. The use of a contract with a colleague to observe a lesson was found to be more acceptable and easier to handle, and for many of the teachers this was a new experience. However, the teachers did express the view that this procedure had potential and should be developed further.

There was considerable anxiety with the analysis of the data the teachers collected. Many of them collected too much data and found it difficult to handle. At times isolating what was really relevant proved to be a problem. Too much data was simply confusing and the teachers did not know which way to proceed with their investigations. In the booklet outlining research techniques for use in monitoring teaching, the analysis of data was omitted because it was felt that the research project team and the co-ordinators would provide assistance. This was found to be more complex than we had anticipated: it was simply too big a task to provide the necessary support. Consequently, this lack of support showed us quite clearly how important it is to provide detailed training in research procedures to monitor teaching. It is obvious from the teachers in the project that their training in University or College did not provide them with the expertise or knowledge to monitor their own teaching.

Before the project, the teachers did not appear to experience problems in their teaching; at least they did report any and they did not perceive the teaching of games as problematic. Even though observers may suggest that problems do exist, teachers are reluctant to admit that there are problems in teaching. Of course they recognise practical problems like poor facilities, lack of sufficient equipment or poor motivation of pupils, but they are centred outside the teacher and are seen as beyond their control. It is the exceptional teacher who believes that teaching is problematic or that how one works with young people to foster learning and an interest in an activity is open to many interpretations.

By asking teachers to reflect critically on their practice they became more conscious to their teaching, and all the teachers expressed the view that monitoring their practice enabled them to learn more about teaching, their pupils, and games. This is a very important finding and represents a very strong claim for encouraging all teachers to engage in monitoring their practice, even if for only a short period of time.

Finding time to engage in monitoring proved to be the most difficult task. It was difficult to find time during the day to sit and reflect because morning and lunch-time breaks were often busy times for teachers of physical education. The bustle and constant pressure of things to do made it difficult to create periods of time for reflection, to write field notes, or interview pupils. In addition, at certain times during the school year there were simply too many tasks to be accomplished in addition to curriculum commitments. For this reason, the autumn term has been chosen to undertake an investigation because earlier research Almond, 1982) has shown that this is a suitable period to fit in a small-scale research project.. Nevertheless, the teachers found the project time consuming and expressed concern at how difficult it was to find the time. This is understandable because in the author's experience the teachers need an opportunity to learn how to fit monitoring into their teaching routines. This was clearly borne out in this project and the teachers found that their second attempt during the school year was much easier - they were beginning to learn. Besides finding the time to fit monitoring into one's teaching routines, the analysis of data requires additional time and many teachers did not realise how much time would be required.

Reflections and Speculations

Innovation of an idea

During the course of developing 'teaching for understanding' a detailed review of literature was conducted on innovations in physical education, but it proved difficult to find any reference which provided an historical perspective to an innovation. The sad truth appears to be that innovations in physical education are not documented in a form which makes them accessible to research or in a form which provided guidelines on how ideas can be developed in practice. However, if one reads the literature on the teaching of physical education there are numerous examples of new innovations emerging in schools. This would suggest that as a research area there is indeed scope for future development.

In this project the use of case studies may provide a medium in which research about innovation can be conducted. If we are systematic in the process of carefully documenting an innovation, it may be possible to provide archive material accessible to teachers and researchers which would help us to learn about the nature of innovations in teaching. The documentation of an innovation is important, and it was interesting to note that in 'teaching for understanding' in games, the rationale for this focus only emerged after it had been introduced to teachers -- a period of about five years, In the early stages, there was only a small input of ideas being generated and tried out in schools, but this increased as more teachers became involved. With increased involvement came a demand for justification and explanation, and at this point the need for a rationale emerged.

The construction of a rationale and a critical debate within the project helped to clarify the thinking of the group and as a result an important step was taken.

Because the idea of 'teaching for understanding' is seen as an innovation, the presentation of the idea is crucial. During the course of the project and in subsequent courses with teachers it became apparent that the presentation of an idea challenged a teacher's existing framework for conceptualising games. Consequently, there is a need to demonstrate why a different focus is necessary and to show that problems exist within the current view of how games should be taught. Teachers will have to abandon their existing frame of reference if they take on a new idea, but they will only do this if the new framework is seen to be practically feasible. We found that in order to help teachers reconstruct a new framework it was necessary to present ideas in a medium they understood and were familiar with. As a result, we believe that new ideas should be experienced in a practical form and seen through the framework of the teachers' existing ideas. Thus, in the induction courses, the game of badminton was used to illustrate what the game was all about and what the key features of the game were, tactically.

The adequacy of the new framework needs to be tested in the teacher's own setting and opportunity for further practical work and discussion needs to be available. When you take part in a practical session for the second and third time, you see new things, and existing ideas are re-inforced or made clear.

However, teachers need practical guidelines about:

1. Exactly what is involved in the new idea
2. A copy of the practical session they participated in with a clear identification of the key ideas
3. Alternative ways of developing the work further.

This creates a paradox because teachers appear to need clear guidelines and yet they want to feel that they can be involved in developing further guidelines.

Support Structures

Teachers appear to want quite explicit help in what to teach and how it should be organised. They appear to be collectors of ideas, or want tips about what to do, and they copy what they have experienced and read. However, when this is exhausted, some teachers are clearly out of their depth; they are unable to develop ideas further. This observation suggests that their initiation into teaching has not provided them with the facility for developing ideas on their own. It may be that initial training encourages teachers to be passive recipients of ideas and not active constructors and developers of ideas. This point ought to be investigated because it has implications for the professional development of teachers. A counter point to this, however, could be that the constraints of teaching and daily pressure of constantly performing and projecting inhibits a teacher's facility for developing ideas.

A further point arises in the training of teachers, because the teachers in this project were not familiar with research techniques for monitoring teaching and their own practice. They had not been given the opportunity to explore such techniques in their training which had included courses on research design and techniques. Their previous experience and knowledge with research procedures had been inappropriate for use in practical teaching situations, though it may have been appropriate for certain types of research relevant to situations other than classrooms. The question needs to be asked whether existing research courses are relevant for practising teachers to examine their own practice. The lack of research literature concerned with classroom research by teachers would tend to support this point of view.

Group Meetings

Teachers see group meetings as important social events because they provide an opportunity to share ideas, to listen to problems that other teachers are facing as well as themselves, and to learn about monitoring techniques and games. They provide an important support structure. However, I doubt if in their present form they can be regarded as real learning opportunities. This is important because the teachers only made real progress when they explained their work with someone from the project team.

Group meetings are essential if we are to provide a forum for critical reflection on teachers' work, but at present they are seen only as a social event, although important. This concerns me, and I can only speculate that involvement in the games project was the first stage for learning how to use a group meeting as a learning medium. With further experience and more detailed study of how teachers use meetings, it may be possible to create a forum of emancipatory action research (Kemmis, 1980) where teachers can accept responsibility for investigating their own practice and engage in a critique of teachers' practical constructs. At the present moment this is impossible and represents an ideal worth working towards.

Collaborative Research

The previous point raises questions about the role of professional educators in Institutes of Higher Education. If teachers are to be supported and encouraged in their endeavours to monitor practice, then Institutes of Higher Education could play a critical role. One of the spin-offs from this project has been the development in England of a number of Curriculum Development Centres in different parts of the country which are providing a support service for teachers. These Centres form a network which will attempt to make accessible the case studies of teachers monitoring their practice, and a framework in which ideas can be incorporated into a teacher's practice in schools. Their potential as a support agency for encouraging research-based teaching is just beginning to be realised.

Research-Based Teaching

Teachers who examine their practice critically and engage in research based teaching all claim that it enables them to learn more about their pupils, their teaching, and games. This is significant because it clearly demonstrates the value of this approach in developing a better understanding of one's practice. However, it is time-consuming and we need further information about how teachers can incorporate research based teaching into their teaching routines and the school calendar. This project has shown also that we are only in the early stages of understanding its potential and its limitations. Teachers who volunteer for a project are atypical. Does research-based teaching provide the average teacher, who may only have a small amount of time to give or who may lack the will and motivation to question their practice, with the facility to understand, to develop, and to change untested assumptions and habitual teaching behaviour? I do not know.

Games Teaching

The project team have organised over 36 courses with teachers and many of the education authorities have initiated their own small-scale projects to re-examine games teaching. Two editions of the Bulletin of Physical Education have been devoted to Games Teaching and have been in great demand. A collection of articles on 'teaching for understanding' has been edited by Lynne Spackman at Cheltenham.

Debate about 'teaching for understanding' has generated a notion of 'intelligent performance' which claims to subsume the idea of skill which has dominated our thinking in physical education for so long (Kirk, 1983). A number of Governing Bodies of Sport in England have endorsed this focus on games teaching and incorporated it into their publications.

This changing focus within games teaching started as a reaction to problems with the way games were being taught and the lack of understanding that young people appear to have. It has started to grow and has captured the imagination of teachers who are prepared to invest time and energy in trying it out. But, how is an innovation transformed and absorbed into the culture of teaching? This project has only been a beginning.

References

Almond, L. (1982), 'Containable Time', in Open University Course E364 Curriculum Evaluation and Assessment in Educational Institutions, Milton Keynes: Open University Press.

Boyall, J. (1983), 'Towards an Analysis of the Teacher as Researcher', unpublished M.Phil. dissertation, University of Technology, Loughborough.

Brackenridge, C. (1979), 'Games: Classification and Analysis', Paper presented to the Kirklees District Teachers Course, May 2 1979.

Kemmis, S. (1980), 'Action Research in Retrospect and Prospect', Paper presented at the Annual Meeting of the Australian Association for Research in Education, Sydney, November 6-9.

Kirk, D. (1983), 'Understanding: A Focus for our Conceptualisations of Physical Performance in Games', Paper presented to the Philosophic Society for the Study of Sport, Annual Conference, King's College, London, July.

Thorpe, R. and Bunker, D. (1982), 'A model for the Teaching of Games in Secondary Schools,', Bulletin of Physical Education, Vol. 18, 1, 5-9.

Thorpe, R. and Bunker, D. (1983), 'Issues that Arise when Preparing to "Teach for Understanding"', Bulletin of Physical Education, Vol. 19, 1, 9-12.

Williamson, T. (1982), 'It's a Different Ball Game', Bulletin of Physical Education, Vol. 18, 1, 23-31.

2

Games Classification Systems as a Foundation for Curriculum

Steve Mitchell, Kent State University

Introduction

Games have long been considered an important component of the Physical Education curriculum. Dating back to the 1960s, proponents argued for the inclusion of games for physical, social, moral and intellectual reasons (Maulden & Redfern, 1969). So began consideration of how best to organize the teaching of games in schools and of how to classify games for inclusion in the curriculum. Scholars including Len Almond (1986) gave thought to these questions for the next twenty years and, in the book *Rethinking Games Teaching*, Len reviewed alternative approaches to classifying games by comparing two different models and commenting on how these models could be used for the selection of games content for the school curriculum. In this chapter I review these, and other classification approaches, and expand on Len's ideas for bringing such classification systems to life in the process of curriculum development. I also suggest that Len's preferred approach to classifying games according to their tactical components lay the groundwork for further development of games education curricula. I conclude the chapter by describing how Len's thoughts have influenced my own work in games education and the games curriculum.

Forerunners in Games Classification Systems

Initial intent to categorize games is seen in the work of Maulden & Redfern (1969, 1981) in primary level Physical Education in the UK. Grouping games based on skills and movements used, they identified the categories of net, batting and running games as a way of addressing similarities and analyzing game play. Len Almond's initial purpose in categorizing games came as a result of a series of seminars in 1983, in which the need for a classification system was identified as a way of providing a basis for selecting the games for inclusion in the Physical Education curriculum. Len suggested the categories of Invasion, Net/wall, Fielding/run-scoring, and Target games. The full classification system is presented in Table 1.

Table 1. Almond's (1986) games classification system.

INVASION		
1. Handball	**Football**	**Stick-ball**
Basketball	Soccer	Hockey (field)
Netball	Rugby (Union/League)	Lacrosse
Team Handball	Gaelic football	Shinty
Korkball	Australian rules football	Hurling/Camogie
Tchouk-ball	American football	Ice hockey
Ultimate frisbee	Speedball	Roller hockey
Waterpolo	Touchball (Finnish rugby)	Cycle polo

2. Games which have: a) Focused target   b) Open end target

NET/WALL		
1(a). Net/racquet	**1(b). Net/hand**	**1. Wall**
Badminton	Volleyball	Squash
Tennis		Handball (court)
Table tennis		Rugby fives
Paddle tennis		Paddle ball
Platform tennis		Racquet ball
		Jai Alai

FIELDING/RUN SCORING		
	Rounders	
Baseball	Cricket	
Softball	Kickball	

TARGET GAMES		
Golf	Boules	Billiards
Croquet	Ten (5 or 9) pin bowling	Snooker
Bowls	Duckpin	Pool
Curling	Pub skittles	

Len's system combined elements of games tactics and techniques to create a mechanism through which teachers and curriculum designers could select balanced games content for inclusion in school physical education programmes. Len's idea was that the games education experience should enable learners to sample a range of games with differing tactical and technical requirements. Simply put, if teachers selected games from each category and sub-category, learners would receive the broadest and, therefore, most balanced games education possible.

Len's work was preceded by that of Margaret Ellis (1983), though in reality these two visionaries spent time discussing and collaborating on their work. Ellis developed a classification system with the purpose of providing an understanding of the similarities and differences among games. As with Len's system, Ellis's classifications reflected game tactical and technical similarities and differences, but also areas of play. Ellis's four categories were each divided into two sub-categories, and were as follows:

1. Territory
    a) Goal (e.g. basketball and soccer)
    b) Line (e.g. rugby and flag football)
2. Court
    a) Divided (e.g. badminton and tennis)
    b) Shared (e.g. racquetball and squash)
3. Target
    a) Opposed (e.g. bocce and croquet)
    b) Unopposed (e.g. golf and bowling)
4. Field
    a) Fan shaped (e.g. softball and rounders)
    b) Oval shaped (e.g. cricket and stoolball)

While the classification systems of Maulden and Redfern, and later Ellis, were forerunners to Len's work, it is his categories of Invasion, Net/wall, Fielding/Run scoring, and Target games that have come to form the basis for the games education components of many contemporary curricula. These categories are seen as providing a clear distinction for the organization of a games curriculum that is taught with a focus on understanding the tactical components of game play (Bunker and Thorpe, 1982; Mitchell, Oslin and Griffin, 2003, 2013).

Contemporary Adaptations of Almond's System

Mitchell, Oslin and Griffin (2003, 2013) further refined Len's system by more clearly incorporating the features of fixed and open-ended targets into the Invasion games category. Our adaptation of Len's system is presented in Table 2 below.

Table 2. Mitchell et al (2003, 2013) adaptation of Almond's classification system.

INVASION	NET/WALL	FIELDING/ RUN-SCORING	TARGET
Basketball FT*	**Net**	Baseball	Golf
Netball FT	Badminton I**	Softball	Croquet
Team handball FT	Tennis I	Rounders	Ten pin bowling
Water polo FT	Table tennis I	Cricket	Lawn bowls
Soccer FT	Pickle ball I	Kickball	Pool
Hockey FT	Volleyball H		Billiards
Lacrosse FT			Snooker
	Wall		
Speedball	Racquetball I		
FT / OET	Squash I		
	Fives H		
Rugby OET			
Football OET	**		
Ultimate Frisbee OET	I = Implement		
	H = Hand		
*			
FT =			
Focused target			
OET =			
Open end target			

From the perspective of curriculum design, Len's purpose in developing his classification system was to enable teachers to sample content selections from across the categories and, in doing so, present a balanced and broad games education for primary and secondary aged children. While Mitchell et al (2003, 2013) also valued the breadth of a games curriculum based on sampling, our concern was for a lack of depth of learning in that learners would not have sufficient time to develop knowledge and skill. Our suggested approach (Mitchell et al, 2013) was to select content from within each category and provide a deeper learning experience without sacrificing breadth of content. For example, successive units of instruction of soccer, field or floor hockey, and ultimate frisbee, all invasion games, would enable deeper learning of the tactical components of invasion games since these games are very similar tactically, but also a breadth of technical learning because they require different techniques. A similar argument can be made for sequencing instruction in badminton and pickleball or tennis.

Additional variations of Len's system are evident in the work of Wall and Murray (1990), Hopper (2000), and Launder (2001). Wall and Murray suggested three categories of games based on degrees of overall complexity and skills used. Low-organization games, including a variety of tag games, often use only locomotor and non-locomotor skills such as running, dodging, swerving and turning, and bear little resemblance to more formal sport related games. By contrast, Lead-up games are more complex and resemble more formal games. By design these games will lead to a more mature and formal version. For example, a game-like attack versus defense (3v2) situated practice might be viewed as a lead-up game in any Invasion game. Lastly, Formal games are the natural extension to Lead-up games as children's skill levels and understanding develop to a point where a more mature form of a game is possible. Interestingly, Wall and Murray, citing the influence of Maulden and Redfern (1969) further divide their formal games category into Target, Net, Batting and Running games.

Describing curriculum development efforts in British Columbia, Canada, Hopper reports the use of categories based not only on the similarities between games, but also on the body management (locomotor skills) and equipment handling (manipulative skills) used in games. The categories include:

1. Target games such as golf and bowling, with balancing as an essential body management skill and sending away by throwing or striking as essential equipment management skills.
2. Batting and fielding games such as cricket and softball, with running, jumping, and turning as essential body management skills and sending away (throwing and striking) and receiving (collecting and catching) as essential equipment handling skills.
3. Net/wall games such as tennis and volleyball, also with running, jumping, and turning as essential body management skills and sending away and preparing to receive as essential equipment handling skills.

4. Territory games such as soccer, rugby, and basketball, again with running, jumping, and turning as essential body management skills and sending away, receiving (catching and trapping) and retaining (dribbling and carrying) as essential equipment handling skills).

Hopper's system is a small adaptation of Len's, as is that of Launder (2001). In developing his approach of Play Practice, Launder suggested a classification system that combines tactical components of game play with areas of play, similar to the previously mentioned approach of Ellis (1983). Launder's categories were Field Invasion games (e.g. soccer and rugby), Court Invasion games (basketball and team handball), Court Divided games (e.g. tennis and volleyball), Striking and fielding games (e.g. cricket and softball), and Target games (e.g. golf and archery).

Personal Influences

As mentioned above, my own work, along with that of my good friends and colleagues Judy Oslin and Linda Griffin, made use of Len's ideas for games classification systems as we sought to develop practical teaching ideas for teachers. In particular, we used Len's games categories as the basis for advocating a thematic approach for the primary/elementary school games education curriculum (Mitchell et al, 2003, 2013). At this level we have advocated teaching not discrete games, such as soccer, volleyball, softball, etc, but instead teaching units of invasion games, net games, striking/fielding games, and target games centered around the solutions to specified tactical problems. Of course, our first task was to identify the tactical problems, and solutions to these problems, associated with each game category. Initial identification of such problems was easy in that all games revolve around the main problems of offense/attack (i.e. scoring), defense (i.e. preventing opponents from scoring), and restarting play when necessary. But this surface level breakdown does not help teachers identify and sequence appropriate instructional content, so we needed to delve deeper and get inside these broad problems. Again, following discussion and thought, we concluded that games within each category had similar, more specific, problems. For example, after much discussion, in Invasion games we identified the following tactical problems:

Offense/Scoring
- Keeping possession of the ball
- Penetrating the defense and attacking the goal
- Transition

Defense/Preventing scoring
- Defending space
- Defending the goal
- Winning the ball

Starting/restarting play
- Beginning the game
- Restarting from the sideline
- Restarting from the endline
- Restarting from violations

Having identified tactical problems, the next logical task was to specify solutions to the problems, these solutions then becoming the basis for selecting specific instructional content in the form of learning activities and tasks. So we developed what we called "Tactical Frameworks," our attempt to breakdown each games category from a tactical perspective and so provide the "scope" of games instruction for any particular category. An example of a tactical framework for invasion games is presented in table 3.

Solutions in this invasion games tactical framework are in the form of decisions to be made, on-the-ball skills and off-the-ball movements, and these solutions represent the content of a thematic approach to games instruction at the elementary or primary school level. For example, in teaching invasion games you might teach young students to keep possession of a ball (the theme) by passing, receiving and supporting in soccer, hockey, and basketball. In this way, novice performers learn to address tactical problems of invasion games play rather than looking only at the skills of a specific game in isolation. This approach is intended to develop more knowledgeable and adaptable games players at the elementary level, players who can switch easily between different invasion games, or perhaps between different net games and retain a degree of understanding (of game play) that transfers from one game to another (see Mitchell et al, 2013 for additional frameworks). For example, because of the similarity between invasion games, students should be quite able to move from soccer to hockey and retain a degree of understanding of game tactics.

Table 3. A tactical framework for content in invasion games.

Tactical Problems	Decisions and Movements	Skills
Offense/Scoring		
Keeping possession of the ball	Supporting the ball carrier. When to pass.	Passing and receiving the ball.
Penetrating the defense and attacking the goal	Using a target forward. When to shoot and dribble.	Moving with the ball. Shooting. Feinting.
Transition	Moving to space.	Quick passing.
Defense/Preventing scoring		
Defending space	Marking/guarding. Footwork. Pressuring the ball carrier.	Clearing the ball. Quick outlet passes.
Defending the goal	Goalkeeping - positioning. Rebounding - boxing out.	Goalkeeping - stopping and distributing the ball. Rebounding - taking the ball.
Winning the ball		Tackling and stealing the ball.
Starting/restarting play		
Beginning the game	Positioning.	Initiating play.
Restarting from the sideline	Supporting positions.	Putting the ball in play.
Restarting from the endline	Supporting positions.	Putting the ball in play.
Restarting from violations	Supporting positions.	Putting the ball in play.

Naturally the question then arose as to how the progression of content might look. In considering this we decided to identify levels of "game complexity" as a means of suggesting when specific content might be taught and learned, thus adding "sequence" to the scope provided by the tactical frameworks. These levels of game complexity for invasion games are presented below in table 4. Taken together, the framework and levels of game complexity provide developmentally appropriate scope and sequence of invasion games content for elementary children. Ideally, game play should be of no larger than 3v3 at first, progressing to a maximum of 6v6 in games such as soccer and hockey.

LIFETIME CONTRIBUTIONS IN PHYSICAL EDUCATION

Table 4. Levels of game complexity for invasion games.

Tactical Problems/ Concepts	Game Complexity Level I 3-a-side maximum	Game Complexity Level II 4-a-side maximum	Game Complexity Level III 6-a-side maximum
Offense/Scoring			
Keeping possession	Pass, receive, footwork. When to pass.	Pass, receive, footwork. Support play.	
Penetration/attack	Shooting, moving with the ball (dribbling). When to dribble and shoot.	Shooting, feinting.	Using a target. Forward, shooting, feinting, change of speed, moving with the ball.
Transition			Moving to space, quick passing.
Defense/Preventing scoring			
Defending space		Marking/guarding, pressure. Footwork (stance).	Clearing the ball, quick outlet pass.
Defending the goal		Goalkeeper positioning.	Goalkeeper shot stopping and distribution, rebounding.
Winning the ball			Tackling and stealing the ball.
Starting/restarting play			
Beginning the game	Initiating play.	Positioning in a triangle.	
Restarting from side and end line	Putting ball in play.	Positioning.	Quick restarts.
Restarting from violations	Putting ball in play.	Positioning.	Quick restarts.

Summary and Conclusion

To conclude, though there have been variations on Len Almond's work in games classification systems (see summary table 5), it is his categorizations based on game similarities and differences that have been most influential in the design of games education curricula in many countries.

Table 5. Comparison of games classification systems.

Author(s)/Category				
Maulden & Redfern (1969, 1981)	Running games	Net games	Batting games	
Almond (1986); Mitchell, Oslin & Griffin (2003, 2013)	Invasion games	Net/wall games	Fielding/Run scoring game	Target games
Ellis (1983)	Territory games	Court games	Field games	Target games
Wall & Murray (1990)	Low organization games	Lead up games	Formal games: Target Net Batting Running	
Hopper (2000)	Target games	Batting and fielding games	Net/wall games	Territory games
Launder (2001)	Field invasion games	a) Court invasion games b) Court divided games	Striking and fielding games	Target games

The language of Invasion, Net/wall, Fielding/run-scoring, and Target games has been useful in enabling teachers and curriculum designers to convey purpose to the selection and sequencing of games content for instruction. Len's work has greatly influenced that of my colleagues and I, and indeed this language has made its way into formally approved curriculum documents from Singapore (Singapore Ministry of Education, 2014) to the United States (SHAPE America, 2013), and has become the language of choice for many other teachers world-wide. For this we have Len to thank!

References

Almond, L. (1986). Reflecting on Themes: A Games Classification. In R. Thorpe, D. Bunker, & L. Almond (Eds.) *Rethinking games education*, (pp.71-72). Department of Physical Education and Sports Science, University of Technology, Loughborough, Leicestershire.

Bunker, D. and Thorpe, R. (1982). A model for the teaching of games in secondary schools. *Bulletin of Physical Education*, 18(1), 5-8.

Ellis, M. (1983). *Similarities and differences in games: A classification system.* Paper presented at the AIESEP conference, Rome, Italy.

Hopper, T. (2000). Games classification system: Teaching strategic understanding and tactical awareness. *CAHPERD Journal*, 66(4), 14-19.

Launder, A. (2001). *Play practice: The games approach to teaching and coaching sports.* Champaign, IL: Human Kinetics.

Maulden, E. & Redfern, H.B. (1969). *Games teaching: A new approach for the primary school.* London: MacDonald and Evans.

Maulden, E. & Redfern, H.B. (1981). *Games teaching.* London: MacDonald and Evans.

Mitchell, S.A., Oslin, J.L. & Griffin, L.L. (2003). *Sport foundations for elementary physical edcuation: A tactical games approach.* Champaign, IL: Human Kinetics.

Mitchell, S.A., Oslin, J.L. & Griffin, L.L. (2013). *Teaching sport concepts and skills: A Tactical games approach.* 3rd Edition. Champaign, IL: Human Kinetics.

SHAPE America (2013). *National Standards for K-12 Physical Education* (2013). SHAPE America – Society of Health and Physical Educators: Reston, VA.

Singapore Ministry of Education (2014). *Physical Education Teaching and Learning Syllabus:* MOE Singapore.

Wall, J. and Marray, N. (1990). *Children and Movement: Physical Education in the elementary school.* Dubuque, IA. Wm. C. Brown.

3

Physical Literacy and Human Flourishing

Elizabeth Durden-Myers & Margaret Whitehead

For many years Len was very interested in what it is to be human and understanding and exploring human experience. Physical literacy often featured in his exploration of these themes. As a result of this Len introduced ideas such as vitality, becoming energised, having meaningful experiences, positive functioning and being authentically engaged in physical activity. In sum, he was very keen to unpack the relationship between physical literacy and human flourishing from an experiential point of view.

While the physical literacy community were contemplating and considering the definition and nature of the concept Len was looking more widely, working to locate physical literacy in relation to the wider perspective. The outcome of this is clear to see, in response to his passion to unravel this area members of the International Physical Literacy Association (IPLA) were challenged to join him in his enquiry. As a result, the area of physical literacy and human flourishing featured in a Paper in the special edition of the Journal of Teaching in Physical Education (Durden-Myers, Whitehead and Pot, 2018) and generates two chapters in the forthcoming book Physical Literacy across the world (Durden-Myers and Whitehead, 2019a; 2019b).

The following passages are taken from an unfinished and unpublished paper by Len, entitled *'Eudaimonia and Modern Psychology'*. We will use this text to reflect on his contribution and development of physical literacy in relation to human flourishing. Len in his paper draws attention to Ryff's (1989) eudaimonia six-factor model and discusses two of these areas in more detail (self-acceptance and purpose in life). Thereafter, Len discusses eudaimonia in adolescence. Each of these areas is then the subject of our consideration. Extracts from Len's unpublished work are set out first and these are followed by a series of discussions that develop some of Len's themes.

Eudaimonia and Modern Psychology (Unpublished Paper)
Len Almond

Introduction

Ryff and Singer (2008) highlights the distinction between eudaimonia wellbeing, which they identify as psychological well-being, and hedonic wellbeing which they describe as pleasure attainment. Building on Aristotelian ideals of belonging and benefiting others, flourishing, thriving and exercising excellence, an eudaimonia six-factor structure is proposed by Ryff (1989):

1. Autonomy
2. Personal growth
3. Self-acceptance
4. Purpose in life
5. Environmental mastery
6. Positive relations with others

Ryff's (1989) six-factor model of eudaimonic well-being describes the six aspects of positive functioning that an individual who strives to lead a fulfilled life must endorse. Ryff (1989) argues that he pursuit and acquisition of positive relationships is an intrinsically motivated desire that is endorsed cross-culturally as a route to being void of ill-being as well as leading a meaningful life.

The results of a study conducted in the 90s exploring the relationship between well-being and those aspects of positive functioning that were put forth in Ryff's (1989) model, indicate that persons who aspired more for financial success relative to affiliation with others or their community scored lower on various measures of well-being (Ryff and Keyes, 1995). Individuals that strive for a life defined by affiliation, intimacy and contributing to one's community can be described as aspiring to fulfil their intrinsic psychological needs. In contrast those individuals who aspire for wealth and material, social recognition, fame, image or attractiveness can be described as aiming to fulfil their extrinsic psychological needs. The strength of an individual's intrinsic (relative to extrinsic) aspirations as indicated by rankings of importance correlates with an array of psychological outcomes. Positive correlations have been found with indications of psychological well-being: positive affect, vitality, and self-actualization. Negative correlations have been found with indicators of psychological ill-being: negative affect, depression and anxiety.

Self-Acceptance

Self-acceptance is one of the six factors in Ryff''s (1989) structure for eudaimonic well-being. It can be defined as:

- the awareness of one's strengths and weaknesses
- the realistic (yet subjective) appraisal of one's talents, capabilities, and general worth
- feelings of satisfaction with one's self despite deficiencies and regardless of past behaviours and choices

A person who scores high on self-acceptance:
- has a positive self-attitude
- acknowledges and accepts all aspects of themselves (including the good and bad),
- is not self-critical or confused about their identity
- does not wish they were any different from who they already are

Some psychological benefits of self-acceptance include mood regulation, a decrease in depressive symptoms, and an increase in positive emotions. Other psychological benefits include:

- a heightened sense of freedom
- a decrease in fear of failure
- an increase in self-worth
- an increase in independence (autonomy)
- an increase in self-esteem
- less desire to win the approval of others
- less self-critique and more self-kindness when mistakes occur
- more desire to live life for one's self (and not others)
- the ability to take more risks without worrying about the consequences

Self-acceptance is also thought to be necessary for good mental health.

Purpose in Life

Purpose in life refers broadly to the pursuit of life satisfaction. It has also been found that those with high purpose in life scores have strong goals and sense of direction. They feel that there is meaning to their past and present life and hold beliefs that continue to give their life purpose. Research in the past has focused on purpose in the face of adversity (what is awful, difficult, or absurd in life). Recently, research has shifted to include a focus on the role of purpose in personal fulfilment and self-actualisation. Identified here are three theoretical approaches to purpose in life, including:

1. Terror management theory
2. Self-control
3. Intrinsic motivation

Terror management theory (TMT) was originally proposed by Greenberg, Pyszczynski and Solomon (1986) based on the work of Becker (1973). The TMT proposes that we are driven by fear caused by an awareness of our own mortality. The self-control approach focusses on exercising self-control to achieve self-esteem by fulfilling goals and feeling in control of our own success. This is further reinforced by a sense of intentionality in both efforts and outcomes. Frankl (2011) argues that the intrinsic motivation approach emphasis finding value in three main areas: creative, experiential, and attitudinal. Creative values are expressed in acts of creating or producing something. Experiential values are actualised through the senses and may overlap the hedonistic view of happiness. Attitudinal values are prominent for individuals who are unable to pursue the preceding two classes of values. Attitudinal values are believed to be primarily responsible for allowing individuals to endure suffering with dignity.

A personal sense of responsibility is required for the pursuit of the values that give life meaning, but it is the realisation that one holds sole responsibility for rendering life meaningful that allows the values to be actualised and life to be given true purpose. Determining what is meaningful for one's self provides a sense of autonomy and control which promotes self-esteem. All three of the above theories have self-esteem at their core. Self-esteem is often viewed as the most significant measure of psychological well-being, and highly correlated with many life-regulating skills. Purpose in life promotes and is a source of self-esteem; it is not a by-product of self-esteem.

Eudaimonia in Adolescence

There has been a significant focus in past research on adulthood, in regard to well-being and development and although eudaimonia is not a new field of study, there has been little research done in the areas of adolescence and youth. Research conducted with this age group had previously explored more negative aspects, such as problem and risk behaviours (i.e. drug and alcohol use/misuse). Adolescents rapidly face cognitive, social and physical changes, making them prime subjects to study for well-being and development.

Previous research (no reference found) on positive youth development and the eudaimonic identity theory identify three developmental elements: *self-defining activities, personal expressiveness and goal-directed behaviours*. Research (no reference found) determined that adolescents sample multiple *self-defining activities;* these activities aid in identity formation, as individuals choose activities that they believe represents who they are. These self-defining activities also help determine the adolescent's social environments. For example, an adolescent involved in sport and physical activity, would likely surround themselves with like-minded active and competitive people. *Personal expressiveness*, are the activities that we choose to express and connect with our *"daimon"* through subjective experiences. Finally, *goal-directed behaviours*, are developed through goal setting, where individuals work towards identity establishment. Adolescents recognise their passions, abilities and talents and aim to fulfil their goals and behave in a way that appeases their true self.

References

Becker, E. (1973). *The Denial of Death*. New York: Simon & Schuster.

Frankl, V. E. (2011) *Man's Search for Ultimate Meaning*. Reading, UK: Rider.

Greenberg, J., Pyszczynski, T. & Solomon, S. (1986). The causes and consequences of a need for self-esteem: A terror management theory. In R.F. Baumeister (ed.) *Public Self and Private Self* (pp. 189-212). New York: Springer-Verlag.

Ryff, C. D. (1989b). Happiness is everything, or is it? Explorations on the meaning of psychological well-being. *Journal of Personality and Social Psychology*, 57, 6, p. 1069-1081.

Ryff, C. D. & Keyes, L. M. (1995) The Structure of Psychological Well-Being Revisited. *Journal of Personality and Social Psychology*. 69, 4, p.719-727.

Ryff, C.D. & Singer, B.H. (2008) Know Thyself and Become What You Are: A Eudaimonic Approach to Psychological Well-Being. *Journal of Happiness Studies*. 9, 13. DOI: https://doi.org/10.1007/s10902-006-9019-0

Building from Len's reading, study and views.

Reflections on Human Flourishing, Eudaimonic Well-being and Physical Literacy

Considering physical literacy alongside human flourishing had not been a significant area of development for the IPLA, however following Len's investigations and thinking in this field a considerable amount of work has been undertaken. Subsequently the area featured in both the special edition of the Journal of Teaching in Physical Education (2018) and in the publication Physical Literacy across the World (2019).

Following Len's reference recommendations, it was recognised that physical literacy shared a number of constituents with human flourishing. Using Ryff's analysis it became clear that, in respect of Autonomy, Personal growth, Self-acceptance, Purpose in life, Environmental mastery and Positive relationships with others, there was an immediate synergy between these two concepts.

Autonomy is seen as relating to independence, self-determination, agency, responsibility, freedom and liberty. Physical literacy aims to encourage individuals to be responsible for adopting a physically active lifestyle. This is seen in the second part of the definition which reads '….to value and take responsibility for engagement in physical activities for life.' In this context participants are encouraged to take ownership of their involvement in physical activities, indeed promoting individual autonomy is an aspiration embedded within physical literacy.

Personal growth is understood as encompassing having a positive attitude to learning, enquiry and exploration of new opportunities. Individuals exhibit ambition and forward thinking. Physical literacy aims to develop motivation and confidence through progressive achievement appropriate to age and endowment. These two areas of the affective domain are, again, spelled out in the definition. Growth and accomplishment are realised in developing physical competence in physical activity in a wide variety of environments. This depends on individual initiative and imagination as well as application of movement patterns. Personal growth is a very significance aspect of all work to foster physical literacy.

Self-acceptance is taken to cover realistic and positive self-perception. This includes the acceptance of, and contentment with, personal potential and the awareness of strengths and weaknesses. These personal traits issue in sound self-esteem and a robust self-concept. Those advocating physical literacy strongly support showing respect for each person as unique, with individual potential. This approach springs from phenomenological principles underpinning physical literacy. Realistic self-perception is fostered through developing motivation and self-confidence. The mode of 'assessment' of physical literacy is designed to re-enforce self-acceptance in that it is ipsative, that is, based on previous performance. Pupils are encouraged to set their own goals and evaluate how far they have achieved these. Self - acceptance permeates the work in physical literacy not least in celebrating steps individuals take in realising their individual potential and developing a positive sense of self.

Purpose in life is seen to include having a clear sense of direction, commitment and perseverance. It also encompasses personal clarity relating to values by which to live and a considered vision of the future. Proponents of physical literacy see involvement in physical activity as providing a rich variety of opportunities that can play a part in defining life. Physical activity offers new horizons and can feature in mapping life experiences for the future. It is believed that engagement in physical activity in the context of physical literacy can add meaning and purpose to life. The strap line of the IPLA is 'Choosing physical activity for life' thus clearly signalling the potential of physical activity to feature in a purposeful life.

Environmental mastery is understood to describe productive relationships within a wide range of environments. This will involve astute perception, clear understanding and imagination. Significantly responses to new environments will build from previous experiences. Progress is made where earlier learning informs new challenges. Physical literacy is grounded in existentialism which identifies that interaction with the world is the seedbed of all development. Human embodiment is involved in most interaction and thus meaningful involvement in physical activity in a range of situations and environments are central to the concept. In all writing about physical literacy the need for rich and varied experience is described as lying at the heart of the enterprise.

Positive relationships with others embraces good interpersonal skills of listening, understanding and empathising. Also included would be the establishment of mutual trust and a caring and responsive attitude towards fellow participants. These sensitive and perceptive inter-personal skills mean that the individual makes a positive contribution to group enterprises. Much engagement in physical activity takes place alongside others and indeed many activities rely on the actions of others. To achieve effective participation individuals are guided to develop mutual respect, empathy and responsiveness in relation to others. Willingness to learn from others and a positive inclusive attitude are also nurtured. The fostering of physical literacy undoubtedly includes the realisation of positive relationships with others. This issues in making the experiences genuinely meaningful and rewarding for all.

Considering the above and Len's article the chapter explores in more detail self-acceptance, purpose in life and eudaimonia in adolescence.

Self-Acceptance and Physical Literacy

Self-acceptance is one of the six factors in Ryff''s (1989) structure for eudaimonic well-being. These factors have been fleshed out briefly above. However, Len highlighted the importance of self-acceptance and clearly sees the contribution that physical literacy can make to individuals' achieving well-being. His concern for this area has influenced the IPLA in their thinking about the implications of physical literacy to practice. Working from Len's three lists set out in his writing, the notion of promoting self-acceptance has been woven into IPLA's recommendations for practitioners. Examples considered here are practitioner feedback, differentiation and providing opportunities for decision making. The table below describes how a focus on developing self-acceptance highlights aspects of work to promote physical literacy.

Table 1: Self-Acceptance and Physical Literacy

Potential benefits of fostering self-acceptance	Broad learning/teaching approach in line with developing physical literacy	Practitioner action in fostering physical literacy and within this growth of self-acceptance
Development of self esteem. Increase in self worth. Secure attitude to self. Identity. Accept self as they are.	Via the use of appropriate feedback.	Feedback is personal and private. Practitioner knows learner as an individual and respects individual potential. Effort, progress and achievement recognized and celebrated.
Loss of fear of failure. See tasks as personal matter. Have no fear of degrading comparison. Less concerned to win approval of others.	Via appropriate differentiation.	Set tasks that are challenging but within reach, thus bringing the satisfaction of success. Practitioner uses differentiation by task, outcome and mode of learning/teaching.
Confidence to take more risks. Appreciate life is for one's self. Develop a sense of freedom. Increase in independence.	Via providing opportunities for choice.	Setting own goals, evaluate own progress, opportunities to create own ideas and solutions.

It is suggested that the promotion of self-acceptance should be taken seriously in the aspiration of fostering physical literacy. Physical literacy is nurtured in the myriad of experiences that the individual encounters in the field of physical activity. It is the combined effect of these experiences that influence the development of motivation, confidence, physical competence and knowledge and understanding that are crucial both to physical literacy and to self-acceptance in respect of physical acuity. Hence to ensure that experiences are constructive, thought needs to be given to aspects of participant/practitioner interaction. The aspects of feedback, differentiation and choice have been singled out above as examples of practices that can enhance self-acceptance. These views are commensurate with Len's interest to interrogate what he called 'the pedagogy of engagement'.

Purpose in Life and Physical Literacy

Psychologists and philosophers have long been interested in the human experience of meaning and purpose in life (Martela & Steger, 2016; Yalom, 1980). Hooker, Masters and Park (2018) describe meaning in life as a multidimensional construct with three key aspects: comprehension (feeling as though one's life makes sense), purpose (feeling directed and motivated by valued goals) and mattering (feeling that one's existence is significant). One aspect, purpose, is often used interchangeably with meaning in the literature (George & Park, 2013). Purpose however, refers to behavioral engagement in life goals and valued activities (McKnight & Kashdan, 2009). Previous research has shown that purpose in life, the belief that one's life is meaningful and goal-directed, is associated with greater engagement in self-reported physical activity (Hooker and Masters, 2016). The reverse correlation is also found. Physical activity engagement can promote a greater sense of purpose in life, and the belief that one's life is meaningful.

Len also saw this connection and drew our attention to the shift in research to include a focus on the role of purpose in personal fulfilment and self-actualisation. It could be argued that the actualising of human potential can facilitate the nurturing of purpose and meaning in life. This is where the capability approach proposed by Nussbaum (2000/2011) could be used to describe and signpost what it is to be human in the identification of human capabilities. Len himself read widely about capabilities – both from Nussbaum's perspective and from the parallel work of Sen (1994). One issue that initiated significant debate was whether physical literacy could legitimately claim to be a capability in its own right or was best seen as contributing to most other capabilities. Nussbaum identifies ten central capabilities to human life. These are outlined in the table below. Each capability is expanded in relation to its relationship to human rights and the way it can be realised more fully by a contribution from embodied acuity. Following further debate in the IPLA, physical literacy as a unique aspect of human nature is proposed as an eleventh central capability. We feel that Len would be likely to support this dual approach to the relationship between capabilities and meaning in life, that is, as a valuable contributor and as of value in itself.

Table 2: Capabilities Approach Table from Whitehead (2019)

Central Capability	Rights from Nussbaum (2000/2011)	Suggested Contribution of Embodied Acuity
Life	Right to life of a normal length.	Right to be involved in physical activity to prolong life.
Bodily health	Right to adequate food and shelter.	Right to be involved in physical activity to maintain health.
Bodily integrity	Right to freedom of movement and having body boundaries treated as sovereign.	Right to freedom to move from place to place. Right to ownership of own living-body/body-as-lived. Right to have embodiment respected.
Senses, imagination	Right to use senses to imagine, think, and reason. Right to freedom of expression.	Right to be involved in physical activity to use embodied dimension to develop creativity, imagination and rationality.
Emotions	Right to have attachments to things and people. Right to love, grieve, show gratitude and anger, right not to have emotional development blighted by abuse or neglect.	Right to show expression of emotion through all aspects of non-verbal communication. Right to have freedom for emotional development in participating in physical activity.
Practical reason	Right to decide oneself on what is good and to engage in critical reflection regarding planning one's x.	Right to be involved in physical activity as an option for life-style planning.
Affiliation	Right to engage in various forms of social-interaction. Right to develop self-respect as of equal worth as others.	Right to engage with others in physical activity contexts and to be respected for this involvement. Right to engage in culturally valued activities.

Affiliation	Right to engage in various forms of social-interaction. Right to develop self-respect as of equal worth as others.	Right to engage with others in physical activity contexts and to be respected for this involvement. Right to engage in culturally valued activities.
Other species and the natural world	Right to demonstrate concern for nature.	Right to be involved in physical activity to experience interaction with the world of nature.
Play	Right to laugh, play and enjoy recreational activities.	Right to be involved in physical activity as a rewarding, self-affirming experience and as a recreational activity.
Control over one's environment	Right to participate in political choices including free speech. Right to own property. Right to seek employment.	Right to have a say in decisions about provision of facilities and practitioner support in relation to physical activity.
Physical Literacy	Right to develop embodied acuity, embracing embodied potential as of value in its own right, affording the interaction with the world that is unique to this human domain.	

Further study would reveal that significance of embodied acuity varies in respect of different central capabilities. The realisation of embodied acuity alongside the agency to draw on this human potential can be described as Physical literacy. In this context every individual has the right to develop physical literacy described as a positive disposition to engage in life-long physical activity.

Len continually made new links to concepts that furthered the merit of physical literacy. In his exploration of purpose and meaning in life he encouraged us to find yet another field that draws correlations between engagement in physical activity and increased purpose and meaning. This research supports the credibility and need for physical literacy as a concept that not only nurtures engagement in physical activity for life but also as a concept that capitalises on the relationship between physical activity, meaning and purpose and thus is central in promoting human flourishing.

Eudaimonia in Adolescence and Physical Literacy

Eudaimonia and adolescence are two terms that many might find hard to associate with one another. Adolescence is an incredibility complex and multidimensional developmental period in an individual's life. Adolescents rapidly face cognitive, social and physical changes, making them popular subjects to study for health, well-being and development. Creating environments whereby individuals navigating adolescence can thrive and flourish both during and beyond this period is worthy cause for research. Len drew our attention to positive youth development and the eudaimonic identity theory which identifies three key developmental elements: self-defining activities, personal expressiveness and goal-directed behaviours. However if any of these elements are to come to fruition individuals must first have a sense of autonomy. Autonomy is key in being able to pursue self-directed/defining activities, being able to freely express oneself and take action towards personal goals.

Autonomy supportive environments induce greater intrinsic motivation, curiosity and a desire for challenge, whilst students who are overly controlled lose initiative and learn less well (Ryan and Deci, 2000; Reeve, 2002). Autonomy supportive environments provide opportunities to co-construct learning experiences responding to student voice and encourages learners to take responsibility for and become actively engaged in their own learning.

Encouraging individual autonomy during adolescence enables individuals to flourish in two ways, firstly by providing opportunities for individuals to pursue self-defining activities, personal expressiveness and goal-directed behaviours. And secondly, by promoting the taking of responsibility and therefore the valuing of engagement in physical activity for life. The contribution that practices in physical education can make to enhancing quality of life during this critical period of life has perhaps attracted insufficient attention by the IPLA, however, building on Len's views, the Association should consider this area further in its recommendations for learning /teaching approaches with these young people.

Conclusion

The purpose of this chapter was to pick up a number of areas of study on which Len was working. In this chapter we focus on human flourishing. We took a broad perspective at the start of our piece and then homed in on particular aspects such as self-acceptance, purpose in life and eudaimonia in adolescence. There is no doubt that Len's fertile thinking and challenging views have been and still are influencing the work of the IPLA and the development of the concept of physical literacy.

References

Durden-Myers, E. J. & Whitehead, M. E. (2019a) Physical Literacy Across the World. Routledge: London.

Durden-Myers, E. J. & Whitehead, M. E. (2019b) Physical Literacy Across the World. Routledge: London.

Durden-Myers, E. J., Whitehead, M. E. & Pot, N. (2018) Physical Literacy and Human Flourishing. *Journal of Teaching in Physical Education*. 37, 3, p. 308-311.

Hooker, S. A., & Masters, K. S. (2016). Purpose in life is associated with physical activity measured by accelerometer. *Journal of Health Psychology*, 21(6), 962-971. DOI: https://doi.org/10.1177/1359105314542822

Hooker, S. A., Masters, K. S. & Park, C. L. (2018) A Meaningful Life Is a Healthily Life: A Conceptual Model Linking Meaning and Meaning Salience to Health. *Review of General Psychology: American Psychological Society*. Vol. 22, No. 11-24. DOI: http://dx.doi.org/10.1037/gpr0000115

George, L. S., & Park, C. L. (2016). Meaning in life as comprehension, purpose, and mattering: Toward integration and new research questions. *Review of General Psychology*, 20, 205–220. http://dx.doi.org/10.1037/ gpr0000077

George, L. S., & Park, C. L. (2013). Are meaning and purpose distinct? An examination of correlates and predictors. The Journal of Positive Psychology, 8, 365–375. http://dx.doi.org/10.1080/17439760.2013.805801

Martela, F., & Steger, M. F. (2016). The three meanings of meaning in life: Distinguishing coherence, purpose, and significance. *The Journal of Positive Psychology*, 11, 531–545. http://dx.doi.org/10.1080/17439760.2015.1137623

McKnight, P. E., & Kashdan, T. B. (2009). Purpose in life as a system that creates and sustains health and well-being: An integrative, testable theory. *Review of General Psychology*, 13, 242–251. http://dx.doi.org/ 10.1037/a0017152

Reeve, J. (2002). Self-determination theory applied to educational settings. In E.L. Deci & R.M. Ryan (Eds.), *Handbook of Self-Determination Research* (pp.183-203). Rochester, NY: The University of Rochester Press.

Ryan, R.M. and Deci, E.L. (2000b) 'Self-determination theory and the facilitation of intrinsic motivation, social development, and well-being', American Psychologist, 55(1), pp. 68-78.

Sen, A. (1994) Capability and well being. In Nusbaum, M. and Sen, A. eds *The quality of life* pp30-53 New York: Oxford Clarendon Press

Yalom, I. D. (1980). *Existential psychotherapy*. New York, NY: Basic Books.

4

Physical Literacy and the Primacy of Movement

Margaret Whitehead & Elizabeth Durden-Myers

Len was passionate about the inherent nature of movement and human development. In his research he came across the concept of the primacy of movement and championed its usefulness in substantiating the value of physical literacy. In relation to this he was also very interested in the neuroscientific research that related to the monist characteristics of human nature. In 2017 Len in collaboration with Elizabeth wrote the following article for PE Matters. After this article a reflection discusses the history of the move from dualism to monism and then how the primacy of movement, as highlighted to us by Len, has been significant in promoting the development of physical literacy.

Physical Literacy and the Primacy of Movement: Implications for Early Years.

Len Almond and Elizabeth Myers (2017) Physical Education Matters. 12(1) P19-21

Introduction

The concept of physical literacy is now being seriously considered across the globe and is becoming readily accepted in some countries worldwide. In particular over the last two years Canada, Australia and USA have seen a major interest in the notion of physical literacy with the publication of many new documents outlining its relevance. Within these countries physical literacy has become a new slogan for change, yet close analysis of these published documents supporting this position raise many questions regarding the understanding and interpretation of physical literacy. These new documents appear to be "old wine in a new bottle", a slogan, with a literacy label, that carries a message of respectability and significance. As Jurbala (2015) states, the concept of physical literacy can be employed to stimulate interest in participation in physical activity, but simply using the term physical literacy to stimulate interest whilst not fully understanding the concept has the potential to significantly damage the cause in the long run.

This recent and sustained interest from a number of countries worldwide has failed to recognise the conceptual framework that underpins the idea and many people simply see it as another name for physical education. In addition, there is a tendency to ignore a key aspect of children and young people's early development – the early years (babies to pre-school) – and the richness and depth of its relevance to future participation in culturally valued physical pursuits and optimal holistic development. The early years of life tend to be overlooked in policy documents, which appear to focus only on age 5-18. In addition, policy documents have been slow to recognise and respond to the UK Physical Activity Guidelines for Early Years and use them as a stimulus to reduce the scandalous case of 91% of young children failing to meet these guidelines. If this happened in other age groups, it would be seen as a major disaster. Another common misconception is that physical literacy is being interpreted as fundamental movement skills or purely physical competency, this failure to acknowledge the holistic nature of physical literacy demonstrates a clear lack of understanding essential in order to embody the concept in both policy and practice.

It is this position that has prompted a group of physical literacy advocates to focus their attention on the early years as a starting point for rethinking what it entails and using this work to build a progressive developmental framework for consideration within the profession. Therefore, this article will outline two areas that we need to explore in more detail – the primacy of movement and self-regulated learning.

Primacy of movement
The moving body is essentially how we experience the world in which the roles of perception and cognition play a big part. Self-movement is fundamental to life and its meaning. This is why we need to examine seriously how it is that babies who cannot walk or talk are able to become toddlers who can do both. From infancy we are all involved in self-organised and self-regulated learning in developing our movement capabilities and in the interrelationships of movement and meaning. Humans are attracted to movement from when we are born, we have a curiosity and a desire to

move, to not only make sense of the world but also to be able to interact and engage within it.

A child moves regularly to energise their life, build robustness, vitality and dynamism without which the child would not be able to sustain their very active lifestyle. The child's urge to move provides the very source of their capacity for optimal development and the enhancement of their health. This is a point in which all adults can learn a significant lesson – moving regularly generates a source for being energetic and a sense of vitality and dynamism. Also, the child's exploration of their world through movement and their efforts at making sense of this world provide the ideal platform for them to learn ways in which they can enrich their lives. This early development in relation to a child exploring the world through movement and enriching its life by moving is the very first step in developing a disposition whereby an individual may become physically literate. As Whitehead states (2010, p.13) *"[physically literate] individuals will have a well-established sense of self as embodied in the world. This together with an articulate interaction with the environment"*. Therefore, to be embodied is to have the capacity to interact effectively within and with the environment and make sense of oneself within ones' environment, this is something that is an innately human capacity as babies themselves without instruction begin their own embodied development by exploring the world through movement.

Neuroscience and the primacy of movement
This position is supported by recent thinking in neuroscience where Wolpert and Moravec's paradox have challenged current ideas.

Daniel Wolpert[1] (University of Cambridge) tells us:
"We have a brain for one reason and one reason only - that's to produce adaptable and complex movements. Movement is the only way we have of affecting the world around us...I believe that to understand movement is to understand the whole brain. And therefore it's important to remember when you are studying memory, cognition, sensory processing, they're there for a reason, and that reason is action".

Moravec's paradox is the discovery by artificial intelligence and robotics' researchers argue that, contrary to traditional assumptions, high-level reasoning requires very little computation, but low-level sensorimotor skills require enormous computational resources. The principle was articulated by Hans Moravec (whence the name of the paradox) and others in the 1980s.

Hans Moravec (1998) makes a very telling point when he explains that:

"Encoded in the large, highly evolved sensory and motor portions of the human brain is a billion years of experience about the nature of the world and how to survive in it. The deliberate process we call reasoning is, I believe, the thinnest veneer of human thought, effective only because it is supported by this much older and much powerful, though usually unconscious, sensorimotor knowledge. We are all prodigious olympians in perceptual and motor areas, so good that we make the difficult look easy. Abstract thought, though, is a new trick, perhaps less than 100 thousand years old. We have not yet mastered it. It is not all that intrinsically difficult; it just seems so when we do it."

When we examine the significance of these statements and consider how babies are able to learn to walk (and talk) through their own efforts because they move to explore, move to learn (and learn how to learn) and move to make sense of their world, it raises important questions that should challenge our conception of learning and acquisition of complex movement patterns and synergies in young children. Children have always explored their movement potential in different environments accessible to them and in this self-directed world they acquired behavioural flexibility within the freedoms they were allowed and the opportunity (without adults) to make decisions on their own. They are acquiring a movement capability that can enrich their lives, have a major impact on brain development and at the same time energised their lives. There is a unity of mind, body and emotions, very different from the dualism of Physical Development in the early years and Physical Education thinking.

From this position we would argue that there is an urgent need to absorb this thinking about the primacy of movement in children's lives and carefully consider its relevance in how we work with young children in early years settings. Babies, toddlers, pre-school and reception children represent a wide range of very different needs therefore we need to carefully consider how we build on children's emerging movement capabilities. This requires the development of environments that can facilitate the widening and enrichment of experiences and provide a platform for future developments in a wide range of contexts and the acquisition of complex movements, competences and meaningful experiences. As Whitehead (2010) argues movement competency can be facilitated by encouraging fluent interaction with a wide range of environments. Therefore, it is important we as adults consider what environments are made accessible and how we can encourage and facilitate fluent interaction for children within these range of environments.

What does this mean for Physical Education?

In the first instance, the primacy of movement is our starting point – a platform for development - from which we can begin the journey of creating a coherent and progressive range (across the whole school age) of experiences that open up infinite possibilities for engaging in purposeful physical pursuits with the ultimate aim of becoming physically literate and maintaining this disposition throughout life.

The early years provides the platform for five distinct areas to emerge and consider as potential sources for articulating a vision and sense of direction for physical literacy:

- Acquiring a Movement capability
- Valuable 'beings and doings'
- Culturally valued pursuits
- Energising lives
- Enriching lives

However, we need to pose a number of questions because these labels are relatively new to most people and there is a need to develop a clear understanding of:

- What do they entail?
- What are these 'beings and doings?
- What counts as culturally valued pursuits"
- What does energising lives imply?

How can we use these labels to identify relevant purposeful pursuits that are developmentally appropriate and attractive to young people's interests and have the potential to open up avenues for acquiring valuable 'beings and doings' and have great cultural depth and richness? In this process provide opportunities also for [people to energise their lives and enrich living.

Clearly, we cannot use secondary education as our guide as this needs to follow on and not instead be extrapolated down. There is a massive range of 'action possibilities' therefore to make informed choices requires an understanding of different phases of children's development and access to quality research that illustrates potential. In addition, it is vital that this process is centred on a shared understanding of the task and its outcomes and we avoid vested interests and uninformed preferences. We need to approach movement development from a divergent perspective whereby multiple possibilities are encouraged as individuals develop through an initially self-regulated process that is driven by a unique and individual curiosity for movement in a range of different environments.

Our preferences is to utilise the early years as a platform and undertake a project with reception and key stage 1 children and demonstrate what can be achieved. This is currently happening as part of a Physical Literacy project (phase 2 – reception and key stage 1) and its results will be made available early in this New Year. At this point phase 3 (key stage 2) will begin.

This brings us to the second part of this article. The primacy of movement is associated with a different way of learning from both primary and secondary education, which is mainly adult directed. At the present moment there are strong moves to ensure that reception and key stage 1 settings embrace this approach. Yet, the evidence from babies and young children suggests that other forms of learning are powerful and deserve serious consideration because they target other capabilities and attributes other that achievement in exam results and other forms of assessment based on a specified curriculum. An achievement-based curriculum based on tests creates new inequalities. Our diverse and changeable world is not like this and to succeed in this world requires attributes and capabilities that are not being catered for and largely ignored. This is a situation that required serious debate. We must stop viewing infancy from an adult perspective and understand what infants needs from their perspective in order to develop most effectively.

Self-regulated learning

Emerging from a consideration of the primacy of movement is the central driving force of children's self-regulated behaviour starting with their learning to move, moving to learn and moving for enjoyment, which is associated with a form of emotional attachment worth the experience. This behaviour represents a major aspect of their development, yet its significance tends to be overlooked. It forms the basis for empowerment, agency and independence.

If empowerment, responsibility, agency and independence are seen as important aspects of education then we need to seriously pose the question why is it that self-regulation from babies learning how to learn and being agents of their own development tends to be replaced by directed learning?

1. Babies learning to learn and how to move with purpose ⟶ self-regulated learning and responsibility ⟶ empowerment/agency and autonomy.

2. Facilitated learning
- Planned
- Provides a focus
- Sets up enriching environments
- Provides affordances and scaffolding opportunities
- Opportunities for observation of learning
- Opportunity to identify developmental delay
- Modelling/demonstration

3. Directed learning
What is the educational priority (as opposed to efficiency priority)? What is the value of each approach? What is essential in directed learning? Does it add an important dimension?

Advantages:
- Purposeful
- Focussed
- Modelling/demonstrating
- Scaffolding
- Encouraging
- Differentiated
- Further children's thinking

In both facilitated learning and directed learning, it is possible that practitioners may use only a narrow focus, display negative reactions to children's work, pose too many questions (at home children ask the questions whereas in settings it is the practitioners who ask the most questions), interfere with children's ideas, intervene to often and children become more passive.

What is the educational priority (as opposed to efficiency priority)? What is the value of each approach? What is essential in directed learning? Does it add an important dimension? It also isn't just babies that are able to learn important tasks without adult supervision or guidance. For example, the list below illustrates that young people are able to develop highly sophisticated capacities without adult supervision.

- Skate boarders and Long boarders
- Street-dance (with its multiple styles)
- Gamers playing electronic games
- Brazilian boys learning to play football
- Young people learn to play a musical instrument without being taught
- Games making or inventing their own games

We need to consider the gradual process of emerging empowerment, independence and agency as `central to how we nurture children's learning path. There is a need for an urgent debate about the role of self-regulated learning, facilitated learning and the relevance of direct learning in the process of children and young people's development. This discussion highlights a a somewhat larger question that asks what is the purpose of education? Directed learning can be possibly more aligned with pre-defined knowledge transfer whereas facilitated learning and self-regulated learning is more concerned with the exploration of the world and how to exist, respond, interact within it. This highlights the schooling vs education debate about whether we are teaching children for tests or adulthood, is education concerned with process or product?

Final thoughts

Human development in the early years is an incredibly intricate process. Previous dualistic efforts to understand this process has failed to appreciate the intricate and holistic nature of human development, therefore a more monist, inclusive and holistic approach is required to make sense of this significant time and understand how to encourage development during this time.

Central to development during the early years is movement, it is something that happens independently and innately without instruction. This highlights the primacy of movement as a tool for humans to make sense of, interact with and develop the movement capability essential in becoming effective adults. As educators we must embrace the notion of the primacy of movement and self-regulated learning and provide opportunities whereby meaningful interaction can take place naturally nurturing these innate behaviours.

Finally, we have introduced suggestions for developing a progressive programme based on an early year's platform for providing a new vision and sense of direction for physical literacy to encompass attributes and capacities that are currently neglected within physical education. These will be developed in more detail in a new article but by highlighting them now we are providing opportunities for practitioners to explore first of all their own interpretations of what these might entail and what are their implications for physical education.

References

Jurbala, P. (2015) What Is Physical Literacy, Really? *Quest*, 67:4, p367-383. DOI 10.1080/00336297.2015.1084341

Moravec, H. (1998). When will computer hardware match the human brain. Journal of Evolution and Technology, 1.

Whitehead, M. E. (Eds) (2010) *Physical Literacy: Throughout the Lifecourse*. London: Routledge.

[1] The important work of Wolpert can be seen on the following resources:
https://www.cam.ac.uk/research/news/the-man-with-the-golden-brain
https://www.cam.ac.uk/research/news/a-move-towards-understanding
https://www.ucl.ac.uk/news/slms/slms-news/neuroscience/12032902-queen-square-symposium-interview

[2] Self-regulation – We prefer this term at present because it implies more than self-directed.

On reflection

In the paper above Len and Elizabeth refer to monism and the unity between mind, body and emotion. They also mention the way that neuroscience is moving forward in understanding aspects of movement. In respect of working with early years children mention is made of the nature of physical development and the environments that can stimulate this progress. The pieces that follow pick up and develop aspects of these ideas. Firstly the growing acceptance of monism is narrated and then issues in early years development are considered.

Attitudes to dualism and monism

In his reading and writing Len was quick to pick up developments in relation to attitudes towards dualism and monism and the formulation of new theories such as 'Essentially

Embodied Existence' and 'Enactivism'. Monism lies at the heart of physical literacy and so it was important that we followed Len's lead and investigated these new ideas. This initiated a re-evaluation of the gradual move away from dualism towards monism in the Western world. The piece below charts these changes. Of necessity this reflection will have to be something of a whistle stop tour, however in and of itself this reflection has spurred us on to further study.

So, stimulated by Len's work we would like to share with readers our fascination with the role of human embodiment in the context of monism. Firstly, we refer to the earlier work of Sartre and Merleau-Ponty and then touch on the views of others such as Gibson, Gibbs, Clark, Leder, Polanyi and Lakoff and Johnson. Finally, we outline the most recent thinking of writers such as Maiese, Varela, Thompson and Rosch.

The roots of dualism can be found in the work of Descartes who asserted in the 19th century the famous quote 'I think, therefore I am'. This followed from his reasoning that the mind is the only element of himself about which he can be 100% certain. All other aspects of his human nature, including his embodiment, could be subject to doubt as to his being or reality. As a result of these views human embodiment was assigned to a subsidiary role in life. The only value of human embodiment was therefore, to ensure the continued existence of a working mind. Western cultures accepted this view as the truth and this opinion has become a real challenge to refute. For example, Leder (1990) expresses regret that the stranglehold of dualism has resulted in our being trapped inside a picture - a dualist picture that has limited our self-development and self-realisation. And Sheets-Johnston (1994) is forthright in her view that the Cartesian legacy has in essence reduced the body by turns to a static assemblage of parts and to a dumb show of movement.

However, there has been a growing scepticism concerning Descartes' view and dualism from philosophers, cognitive scientists and neuroscientists. For example, in the mid-20th century both Sartre and Merleau–Ponty (1962) cast doubt on dualism. Sartre (1957) wrote that 'For human reality, to be is to act' and Merleau-Ponty expressed the view that 'existence (is) a perpetual incarnation'. Both philosophers were in the vanguard of questioning dualism. A view expressed by many since the turn of the century is that far from the body relying on the mind to organise and plan embodied action, the mind relies on the human embodied dimension to develop a coherent understanding of, and relationship with, the world. For example, Burkitt (1999) writes that prior to the Cartesian 'I think', there is an 'I can' – a practical cogito which structures not only our relationship to the world, but also the ways in which we think about it. Similarly, Gibbs (2006) expresses the view that the traditional disembodied view of the mind is mistaken, because human cognition is fundamentally shaped by embodied experience.

Other thinkers have continued to develop this idea and argue that, not only are our mental capabilities reliant to a considerable extent on our embodied nature, but that human reality is significantly realised in the context of our embodied nature. Lakoff and Johnson (1999) write that for real human beings, the only realism is embodied realism and similarly Burkitt (1999) states that the basis of meaning is not to be located in the rules that order cognition, nor in the grammatical structure of linguistic sentences, but in the bodily pattern and order of active perceptions. Taking a related stance Leder (1990 p17) stresses that perception is not purely a cognitive exercise. He describes all human experience as incarnated and argues that what is perceived is always saturated by the implicit presence of motility.

Some writers propose that the body is at the core of existence. For example, Gill (2000 p45) explains that 'the body is the pivot point of human existence in the world' and again (p 97) that 'our body is the entry point into the world, the medium through and in which our reality is constituted'. Other thinkers do not go as far as this but underline the significant role played by human embodiment in the development of knowledge, rationality and language. These notions are not straightforward as the contributions made to these areas of human potential operate below the level of consciousness. Nietzsche (1885/1971 p61/62) signals this by writing that 'The body is a great intelligence… Behind your thoughts and feelings, my brother, stands a mighty commander, an unknown sage - he is called Self. He lives in your body, he is your body.' This position is developed at length by Polanyi who introduced the notion of tacit knowledge. This knowledge can be described as an appreciation and understanding of the way that our embodied nature retains, stores and uses extensive knowledge about the world and how, as humans we can interact effectively in our environment. This pre-reflective knowledge is a feature of the lived-body, although it is often associated with the living body.

The living body is that mode of the body which, as conscious humans, we can 'divorce' from ourselves and stand back from and describe, consider and train. The lived body is that mode of embodiment which Merleau-Ponty describes as passed over in silence, as we humans navigate and relate to the world around in everyday life. Gill (2000 p54) reports Polanyi's view that, because 'tacit knowledge is the anchor or tether for explicit knowing, it necessarily follows that we always know more than we can tell' or for that matter articulate.

This reference to Polanyi's work opens the next chapter of theories of monism, this being that tacit knowledge is the essential forerunner of explicit knowledge. For example, Gill (2000 p54) explains Polanyi's views which include the assertion that 'tacit knowing is logically prior to explicit knowing and hence is the fulcrum or axis from which the latter acquires its possibility and significance. This view is built on by Johnson (2007) and Lakoff and Johnson (1999). These writers argue that embodied experience is the root of rationality and language. It is worth quoting from the work of Lakoff and Johnson (1999 p82) to clarify this point. They write:

> The vast majority of our concepts, systematic mechanisms, and other cognitive structures operate for us automatically and unreflectively.... for the most part, our conceptual systems operate, as they must, beneath the level of consciousness. The body is crucial at this level, because all of our cognitive mechanisms and structures are grounded in patterns of bodily experience and activity, such as our spatial and temporal orientations, the patterns of our bodily movements, and the ways we manipulate objects. Mental images, image schemas, metaphors, metonymies, concepts, and inference patterns are all tied, directly or indirectly, to these bodily structures of our sensori-motor activities.

Lakoff and Johnson (1999) also go to great lengths to explain how language and rationality depend on embodied pre-reflective experience. As explained in Whitehead (2010) they argue 'that concepts such as *up*, *down*, *above*, *below*, *near* and *far* are not grasped until the corresponding interaction with the world via our embodied dimension has been experienced. And again, far from aspects of movement appreciation being foreign to our language, our speech is imbued with movement metaphors. Individuals talk of being *weighed down* with responsibilities, having *close* friends, feeling *down* when they are depressed and describing a colleague's understanding of a subject as *way ahead* of their own. All the words in italics are metaphors based on movement experiences. Others who support the foundations of language in embodied interaction with the world include Nathan in De Vega (2008 p412) who wrote 'Everything in language comprehension is embodied, not only the meaning of the words, but also the representations of words themselves.' In addition, there is a good deal of writing about the way that human embodiment is the ground for many aspects of human nature. For example, discussions abound concerning, inter alia: Rationality, Reason, Conceptualisation, Understanding can be found in Weiss and Harber (1999); Cognition in Varela et al (1993 p172); Meaning in Nathan in De Vega (2008 p425); Perception in Leder (1990 p17); Mindedness and Sense Making in Maiese (2016).

As can be seen there has been a gradual acceptance of the involvement of the human embodied dimension in life, not as a subsidiary adjunct but as a key player in life as we know it. It is clear that the position now is not 'How can the mind and the body be in contact - but rather how can the mind and the body be disentangled from each other? In these terms, dualism is history and has been sequentially disproved by the relentless search to understand the nature of the embodied human being.

The next development builds from these views and sees the creation of what Claxton (2010 p4) describes as an 'exciting new hybrid science' of embodied cognition. De Vega (2008) clarifies this by explaining that *embodied cognition* is a position in cognitive science and the philosophy of mind, emphasising the role that the body plays in shaping the mind. Furthermore, he explains that *embodied embedded cognition* is a position in cognitive science stating that intelligent behaviour emerges out of the interplay between brain, body and world.

This new hybrid science builds from the work of philosophers, cognitive scientist and neuroscientists and reinforces how monism is supported by complimentary notions such as having an 'essentially embodied existence' and in concepts such as 'enactivism'. Valera et al (1993) explain that the use of the term enactivism emphasises the growing conviction that cognition is not the representation of a pre-given world by a pre-given mind but is rather the enactment of a world and a mind on the basis of a history of the variety of actions that a being in the world performs. Clark entitled his book *Supersizing the Mind* (2001) and argues that cognition should be considered as permeating the human organism as a whole. In support of these views Maiese (2016) refers to the 'Essentially embodied self' and Archer (2000) asserts that being human is characterised by the primacy of practice over consciousness and thought.

One of the outcomes of the accumulation of developing thinking about the nature of humans is the dismissal of a second form of dualism. This dualism relates to the general understanding that the environment and the individual as two 'free standing phenomena'. With the recurring assertion that humans create themselves as they interact with the world and that the environment 'comes into being' as a result of our interaction it can be argued that the environment and the individual are totally dependent on each other. In this respect Lewontin (in Varela 1993 p198) writes 'The environment is not an autonomous process but a reflection of the biology of the species. Just as there is no organism without an environment there is no environment without an organism'. This is endorsed by Varela (1993 p139) who expresses the view that 'This shift requires that we move away from the idea of the world as independent and extrinsic to the idea of the world as inseparable' from human embodied processes.' This notion brings us to the next topic of discussion around the importance of issues related to the primacy of movement and enabling environments.

The primacy of movement, physical literacy and enabling environments

Len drew the IPLA's attention to the primacy of movement as a concept that could support and develop the rationale for the importance of physical literacy. Two areas are discussed in more detail, firstly, the relationship between physical literacy, the primacy of movement, monism and embodiment and secondly, the primacy of movement and enabling environments.

Len through his exploration of the primacy of movement highlights how humans are essentially embodied and no more so is this evident than in the early stages of life where our innate intentionality compels us to explore the world through movement. Intentionality can be described as the innate human urge to relate to and be stimulated by our environment. In the early years these two areas can be linked to ontogenic development which occurs as a child matures as a result of genetics and can be considered as an outcome of nature. And phylogenetic development which occurs as a result of learning which is often environmentally dependant and an outcome of nurture.

In the early years there is a reciprocal relationship between ontological physical development and learning that supports physical competence. Growth opens up new possibilities for developing phylogenetic physical competence while increasing competence and therefore stimulates growth. In this way, at this stage, development and learned competence go hand in hand. Taking into consideration this reciprocal developmental relationship providing environments and experiences that stimulate and promote growth are essential. These enabling environments provide individuals with the opportunity to explore their embodied and movement potential through physical activity. When physical activity experiences are purposeful, engaging, relevant and rewarding they can be considered as meaningful. Meaningful movement and physical activity experiences are frequently referred to as being important in fostering physical literacy. Meaningful experiences could be characterised as opportunities to develop and nurture the motivation, confidence, physical competence and knowledge and understanding required in order to engage in sustained physical activity for life.

Creating meaningful movement experiences that enable growth and development can also be connected with the development of affordances. Affordances are generally described as opportunities for action in the environment. There is a sense in which features in the world 'call for' a particular response. They invite involvement and engagement with the human embodied capability. In other words, features/objects present themselves as 'climbable' or 'requiring a certain amount of power or care in their handling'. Affordances are endowed on features in the world on account of having been involved in previous interaction. Once there has been contact with a feature, this experience becomes part of memory and is drawn on in future encounters. Affordances are not self-generating characteristics they arise from previous interaction.

The concept of affordances was initially proposed by Gibson (1979) but has been picked up and analysed by other writers (e.g. Sanders 1999) who proposes that individuals only respond to perceived affordances in situations that they choose to be the most desirable. Rietveld and Kiverstein (2014) argue for the need to widen the scope of affordances from a focus principally on features of the world to include all aspects of the socio-cultural context. It is interesting to note that the notion of affordances was an element of Merleau-Ponty's work (1968). He created the concept of The Chiasm to describe the intertwining of the human being with the world. In a sense this concept brings together the existential notion of interaction between the individual with the world, the embodied perceptual potentialities of the human, the characteristics of the world and indeed the exploration of affordances. It is a cycle that cannot be taken apart, as that which is understood about the world has been generated by characteristics of the embodied human being. We are through and through beings in the world and of the world, and the world we inhabit is the world we create.

Len was passionate about understanding innate human nature and how this can be harnessed and nurtured by creating conducive and enabling environments. The IPLA has developed an early years working group with Len's thinking and writing continuing to inform their work. Many of the members of this group were introduced to us by Len and they are intent on investigating the issues that Len highlighted for our attention.

Summary

This chapter has considered a range of issues raised by Len that arose on account of his interest in the primacy of movement. Important here are the holistic nature of the individual and the way that relationships with the environment are key to development. It would seem that there have been great strides in understanding the way that human beings draw on many of their capabilities to establish a rich and rewarding life.

There is an irony in the way that the detailed explanations that scientists are formulating issue in ever more new challenges. Having made a strong case for the importance of the role of human embodiment in much of life and beginning to understand the way that body and mind are mutually interdependent, the conundrum of the relationship between the lived body and the living body has reared its head. This is referred to as the mind-body-body problem. Maiese (2016 p5) attempts to unravel this and writes 'When we examine the lived body, our focus is on phenomenology; and when we examine the living body, the focus is on neurobiological processes of self-organisation and adaptive self- regulation. However, there is no sharp division between the lived body and the living body and this is because lived experience and sense-making (cognition) are essentially embodied, enactive, and rooted in the dynamics of certain types of living bodies.' There is still a great deal of work to do to understand the complexity of human life in all its richness. We guess that Len would have relished the challenge to think this through.

Len was aware that we live in exciting and changing times. In his diligence he identified many of these ongoing developments. He was fond of challenging quotations so we end with four, which have emerged from following up his ideas.

'Man is an autopoetic being. That is a being that creates itself' (Maiese, 2016 p14).

'So the self is nothing more and nothing less than a dynamic, minded, living, essentially embodied process – in effect a life form or a form of life' (Maiese, 2016 p xiii).

'The common upshot of all these arguments, then, is a kind of principled body centrism, according to which the presence of humanlike minds depends quite directly on the possession of a human-like body' (Clark, 2011 p155).

'Philosophy itself also turns out to be very different from what we thought before. Instead of being an activity of pure reason, it is an activity of an embodied reason' (Lakoff and Johnson, 1999 p540).

References

Almond, L. & Myers, E. J. (2017) Physical Literacy and the Primacy of Movement. *Physical Education Matters.* 12(1) P19-21.

Archer, M.S. (2000) *Being Human. The Problem of Agency.* Cambridge University Press.

Burkitt, I. (1999) *Bodies of Thought: Embodiment, Identity and Modernity.* London: Sage.

Clark, A. (2001) *Supersizing the Mind.* Oxford University Press.

Claxton, G., Lucas, B. & Webster, R. (2010) Bodies of Knowledge. Edge Foundation. London.

Descartes, R. (1970) Philosophical Letters. trans ed A.Kenny. Clarendon Press Oxford.

De Vega, M., Glenberg A.M. & Graesser. A.C. (eds) (2008) Symbols and Embodiment. Oxford University Press.

Gibbs, R.W. (2006) *Embodiment and Cognitive Science.* Cambridge University Press.

Gibson, J.J. (1979) *The Ecological Approach to Visual Perception.* Boston: Houghton Mifflin

Gill, J.H. (2000) *The Tacit Mode.* New York:State University of New York Press.

Johnson, M. (2007) *The Meaning of the Body.* The University of Chicago Press.

Lakoff, G. and Johnson M. (1999) *Philosophy in the Flesh.* Basic Books. Perseus Group. Basic Books.

Leder, D. (1990) The Absent Body. Chicago and London: The University of Chicago Press.

Lewontin, R. in Valera, F. J., Thompson, E. & Rosch, E. (1993) *The Embodied Mind.* The MIT Press Cambridge, Massachusetts. London, England.

Maiese, M. (2016). *Embodied selves and divided minds.* Oxford, UK: Oxford University Press.

Merleau-Ponty, M. (1962) *Phenomenology of Perception,* trans. C.Smith. London.:Routledge & Kegan Paul.

Merleau-Ponty, M. (1968) *The Visible and the Invisible.* USA: Northwestern University Press.

Nathan, M.J. in De Vega, M., Glenberg A.M. & Graesser. A.C. (eds) (2008) Symbols and Embodiment. Oxford University Press.

Nietzsche, F. (1885) *Thus Spake Zarathustra*. Trans. R.J. Hollingdale (1971) Penguin Classics.

Polanyi, M. in Gill J.H. (2000) The Tact Mode. *Michael Polanyi's Postmodern Philosophy*. State Univeristy of New York Press.

Rietveld, E. & Kiverstein, J. (2014) A rich landscape of affordances. *Ecological Psychology* 26: 325- 352.

Rosch in Valera, F. J., Thompson, E. & Rosch, E. (1993) *The Embodied Mind*. The MIT Press Cambridge, Massachusetts. London, England.

Sanders, J. (1999) Affordances: An Ecological Approach to First Philosophy. in Weiss, G. and Harber, H.F. (1999) *Embodiment. The Intersections of Nature and Culture*. New York and London: Routledge.

Sartre, J-P. (1957) *Being and Nothingness*, trans. H.Barnes. London: Methuen

Sheets-Johnstone, M. (1992) (ed)Giving the body its due. Albany : State University of New York Press.

Thompson in Valera, F. J., Thompson, E. & Rosch, E. (1993) *The Embodied Mind*. The MIT Press Cambridge, Massachusetts. London, England.

Valera, F. J., Thompson, E. & Rosch, E. (1993) *The Embodied Mind*. The MIT Press Cambridge, Massachusetts. London, England.

Weiss, G. and Harber, H.N. (1999) *Perspectives on Embodiment*. London: Routledge.

Whitehead, M.E. (2010) *Physical Literacy throughout the Lifecourse*. London: Routledge.

5

Almond, L. and Ezzeldin, K. (2103). Are Fundamental Movement Skills the Foundation of Physical Education? *Physical Education Matters*. Autumn, 2013

Commentary by Kath Ezzeldin

Throughout his career Len aimed to inspire teachers at all levels to teach high quality lessons which would enthuse and engage their pupils, and later in his career he became particularly interested in how Physical Education is taught to younger children. Len questioned the educational validity of teaching fundamental skills out of context and challenged the links some have made between acquiring movement skills and physical literacy. He called for a framework to support those working with young children to promote greater levels of physical activity. In this paper we bring together Len's thinking on how young children acquire and should be taught movement skills within physical education in their first years in school.

Are Fundamental Movement Skills the foundation of Physical Education?

Len Almond & Kath Ezzeldin

Introduction
The internet has provided a wonderful opportunity to find out what other countries are doing in Physical Education as well as access to wonderfully produced resources. However, this access has meant that we pick and choose what we like and we internalise a common language thinking that we know what it means. This has happened with fundamental movement skills and as a result many (if not all) English-speaking countries have adopted it as a central focus.

In this article we shall attempt to highlight some problems with this approach. There is a vast and growing literature that makes it difficult to provide at this stage a comprehensive review therefore we have identified some key issues surrounding the complexity of this topic. We hope to stimulate a more informed debate and an understanding of what fundamental movement skills have to offer physical education.

Fundamental Movement Skills in Physical Education and Physical Literacy

The new English National Curriculum Physical Education programmes of study (Department of Education, 2013) released in September proposes in the subject content for key stage 1 that:

"Pupils should develop fundamental movement skills, become increasingly competent and confident and access a broad range of opportunities to extend their agility, balance and coordination, individually and with others" (p.199).

A new draft Australian Curriculum, Health and Physical Education: Foundation to Year 10 draft[1] has been released for consultation. One of the strands is 'Movement and Physical Activity' and within this strand it proposes also that:

"The content in this key idea lays the important early foundations of play and fundamental movement skills. It also builds upon these to support lifelong participation and enhanced performance in physical activities" (p.7).

The Australian proposal clearly associates fundamental movement skills (FMS) with promoting lifelong participation together with enhanced performance.

These two countries illustrate exactly what many countries are now appearing to recognise. They see fundamental movement skills as central to physical education and the foundation for competent and confident participation in a range of physical activities. However, this acceptance appears to be an uncritical assumption in all the English-speaking sources that we have read, that the case has been made and there is no need for further debate. Such an assumption needs to be carefully considered and should be open to serious debate. Nevertheless, is there any evidence that clearly establishes that the fundamental movement skills model is the best approach for physical education?

FMS are now seen as the building blocks of long term athlete development and this is can be seen in a factsheet compiled by Sheelagh Quinn for Coaching Ireland (website www.coachingireland.com) on Fundamental Movement Skills and Physical Literacy' where she says that:

"To develop physical literacy a child should first master the fundamental movement skills. Having these skills is an essential part of enjoyable participation and a lifelong interest in an active lifestyle. Physical literacy is the foundation of the LISPA framework and provides children with the tools they need to take part in a wide range of physical activity and sports, much in the same way as numeracy and literacy skills prepare a child for a life of work or study" (p.4).

This quotation illustrates also that Ireland like many English-speaking countries appears to have made a link between fundamental movement skills and physical literacy. A new resource and training programme in England called Start to Move: developing physical literacy aimed at 4-7 year olds makes a clear association with fundamental movement skills. Also, one of their aims is to "teach PE using the same approach used in literacy i.e. learn an alphabet of movement skills, combine them into movement words (multi-skills), and develop movement stories (e.g. a 2v2 game)".

Is this really what literacy in physical literacy means? A careful reading of the literature associated with physical literacy would cast serious doubts about this claim This raises a contentious point because the Start to Move understanding of literacy is at odds with the various meanings of literacy in debates around spiritual literacy, health literacy, economic literacy, media literacy and many others. Frisch et al (2011 undertook a critical analysis of different examples of literacy and Sørensen et al (2012) identified different dimensions of literacy and they provide a very different perspective.

Canadian Sport for Life (CS4L) is a movement to improve the quality of sport and physical activity in Canada. It links sport, education, recreation and health and aligns community, provincial and national programming. Within this development they identify a seven-stage training, competition and recovery pathway that guides an individual's experiences in sport and physical activity from infancy through all phases of adulthood.

The literature on FMS is associated with sport and long term athlete development in Canada and they argue that children need to acquire these skills if they are to progress to sports or activities promoting active living. This separation of sports and 'activities for active living' is problematic. It ignores the point that dance or adventurous activities are just as disciplined a purposeful physical pursuit as any sport and can be just as enriching and fulfilling. In addition, the separation does not acknowledge that sport can also be an active living pursuit.

An examination of the Canadian resources shows that considerable investment has been made in providing comprehensive resources and support structures. Two of these resources reveal some interesting observations. The Canadian Gymnastics resource says that the roots of all gymnastics originate in the body's fundamental movement patterns and they go on to identify 7 movement patterns. This resource deviates from the others by using patterns in the place of skills and implies a different way of thinking that needs to be explored. The Canadian Swimming resource on the other hand in a section on FUNdamentals proposes that:

"The development of a comprehensive repertoire of movement and sport skills – otherwise known as physical literacy - should be considered a requirement for the early stages of sport involvement for a young child. The skills to be developed are the ABC's (Agility, Balance, Coordination, Speed), RJT (running, jumping, throwing), KGB (kinesthetics, gliding, buoyancy, striking with a body part) and CKs (catching, kicking, striking with an implement). In order to develop basic movement literacy, participation in as many sports as possible is encouraged."

This is clearly recognising that a broad based programme of positive experiences in sports is important and by using the word FUNdamentals they are striving to ensure that fun is highlighted. Recognition of the need for a broad based programme is reinforced in a recent Sport England report on how to develop a sporting habit for life (Sport England, 2012).

In our description of how fundamental movement skills is portrayed in the literature, it is quite clear that it is associated with promoting a young person's pathway into sport and it is seen as the central organising concept for physical education. In this process, however, the emphasis on sport detracts from other key aspects of a young person's and appears to marginalise dance and adventurous activities.

We would now like to address a number of concerns that can so easily arise when ideas in well-prepared resources are translated into actual practice. Our concerns focus on the way that teachers pick and choose ideas and absorb them into their practice in what may seem to be an uninformed process. In picking and choosing whatever they like, activities become a resource box that one can pull out and use at any time. However, the use of such a resource can be seen as ideas just to occupy young people and the idea of progression and addressing individual needs is neglected because 'one size fits all'. In our experience this often happens especially when continuing professional development is dropped because there is no money in these days of austerity.

For example, the list of fundamental movement skills in three categories creates a special problem because to some teachers or practitioners the list can be seen as a set of 'I Can' challenges that can be taught in isolation and can be seen as a ready-made physical education programme. In the hands of inexperienced teachers, however enthusiastic and eager they are, there is a potential risk that they will use lists of isolated techniques as the only basis for their teaching. In such an approach, they can be drawn easily into a pedagogy of command, control and correct and they risk a failure to acknowledge that children have different needs, respond in different ways and have different starting points for learning. Would teachers in England see this approach as a representation of a quality physical education programme? It would be interesting to see what kind of responses they make.

Advocates of fundamental movement skills may respond by saying that this is a miss-representation of what they are trying to achieve. Nevertheless, this position does highlight a potential danger for many inexperienced teachers. For them, it provides clarity about what they have to teach and a list of what they have to cover and many teachers will simply be grateful that they have access to ideas that they can put into practice. However, will this approach provide a range of positive experiences for all young people? It highlights also the possibility that the teaching approach in these circumstances will be didactic and negate creative and self-directed learning.

There is a further problem that is highlighted specifically in any discussion on fundamental movement skills. When advocates of FMS focus on skills, they are making a basic error. This is an error that has become common practice because skills and techniques are seen as synonymous and interchangeable. Skills in games represent the ability to apply techniques in game situations and demonstrate intelligent performance. In games we want children to be technically competent and skilful in game situations and to love playing. A focus on isolated techniques and drills is unlikely to develop skilful and intelligent performance in a game and it also unlikely to promote an emotional attachment to a game. In teaching games for understanding (TGfU) the basis of this approach was to avoid such practices that can be associated with turning off many children and can easily deteriorate into mindless practices.

In a different sport such as track and field athletics, are fundamental movement skills are seen as a basic working model (a technical model) that young people are able to use in competitions or to enhance their personal performance. Teachers may well modify specific events to represent the adult form and reduce the demands of the event and as a result make them more accessible to young people, but do they provide also a working model to enable them to perform? Are fundamental movement skills different from the idea of a basic working model in athletics, or fundamental movement patterns in gymnastics? These kind of questions open up a debate about how we represent sports to young people and what kind of a pedagogy is needed. A debate that does not seem to penetrate the commitment to fundamental movement skills. In such a debate it would be useful to hear the views of the dance world as well as those in adventurous outdoor pursuits. Are fundamental movement skills essential for people who walk many miles in open countryside and hills at weekends and holidays?

The Sport England report on how to develop a sporting habit for life (Sport England, 2012) identifies emotional engagement or attachment to playing a sport as an important ingredient of developing a sporting habit. We would argue that this is just as significant for young people who dance or those who take part regularly in adventurous pursuits. In fact, to our mind, this concept of emotional engagement may well be more significant that learning fundamental movement skills in schools or sports club.

Conclusion
The Physical Education profession needs to consider carefully whether fundamental movement skills represent the core and the very essence of what they want young people to experience. It does appear that fundamental movement skills are more concerned with sport and developing a commitment to a sporting pathway from the early years to adulthood. In this case, dance, adventurous activities and purposeful physical pursuits that promote active living need to make their case clearly and more cogently and identify other models for developing a commitment to pursuits that can enrich their lives and become an absorbing interest that rewards and fulfils as well as provides avenues for the enhancement of human potential.

Fundamental movement skills have become a central focus for many new developments but a focus that carries with it a neglect of pedagogy. There is little discussion or recommendations to enable teachers to recognise the educational validity of this focus. When there is little opportunity for continuing professional development in times of austerity, websites offering ideas for fundamental movement skills may well obscure pedagogical concerns and reduce teaching to organising learning in rows with children waiting their turn and a 'one-size fits all' approach.

In writing this article, we hope to stimulate a debate about the very essence of facilitating learning and what practices will promote a love of being physically active in a variety of purposeful physical pursuits and maintaining a commitment and interest in them for many years. To further this debate we welcome criticisms, amendments and new perspectives on our thinking concerning fundamental movement skills.

References

Department of Education (2013) The national curriculum in England
    Key stages 1 and 2 framework document.
Frisch, A-L. Camerini, L. Diviani, N. and Schulz, P.J. (2012) Defining and measuring health literacy: how can we profit from other literacy domains? Health Promot. Int. 27 (1): 117-126.
Sørensen, K. Van den Broucke, S. Fullam, J. Gerardine Doyle, G., Jürgen Pelikan, J. Slonsk, Z. and Brand, H. (2012) Health literacy and public health: A systematic review and integration of definitions and models. BMC Public Health 12:80.
Sport England (2012) How to Develop a Sporting Habit for Life: Final report.

[1] This can be accessed at:
www.consultation.australiancurriculum.edu.au

6

Purposeful Physical Play in the Early Years: a missing ingredient

Len Almond & Kim Lambden

Introduction

In the Early Years Framework, Physical Development is recognised as a Prime Area and practitioners have a responsibility to generate appropriate opportunities for meeting its requirements. Yet the term Physical Development has a very restrictive meaning because it refers specifically to the physical side of children's development and adopts a dualist perspective that separates the physical from cognitive development and sees them as separate products of education. In addition, its focus in the Early Learning Goals is far too narrow and to fails to address the significance of movement in a young child's life. Expressive movement, deep play, outdoor challenges and opportunities to enrich the lives of children are not fully recognised. The major omission is the absence of recommendations to address the UK Physical Activity Guidelines for the Early Years issued by the Chief Medical Officer in 2011. Managers and practitioners in early years settings are unaware of its publication or its significance and because of this they do not see its relevance for children's health and it is not recognised as a priority.

These issues have to be addressed because Physical Development is too narrow as a guide to practice in early years setting. We need to explain an alternative way of thinking. So this article will outline a number of ideas that need to underpin the way that early years setting think about movement literacy and the development of a movement capability.

The Primacy of Movement

Physical Development is too narrow an interpretation of the EYFS Prime area. It separates the physical from the mind: yet the recent work in embodied cognition would see them as inseparable.

Instead of focusing purely on the physical we need to understand that the moving body is essentially how we experience the world. How is it that babies who cannot walk or talk can learn to do so without a manual? Is there something intrinsic in this capacity that we ought to nurture and nourish? All babies have a 'seeking drive' so once a baby is born they are driven to move; they move to explore the world and they move to make sense of it (their intentionality) stimulated by curiosity.

The moving body (whose central role is perception and cognition) is essentially how we have direct contact with the world around us and make sense of it all and this has a major impact on the development of the mind. It is fundamental to life and its meaning. We must not destroy this because meaning is central to life and children learn to value it through their own exploration.

The 'early years' is the period when movement (not physical development), language and emotional development are inseparable and as such represent prime areas. The development of the child is an integrated process that requires a recognition and understanding of what this process requires.

But what does a focus on 'moving,' 'moving to explore the world' and 'moving to make sense of it' entail? The focus is about purposeful physical play that provides opportunities for the young child to energise their life (working towards optimal development) and enrich it with new discoveries that open up the world and helps them to make sense of it. Children may not need a manual but adults and practitioners need to remove obstacles (like prolonged inertia and restraint) to a baby's potential for moving. They can facilitate opportunities for the baby to 'move to explore' and 'move to learn'. As a consequence we need to be asking what sort of experiences enable young children to make sense of their world and facilitate their movement capabilities so that we can develop this process. The idea of movement capabilities within movement literacy is an important concept for the early years.

This approach needs to extend beyond babies to toddlers and children in pre-school because we need to recognise its power and the significance of the practitioner's role. It is about facilitating learning not directing learning because the practitioner or outside trainer wants the children to do something their way. This is why we believe that there is a need to go beyond the narrow focus of Physical Development and provide a more comprehensive vision of what can be achieved.

Addressing the inactivity and sedentary behaviour of young children

First of all, we need to recognise the importance of movement itself that enables optimal development and facilitates vitality and dynamism and energises living: children need to move much more frequently and more energetically.

91% of children in the early years fail to meet the Chief Medical Officer's recommendations in the UK Physical Activity Guidelines (HSE, 2015). It would appear that young children are not experiencing enough physical activity in their lives and this, coupled with the alarming figures of unproductive sedentary behaviour due to too much restraint and prolonged sitting, means that action needs to be taken. (If young children are getting so little physical activity in their lives coupled with the alarming figures of unproductive sedentary behaviour because there is far too much restraint and prolonged sitting in their lives, we need to take action.) This state of affairs has to be addressed because the Physical Development Prime Area is inadequate in this respect.

This failure means that we need a stimulus for urgent action in all settings. We suggest that settings should be supported by establishing what we call the 25% rule as a form of targeted provision and clear guidance is provided about what needs to be done to ensure that they can aspire to meet this aspiration.

This would entail introducing at least 45 minutes of purposeful physical play in the three hours of children's attendance at an EY setting. This is based on 25% of a child's waking day (three hours) and 25% of the recommended 180 minutes of daily physical activity outlined in the UK Guidelines. Thus, in the 3 hours statutory provision in a setting we would like all practitioners to make available opportunities for 45 minutes of purposeful physical play each day.

If children are able to take part in 45 minutes of purposeful physical play within 3 hours at a setting, this leaves parents with 135 minutes in which to satisfy the UK Guidelines of 180 minutes. This is currently not being addressed because many parents believe that it is not their responsibility[1] to get their children more active: that is seen as the job of the setting. In this case, we will never reduce the 91% of children who fail to meet the UK Guidelines or make in-roads into the obesity/overweight issue. This is an urgent problem because only practitioners in early years settings can currently reach parents and help them to understand the need for children to continue to be more active when they are away from the setting. We have to find other ways of engaging with parents so that they can be central to increasing levels of participation. This is the reality of health promotion in the early years because public health has not fully recognised the need to reach parents as well as practitioners in this age group and put in place a programme to meet these needs.

Furthermore, we need to engage with parents to increase levels of health promoting physical activity needs and address the way in which some parents (such as "helicopter" and "lawnmower" parents) socialise their children into sedentary behaviour and inactivity, inhibiting the development of movement capabilities and movement literacy. In addition, some parents try to influence practice in settings preferring their children to stay indoors and to be engaged in formalised learning in preparation for school: once again inhibiting a child's optimal development. This socialisation process breeds dependency, a lack of responsibility and poor self-control. Many practitioners fully recognise this problem and we have seen many examples of excellent work to address it but it must become a priority for all settings.

Enriching Children's Lives

Secondly, from our experience over many years it has become increasingly obvious that children's experience of purposeful physical play is limited and there is no conception of an "entitlement" within movement literacy and purposeful physical play that all children in early years settings should have access to. Because we do not use the word "entitlement" for all children, key areas of experience are being neglected in the early years and a child's movement literacy is substantially reduced. For examples, many children are given little opportunity for outdoor challenges and deep play, the vast scope of expressive movement and dance, running in open spaces, playing games with rules to name just a few. If there is no concept of entitlement important experiences are overlooked or simply ignored and a narrow set of experiences tale their place.

An entitlement needs to address the depth and richness of opportunities that should be available to all children. This means that we need to have a conception of the different domains of purposeful physical play (that generate unique experiences and outcomes) and provide insight into what affordances they can generate.

In our analysis of the research literature and the books that have been written about the value of purposeful physical play a number of specific areas of experience or domains emerge. For us, they are:

- Exercise Play
- Object Play
- Expressive Movement and Dance
- Outdoor challenges and experiences in natural environments

Each one of these domains contains a wealth of action possibilities for purposeful physical play that practitioners can stimulate by creating enabling environments and understanding what they can generate. Two of these domains are associated with Specific Areas in the EYFS Early Learning Goals but they have a very strong association with purposeful physical play.

We also need to consider how we can enrich children's experiences in ways that expand their capabilities and enable them to learn to value them. There is much to address here and each domain or area of experience needs to be spelled out in much more detail (Almond and Lambden, 2016) so practitioners can be aware of their importance and recognise what can be made available: this requires careful thought about the nature of these experiences that can open up a world of challenge and meaning. However, the richness of this "potential" can only be sampled by practitioners because there is such a huge set of possibilities. It is in this spirit that we have identified the idea of four domains and recognise that practitioners will need support in identifying a sample of "possibilities" that they can implement.

Much work has been done to develop this idea and provide very practical ways of putting them into practice (In the East Midlands and London Boroughs) and this needs to be more widely available and accessible in forms that practitioners can relate to.

Independence, responsibility, the learning of self-control and the drive for self-directed learning.

A child's exploration of the world needs to build on the need for growing independence and responsibility, the learning of self-control and the drive for self-directed learning. However, there is a problem that appears to mitigate these aspirations.

When people speak of a need for a balance between self-directed learning and structured learning (by which they mean adult-led and adult directed learning) it is clear that they do not have an understanding of what they are saying. This can easily be seen when outside trainers come into a setting to deliver a session of physical play: these are often people with a sports or coaching background, and their focus is usually on the learning of specific fundamental sport skills (as products) in a very structured and formal manner. They tend to neglect self-directed learning because of their more structured trainer-led approach and their understanding of the need for children's growing independence and taking responsibility together with self-control is minimal.

In many cases there is little energetic physical play because their organisational skills are inappropriate for little ones and we know that children are less active when directed. Consequently, this more structured approach has a limited role in the early years. Dance or movement specialists and people working on play in the outdoors tend to have a different perspective and a better understanding of purposeful play and how it can be presented.

The practitioner and outside-trainer need a much deeper understanding of how to create enabling environments that can stimulate a range of affordances and generate a multitude of action possibilities. In addition, they need to be aware of how they can scaffold the learning process with an enabling attitude. In this way they give the child the freedom(s) to learn and recognise their need for independence. This is an important process that can foster self-directed learning, a growing independence and a love of being active. But first of all, as many practitioners have little understanding of the primacy of movement and its role in a child's development, they need to be supported in how to achieve this.

A very Practical problem.

We need to acknowledge a very practical problem that has hindered the development of purposeful physical play throughout the early years. Very few practitioners have had any form of practical experience of what they could do in an early years setting to promote purposeful physical play and Physical Development. In a survey conducted by the BHF National Centre (2011) only 1% of practitioners had received minimum training in physical development or purposeful physical play for their initial early years qualification. In this year alone, out of 14 training days only 2 people said that they had received some training and that was based in primary schools. As a result, it is little wonder that there is a lack of practical knowledge and understanding of what practitioners can do. In the early years it is very clear that there is:

- No clear Vision of what could be done.
- No sense of direction of what needs to be done
- No sense of what needs to be planned and organised
- No Focus on what can be achieved

In order to address the above there is an urgent need to explore first of all, what kind of vision and sense of direction is needed for the early years and secondly, how we can help them to make sense of planning needs and identify an appropriate focus. There have been some valuable attempts to address this but
they are not readily available to a wider audience so this is an important task to achieve.

Conclusion

In this article we have tried to highlight the inadequacy of the Physical Development Prime area and propose that it needs to be rethought in the light of the following factors:

- The primacy of movement in children's development
- Addressing the inactivity and sedentary problem
- Enriching children's lives
- The promotion of independence, responsibility, the learning of self-control and the drive for self-directed learning for all children.

These factors illustrate the need for urgent action by policy makers, government officers, national associations, local authorities and boroughs as well as early years managers and practitioners.

We believe that the focus for purposeful physical play in the early years should enable children to generate a personal resource that energises and enriches their lives. It should focus on movement literacy and the development of a movement capability so that children are ultimately able to make better sense of the world, recognise its potential, understand the importance of people and acquire attributes that enhance their perspective, cognition and empathy. The idea of creating a personal resource for living well through the development of a movement capability is a more positive way of thinking about health because its roots start in the early years.

[1] This is based on focus groups with parents. This is very disturbing and the issue needs to be seriously explored.

7

Health-Based Physical Education: The Journey from Early Rationale to Established Practice

Lorraine Cale, Sonia McGeorge & Jo Harris

Introduction

It is a privilege to contribute a chapter on Health-Based Physical Education (HBPE) which was a movement Len Almond was so committed to throughout his career. Whilst physical education's association with health is long standing, the 1980s saw renewed interest in health as a key objective of the subject and as 'a solution to the problem of improving the healthy lifestyles of children' (Tinning, 2010: 177). In the United Kingdom (UK), the renewed interest at this time was very much instigated by Almond who was a leading advocate and instrumental in driving developments in HBPE. Through his work, Almond achieved numerous positive outcomes for the benefit of researchers, physical education and health practitioners and young people, and he mentored, challenged and inspired each of us in different ways. Consequently, and whilst between us we have taken somewhat different career pathways and journeys, we have continued to work to influence policy and practice in the area. This chapter primarily charts the journey of HBPE and Almond's work in this area from its early beginnings to it becoming an established component of the physical education curriculum. Specifically, it highlights key developments, outcomes and messages which emanated from Almond's work and publications on HBPE, as well as issues and challenges the area has faced, some of which are still pertinent today. To conclude, the chapter considers some of the progress and developments that have taken place more recently in HBPE, and which have arguably drawn and built upon Almond's early work.

Early Beginnings and Developments

Within and beyond the UK, various terms have been adopted to denote this area over the years including, for example, health-based physical education, health-related physical education, or health-related exercise or fitness. It is therefore perhaps useful at the outset to define HBPE. According to Harris (2000), the different terms that have been used reflect the varying influences on health issues within physical education over time. For the purpose of this chapter, the term health-based physical education (HBPE) is adopted throughout with all other variants seen to be synonymous, and it is taken to be:

> 'the teaching of knowledge, understanding, physical competence and behavioural skills, and the creation of positive attitudes and confidence associated with current and lifelong participation in physical activity'
> (Harris, 2000, p. 2).

In the decades leading up to the 1980s, other objectives and notably the acquisition of physical skills had taken priority in the curriculum for many years (Cale & Harris, 2013) but then with the establishment of the HBPE movement, health once again became an important goal and HBPE began to flourish. In the UK, evidence of this was seen in the significant growth in the number of health-related courses which began to feature in physical education curricula. Between 1985 and 1989 Almond (1989) pointed to a virtual tenfold rise in schools incorporating a health-based approach within the subject. During the 1990s, a growing number of researchers and physical educators contributed research articles, reviews and debates to the area (e.g. Almond, 1991; Armstrong, 1990; Sleap, 1990; Fox, 1992; Green, 1994; Harris & Elbourn, 1992a; 1992b; Harris, 1994; 1995; Cale, 1996) providing further evidence of the growing popularity of the movement. Indeed, Fox (1992) acknowledged how great strides had been made in the area and suggested that this signified a general acceptance of the importance of this approach to physical education.

Unquestionably underpinning and providing momentum for the above was the Health Education Authority (HEA) Health and Physical Education Project, of which Almond was the founder and director. Based at Loughborough University, the project was the first of its kind which sought to actively promote health-related work in physical education in schools. The project ran from 1985-1993 and provided an invaluable service for teachers and advisers delivering professional development courses and seminars across the UK and producing resources and regular newsletters to support its work (HEA, 1993). Numerous school-based resources and initiatives emanated from the project and have been developed since, but notable and innovative examples at the time included the 'Exercise Challenge' (McGeorge, 1993) and the 'Active School' (Almond & McGeorge, 1995). The Exercise Challenge was a curriculum-based scheme which encouraged young people to be more active and supported delivery of the health requirements of the National Curriculum (McGeorge, 1993), whilst the Active School initiative aimed to support schools in increasing and enhancing young people's physical activity experiences both within and beyond school through the formulation and implementation of an action plan (Almond & McGeorge, 1995). These initiatives drew on new philosophical principles and approaches, were supported by teacher manuals and a range of support materials, and addressed a real need at the time. The philosophy and approaches informing these and the work of the HBPE Project and HBPE more broadly, is discussed later.

Further cementing the acceptance and importance of HBPE around this time came with the advent of the National Curriculum for Physical Education (NCPE) in England and Wales, within which a statutory place for the subject was secured. At the time of the National Curriculum proposals, proponents of the area were anxiously asking whether HBPE would find a place within the NCPE, and if so, what form and context this would take. Indeed, its inclusion was considered essential to the future development and progress of HBPE in schools (Cale, 1996). Almond was instrumental in ensuring this was the case, strongly lobbying and advocating for HBPE to be a key element. In an Open Statement to members of the NCPE Working Group (the group tasked with advising government on the statutory order), Almond (1991) set out a clear and convincing case for HBPE. This was based on concerns over young people's physical activity levels and the implications for their health, and recognition of school as a critical period and potential influence in fostering a commitment to active living. Whilst Almond (1989; 1991) acknowledged sport, dance and adventure activities to be major elements of the physical education curriculum, he asserted the underlying key to pursuing any type of purposeful physical activity in depth was firstly a commitment to HBPE. He further went on to claim the area to be the 'core' of all physical education 'because it provides the foundation from which excellence or a commitment to purposeful physical activity as an absorbing activity can enhance the quality of one's life..', suggesting it brings with it '…a number of major short and long term benefits' (Almond, 1991, p. 29). For example:

- It enables people to lead full and active lives
- It can decrease the risk of heart disease and osteoporosis
- It enables people to recognize the influence of exercise on daily energy balance
- It can modify the effects of existing disease (e.g. asthma, diabetes) and assist with their management (Almond, 1991, p. 29).

Importantly, in his Open Statement Almond (1991) went on to identify the features and knowledge base he viewed to be critical for HBPE across Key Stages 1-4 (i.e. ages 5-16). Whilst not all of this detail and his recommendations found their way into the statutory order, certainly many elements and the essence of what Almond was advocating did. Health was included as a compulsory component of the NCPE in all Key Stages and as a cross-curricular theme of health education (Department for Education and the Welsh Office, 1995; National Curriculum Council, 1990). This development was significant as it gave HBPE a formally recognised, clearly defined knowledge base and place in the curriculum (Cale & Harris, 2005), thereby raising its status. Harris (1995) noted how, following the NCPE, physical education's contribution to health changed from being previously implicit and more incidental, to being explicit, and a planned learning outcome, whilst Fox (1992) surmised that the NCPE covered almost all the components of an admirable health-related PE curriculum. Since, health has furthermore become increasingly prominent and assumed a stronger position within successive versions of the NCPE. For example, in the current National Curriculum for England ensuring that all pupils 'lead healthy, active lives' and 'are physically active for sustained periods of time' represent two of the main aims of the subject (Department for Education, 2013, p. 1). Despite these aims, curiously references to health-related learning and to health-related activities in the actual programmes of study are still 'somewhat limited and more implicit' (Cale & Harris, 2018, p.281). How specifically the NCPE aims are to be achieved, and the programmes of study addressed such that pupils have the requisite knowledge and skills with respect to healthy active lifestyles, is thus still open to debate (Cale, Harris & Hooper, in press).

Philosophy and Principles

Alongside developing a rationale, impetus, support, and place for HBPE in the curriculum, and as alluded to earlier, Almond established a clear philosophy for the area. For HBPE to be effective, it was recognised that delivery needed to involve not only acquisition of a new knowledge base for many teachers, but a different philosophical approach or emphasis to delivery as well (Cale, 1996). In an article entitled 'Learning to Care', Harris and Almond (1991, p.6) highlighted how central to HBPE was 'every child' and the notion that 'everyone can be good at exercise' (i.e., there are no obstacles to anyone participating and succeeding with HBPE), and 'everyone has the right to positive experiences of exercise.' Other and related philosophical principles or messages which have been since adapted from Almond's earlier work include:

- Physical activity is for all.
- Physical activity is for life.
- Everyone can benefit from physical activity.
- Excellence is maintaining an active way of life.
- (adapted from Cale & Harris, 2009a and cited in Harris & Cale, 2018, p.78).

To achieve the above, Harris and Almond (1991) called for the physical education profession to humanise and personalise physical activity experiences to ensure they are satisfying, enjoyable and relevant to the future lives of young people. Almond saw the teacher's task as to help young people to learn to love being active, and through this and a commitment to active living, flourish as individuals. To support teachers in this endeavor and in creating positive, rewarding and meaningful experiences for young people, Harris and Almond (1991) identified a number of enabling principles of practice and equally some inhibiting practices which should be refrained from. Examples of both included:

Enabling Practices	Inhibiting Practices
setting attainable tasks	exposing anyone to incompetence
setting challenging tasks	monotonous, repetitive drills
rewarding effort	rewarding performance only
valuing pupils' contributions	treating pupils as 'empty vessels'
moving towards independence	keeping pupils dependent on the teacher
asking if pupils wish to share work	demanding displays of pupils' work
providing fair competition v others	permitting unfair competition v others

(adapted from Harris & Almond, 1991, p. 7)

The enabling principles were simply seen to be ethical and grounded in a commitment to providing learning opportunities which demonstrate equity, fairness, respect for persons and consideration for others (Harris & Almond, 1991). In conflict with and hampering the above however, was the performance-oriented philosophy which reportedly dominated physical education during this era (Almond, 1989). Almond (1983, p. 9) claimed 'The physical education curriculum is really competitive sport for many teachers', suggesting that this new and more child-centred philosophy and 'caring pedagogy' was likely to have been quite different to what many teachers were accustomed to. In support of Almond's work and HBPE, Cale (1996, p. 10) purported that only by adopting such a philosophy though, would physical education lose the 'aversion therapy' image of the past which drives many young people away from physical activity. Whilst we appreciate real 'philosophical' strides in physical education have been made since this time and would like to think that enabling principles and practices are commonplace and routinely accepted as just good, inclusive practice, evidence suggests that challenges remain. For example, it is contested that the PE profession is resistant to change (Alfrey & Gard, 2014; Kirk, 2010) and a performance-oriented philosophy and approach to physical education is still prevalent (Alfrey & Gard, 2014; Green, 2009; Kirk, 2010; Trost, 2006). This and other such challenges are addressed in more detail later.

Approach, Delivery, and Content

Additionally, in terms of pedagogy, Almond (1990) was a firm advocate of practical and experiential learning and of the acquisition of a practical knowledge base through HBPE. In other words, developing health knowledge and skills through active participation in a range of activities and via a combination of understanding, experiencing, decision making and evaluating (Cale & Harris, 2013; Cale, 2017). Thus, Almond challenged the practice of some who had opted for classroom-based delivery of health. Speaking about HBPE programmes, Almond (1983, p. 8) explained '… young people must not equate these new courses with the usual classroom type lessons…', and asserted that the area needed be taught 'in a practical and experiential way and NOT as some kind of theoretical lesson' (Almond, 1990, p.20). Indeed, in support of Almond's approach, the limitations, didactic and sedentary nature, and ineffectiveness of classroom-based delivery of health and health-related concepts and information has since been recognised (Cale, 2017; Cale & Harris, 2006). In contrast, a practical and experiential approach is reflective of the physical context of the subject and importantly helps to contribute to young people's overall physical activity levels (Harris, 2000; Harris and Cale, 2018). Furthermore, it encourages and facilitates the adoption of a more socially-critical perspective to teaching and learning about health, the need for which is increasingly being recognised (Burrows et al., 2009; Haerens et al., 2011; Quennerstedt, 2008). Given that young people today are bombarded with health-related information and messages from various sources and the power of the media and social media in particular in this regard (Goodyear & Armour, 2018), there is a growing need for practical approaches within HBPE which encourage and equip young people with the knowledge and skills to make critically informed decisions about health information, messages and about their own health and health behaviours (Cale, 2018). This is an explicit and firmly embedded aspect of the Health and Physical Education curriculum in Australia (ACARA, 2012) and we could learn much from others in this regard in the UK.

In advocating practical and experiential learning, Almond equally found himself having to defend and clarify this position and challenge other misconceptions associated with the delivery of HBPE. Myths that HBPE involved little more than engaging children in vigorous activity (Oxley, 1994), or that it was all about fitness testing, was anti-competition, anti-games, just about aerobics, circuit training and cross country (Harris & Elbourn, 1992b) or involved 'drill' or 'running children hard' (Harris, 1995) reportedly plagued the subject in the early years. Although to some practitioners these activities may have seemed appealing 'quick fix' solutions to address concerns over children's health and fitness and achieve short-term fitness gains, they are fraught with potential issues. For example, they are narrow in focus, directed and repetitive and may lead to unappealing, undesirable and inappropriate practices which limit learning and become counterproductive to the promotion of active lifestyles (Cale & Harris, 2009b; Cale, Harris & Hooper, in press). On a more positive note, the findings from a national survey of HBPE in secondary schools one year after the initial introduction of the NCPE (Harris, 1995) suggested a more encouraging picture. Harris (1995) reported teachers to generally have a broader understanding of what the area entailed and the vast majority to have forsaken such simplistic notions. Over 90% of schools surveyed taught predominantly practical units of work with most including explicit learning opportunities covering various relevant topics (e.g. stamina, suppleness and strength (Harris, 1995). That said, the survey findings did reveal some significant weaknesses which are outlined later.

In his on-going efforts to address misconceptions and promote and advance HBPE as a valued component of the curriculum, Almond (1983; 1989) challenged various aspects of traditional physical education practice and identified a number of ways in which he felt teachers needed to change their practices to achieve health-related learning goals. He questioned both the content and quality of the curriculum encouraging teachers to examine their physical education programmes to see whether lifetime activities and sports were included, that fitness programmes were not sport oriented, and that lessons did not involve 'mindless repetition of outdated training type activities' with minimal or no learning (Harris, 1993, p. 6). Indeed, he called for 'radical changes' (Almond, 1983, p. 6) in developing HBPE, spanning content, curriculum design and organisation, and extra-curricular provision. With regards content, Almond valued all forms of 'purposeful' physical activity including sport (lifestyle sports, play sport and competitive sport), dance, outdoor adventure, and individual activities, in terms of its potential to contribute to an active lifestyle and transform and enrich people's lives. Consequently, he argued that some aspects of health-related learning could not be taught in a traditional activity focused curriculum (e.g. comprising athletics, gymnastics swimming, games, dance etc) (Almond, 1990). He was keen to move away from a purely activity based curriculum and proposed new modules or units on health in their own right which could incorporate a broader range of activities such as fitness-related activities, aerobics and circuit training as well as other aspects such as lifestyle management, goal setting, and planning an exercise programme (Almond, 1990). Consequently, HBPE broadened the traditional, competitive team-sport orientated physical education programmes in place at the time to include education about lifetime physical activity (i.e. activity that can readily be carried over into adulthood), lifetime physical activities (Harris, 2010) and lifestyle skills. Beyond HBPE, Almond also recognised cross-curricular links and working with other subject areas as well as the role of wider aspects of the school (e.g. school breaks/lunchtimes and special events) and whole school approaches to be key in promoting health and health-related learning (Almond, 1990; 1991).

Challenges, Concerns and Solutions

Despite the many positive developments and the vision and clarification Almond offered with respect to HBPE, he identified a number of constraints which he believed hindered teachers' ability to embed good practice in their schools (Almond, 1983; 1989). Almond cited lack of time, the dominance and even preoccupation with competitive sport in the curriculum, lack of teacher resources and a lack of knowledge of 'how to start' as barriers posing real challenges and constraints to progress. Likewise, concerns over the position, interpretation and expression of HBPE in the curriculum were recognised by others (Fox 1992; Harris, 1994) and were reinforced by some of the less positive findings from Harris' national survey which revealed the teaching of the area to be characterised by confusion, lack of coherence, limited systematic expression and variation in practice (Harris, 1995). Moreover, these issues were seen to stem from teachers' lack or limited knowledge and understanding of HBPE and from inconsistent guidance and insufficient professional development in the area (Almond

& Harris, 1997; Cale, 1996; Fox, 1992; Harris, 1995). Further compounding concerns may also have been the disappointment of many that the area was not afforded the status of a separate programme of study in the NCPE when introduced in 1992, and fears that without which, the area could easily be marginalised or overlooked (Cale, 1996; Fox, 1992; Penney & Evans, 1997). Fox (1992) argued then that 'without a formal programme of study there is a grave danger that exercise and fitness education will be given a lower priority at a time when it needs more help than the well established areas.' (Fox, 1992, p.11). No individual activities are given this status in their own right in the current NCPE, but in essence the same argument could still made in that, despite its aims, the emphasis on health and physical activity in the programmes of study is still limited (Cale & Harris, 2018), certainly relative to other areas.

In response in 1997, a working group was established to achieve consensus on health-related learning within the subject (Cale & Harris, 2018) as well as support the interpretation and delivery of the health requirements within the NCPE (Harris, 2000). The group included Almond, other academics, plus representatives from schools and key national sport, health and physical education organisations. The main task of members was to produce national guidance, including good practice guidelines for teachers and health-related outcomes for children aged 5 to 16 in the form of a curriculum resource (Harris, 2000). The outcomes, which have recently been updated (see Harris & Cale, 2018), included cognitive (knowledge and understanding), affective, and behavioural components and were presented in four categories or areas of learning: safety issues; exercise effects; health benefits; and activity promotion. To illustrate their scope and progression in learning they were also organised by Key Stage or age group (i.e. 5-7 years (KS1); 7-11 years (KS2); 11-14 years (KS3) and 14-16 years (KS4)). As Cale and Harris (2018, p. 282) explain, for individuals to successfully engage in physical activity for life, it is important that they know and understand i) how to take part in physical activity safely and effectively (safety issues); ii) the body's response to participating in physical activity (exercise effects); iii) the reasons for participating in physical activity (health benefits), and iv) what (type and volume) physical activity to take part in, where and how (activity promotion).

These outcomes now feature in a new research-informed and evidenced-based resource for teachers on Promoting Active Lifestyles in Schools (Harris & Cale, 2018). The resource draws and builds on Almond's early work alongside the research and/or policy and practical work we have been involved in and developed over many years and presents a holistic perspective on the promotion of health and physical activity in schools. Its development was inspired and triggered by a continued desire to enhance practice in the area and to address the challenges and constraints identified by Almond and which are still commonly highlighted as issues today. A recent critique of these and their implications for practice is offered in Cale, Harris and Hooper (in press), but briefly persistent issues include the relatively low status afforded to health within physical education (Alfrey, Cale & Webb, 2012; Cale, Harris & Duncombe, 2016), the dominance of sport (Alfrey, Cale & Webb 2012; Green 2009; Kirk, 2010) or fitness and fitness-related activities as vehicles for delivering HBPE (Alfrey, Cale & Webb, 2012; Harris and Leggett, 2015), and physical education teachers' limited health knowledge and lack of or limited training or engagement in relevant professional development (Alfrey, Cale & Webb, 2012; Armour & Harris, 2013; Cale & Harris, 2013; Cale, Harris & Duncombe, 2016; Castelli & Williams, 2007; Harris & Leggett, 2015; Hastie, 2017; Kulinna et al., 2008; Keating et al., 2009; McKenzie, 2007; Puhse et al., 2011). In turn, there remains a lack of widespread consensus or understanding of the nature of learning in HPBE (Armour & Harris, 2013; Cale & Harris, 2018). Indeed, Armour and Harris (2013) claim that much of the international physical education community is unclear about the precise nature of appropriate health knowledge to be covered in the subject, whilst Cale and Harris (2018) contend that health-related learning needs to extend beyond the 'basics' and the rather limited knowledge and understanding requirements implied in the NCPE. Promoting Active Lifestyles (Harris & Cale, 2018) strives to address these challenges and to be an informative and accessible resource which equips teachers with the knowledge and ideas to incorporate the area into the curriculum in an informed, planned and progressive manner. As such, it includes explanations of current thinking in the area, tried and tested practical learning activities and ideas, developmentally appropriate practices, and case studies of best practice.

PE-for-Health Pedagogies and Digital Technologies

Given the long-standing challenges and despite the early and more recent efforts and developments in the area, it is perhaps not surprising that knowledge about effective pedagogies for delivering the area, or what has been referred to as PE-for-Health pedagogies, is also lacking (Armour & Harris, 2013; Haerens et al., 2011). Armour and Harris (2013) assert that the traditional approach to the area has been for the curriculum, programmes and activities to drive the educational process but stress that effective PE-for-health pedagogies should place the pedagogical encounter and the needs of the learners at the core. Almond was evidently ahead of his time in this regard and in his commitment to and beliefs concerning pedagogy and child-centred 'caring' pedagogy. However, it seems the influence of his and others' work was, and has been, largely restricted to the promotion and incorporation of health-focussed curriculum activities, ideas and interventions. Calls have therefore been made for alternative methods, strategies or models to teach health-related knowledge (Haerens et al., 2011; Armour & Harris, 2013; Hastie, Chen & Guarino, 2017; Hodges et al., 2017) and there have been some encouraging pedagogical developments both within and beyond the UK worthy of noting in this regard. Examples include the Health-Based Physical Education (HBPE) Model (Bowler, 2019; Haerens et al., 2011), Health Optimizing Physical Education (HOPE) (Metzler et al., 2013), the Promoting Active Lifestyle (PAL) Project (Cale & Harris in press; Harris, Cale & Hooper, 2017), and The Project-Based Learning PBL Model (Hastie, Chen & Guarino 2017). Whilst distinct in their own right, they each uphold Almond's same broad philosophy and values with respect to physical activity and promoting active lifestyles. To focus on just two of these here, the HBPE Model has as its central theme 'pupils valuing a physically active life' (Haerens et al., 2011, p. 321), draws on self-determination theory, the social ecological model and theories of behaviour change, and identifies four goals for HBPE including supporting learners to become habitual, motivated, informed and critical 'movers'. Whilst intended to be used flexibly, the affective domain is prominent in planning for learning and the importance of valuing a physically active life as a sustainable long-term process, knowledge as a significant component, and of focussing beyond the individual to the wider community are all emphasised. Since its first iteration, the model has undergone further development with teachers, teacher educators and pupils resulting in some positive outcomes (Bowler et al., 2015; Bowler 2019). The PAL Project (Harris et al., 2016) represents a principle-based approach to promoting active lifestyles designed primarily to inform schools' and teachers' policies and practices in this area. Informed by the literature and underpinned by social cognitive theory and the social ecological model, experienced and trainee teachers developed and trialled a number of whole-school and physical education-specific PAL principles. Some focus on the development of knowledge and understanding, for instance, 'Teach pupils about the broad range of benefits (physical, psychological and social) of a healthy, active lifestyle, including the role of physical activity in healthy weight management', while others are policy or practice oriented, for example, 'Promote active travel to school (cycling, walking, scooting) and ensure safe storage of cycles/scooters', 'Include assessment of learning and progress in active ways (e.g. show me….; demonstrate….; shadow….) (Harris et al., 2016). Attractive features include their flexibility and simplicity and that they can be incorporated with minimal training and limited resources (Cale, Harris & Hooper, 2017).

Finally, we need to recognise the growing availability, influence and use of digital technologies to support pedagogy in HBPE. Numerous health-related apps, wearables and sites are now available (Goodyear, Kerner & Quennerstedt, 2017; Rich and Miah, 2017) and being used to support health-related teaching and learning within the subject (Casey, Goodyear & Armour, 2017; Gard, 2014). However, despite the potential benefits of such technologies, concerns have been expressed over the potentially negative impact they might have on teachers' practice, pupils' learning and/or pupil wellbeing (Cale, Harris & Hooper, in press). Potential issues with such technologies is their tendency to quantify and limit health-related learning, for example, by measuring, ranking or tracking pupils (Goodyear, Kerner and Quennerstedt, 2017; Lupton, 2016), to reinforce a narrow, fitness focus within physical education (Cale, Harris & Hooper, in press), or promote unhealthy surveillance practices (Rich and Miah, 2017; Williamson, 2015). Given the widespread prevalence of digital technologies and their popularity with young people and within education generally, their use within HBPE is inevitable. Thus, consideration needs to be given to their pedagogical application to ensure that they facilitate appropriate content, appropriate context and effective pedagogy (Elbourn & James, 2013). As noted earlier, there is a growing need for approaches which encourage and equip young people to make critically informed decisions about health information, messages and behaviours (Cale, 2018), and this extends to the digital space.

Conclusion

This chapter has charted the journey of HBPE and the work of Almond, and others, in this area from the 1980s onwards, highlighting key developments, outcomes and messages as well as issues and challenges associated with the area. In this respect, we hope the chapter has done justice to Almond's work and the significant contribution he made to HBPE. In re-visiting his work, it is striking to see how far the HBPE movement has come and what Almond managed to achieve. From its early beginnings, HBPE is now well established as a component of the physical education curriculum within and beyond the UK. Almond's values and commitment to constantly challenging, questioning and examining physical education practice, to caring and inclusive pedagogy, and to supporting all young people to pursue a physically active lifestyle are ones to which we should all aspire today. Furthermore, his philosophy, practices and so many of his ideas have taken hold and are now widely accepted as just good practice. As we have seen, a number of challenges remain and there are still gaps and limitations in our health-related knowledge, understanding and practice. However, the energy, passion and vision Almond had for HBPE should inspire us all to address these and continue to make advancements in the area. He has certainly left a legacy and we have a great deal to be thankful to him for.

References

Armstrong, N. (1990). New Directions in Physical Education. Volume 1. Human Kinetics.

Alfrey, L. & Gard, M. (2014) A crack where the light gets in: a study of health and physical education teachers' perspectives on fitness testing as a context for learning about health, Asia-Pacific Journal of Health, Sport and Physical Education, 5(1), 3-18.

Alfrey, L., Cale, L. & Webb, L.A. (2012) Physical education teachers' continuing professional development in health-related exercise, Physical Education and Sport Pedagogy, Physical Education and Sport Pedagogy, 17(5), 477-491.

Almond, L. (1983) A rationale for health-related fitness in schools, The Bulletin of Physical Education, 19(2), 5-10.

Almond, L. (1989) New wine in a new bottle-implications of a National Physical Education Curriculum, The British Journal of Physical Education, 20(3),123-125.

Almond, L. (1990) A Health-related exercise focus in physical education, The Bulletin of Physical Education, 26(1): 18-21.

Almond, L. (1991) An open statement to members of the PE working group, The Bulletin of Physical Education, 27, 29-33.

Almond, L. & Harris, J. (1997) Does health related exercise deserve a hammering or help? The British Journal of Physical Education, 28(2): 25-27.

Almond, L. & McGeorge, S. (1995) Leicester health - an active schools promotion. Loughborough University, Leicestershire: Exercise and Health Group.

Armour, K. & Harris, J. (2013) Making the case for developing new PE-for-health pedagogies, Quest, 65(2), 201-219.

Australian Council for Health, Physical Education and Recreation. (2004) Australian Fitness Education Award Revised Edition. Teacher Manual (Adelaide, ACHPER).

Australian Curriculum, Assessment and Reporting Authority (ACARA). (2012) The Health and Physical Education Curriculum F-10. Sydney: ACARA.

Bowler, M. T. (2019) Developing a Pedagogical Model for Health-Based Physical Education. Doctoral Thesis, Loughborough University.

Bowler, M., Sammon, P., Kirk, D., Haerens, L., Cale, L. & Casey, A. (2015). Developing a 'prototype' Health-Based Physical Education pedagogical model, Paper presented at the International Association for Physical Education in Higher Education (AIESEP) Annual Conference, Universidad Europea, Madrid, Spain.

Burrows, L., Wright, J. & McCormack, J. (2009) Dosing up on food and physical activity: New Zealand children's ideas about 'health', Health Education Journal, 68(3), 157-169.

Cale, L. (1996) Health-related exercise in schools - PE has much to be proud of!, The British Journal of Physical Education, 27(4), 8-13.

Cale, L. (2017). Teaching about Healthy Active Lifestyles. In C.D. Ennis (ed). Routledge handbook of physical education pedagogies (pp. 399-411). Oxon, UK: Routledge.

Cale, L. (2018) Social media, young people, physical activity and health: The work, the present and the future. In V. Goodyear, and K.M. Armour (eds). Social Media, Young People, Physical Activity and Health. Routledge.

Cale, L. & Harris, J. (2005) (Eds), Exercise and Young People. Issues, Implications and Initiatives, Basingstoke: Palgrave Macmillan.

Cale, L. & Harris, J. (2006) School based physical activity interventions – effectiveness, trends, issues, implications and recommendations for practice, Sport, Education and Society, 11(4), 401-420.

Cale, L. & Harris, J. (2009a) Getting the Buggers Fit. Second Edition, London: Continuum, 138-152.

Cale, L. & Harris, J. (2009b) Fitness testing in physical education - a misdirected effort in promoting healthy lifestyles and physical activity?, Physical Education and Sport Pedagogy, 14(1), 89-108.

Cale, L. & Harris, J. (2013) Physical education and health: considerations and issues. In S. Capel & M. Whitehead (eds) Debates in Physical Education (pp. 74-88). Oxon: Routledge.

Cale, L. & Harris, J. (2018) The role of knowledge and understanding in fostering physical literacy, Journal of Teaching in Physical Education, 37(3), 280-287.

Cale, L., Harris, J. & Duncombe, R. (2016) Promoting physical activity in secondary schools. Growing expectations: same old issues, European Physical Education Review, 22(4), 526-544.

Cale, L., Harris. J. & Hooper, O. (2017) The Promoting Active Lifestyles project. The 30th Australian Council for Health, Physical Education and Recreation (ACHPER) International Conference, University of Canberra, Australia.

Cale, L., Harris, J. & Hooper, O. (in press) Debating health knowledge and pedagogies in physical education. In: S. Capel & R. Blair (eds). Debates in Physical Education. Second Edition. Routledge.

Casey, A., Goodyear, V. A. & Armour, K. M. (2017) Rethinking the relationship between pedagogy, technology and learning in health and physical education, Sport, Education and Society, 22(2), 288–304.

Castelli, D. & Williams, L. (2007) Health-related fitness and physical education teachers' content knowledge, Journal of Teaching in Physical Education, 26(1), 3-19.

Department for Education and the Welsh Office. (1995). Physical Education in the National Curriculum. London: HMSO.

Department for Education. (2013) Programmes of Study for Physical Education. Key Stages 3 and 4 https://www.gov.uk/government/uploads/system/uploads/attachment _data/file/239086/SECONDARY_national_curriculum_-_Physical_education.pdf.

Elbourn, J. & James, A. (2013) Fitness Room Activities for Secondary Schools. A Guide to Promoting Effective Learning about Healthy Active Lifestyles, Leeds: Coachwise.

Fox, K. (1992) Education for exercise and the National Curriuclum Proposals: A step forward or backwards, The British Journal of Physical Education, 23(1), 8-11.

Gard, M. (2014) eHPE: A history of the future, Sport, Education and Society, 19(6), 827–845.

Green, K. (1994) Meeting the Challenge: Health Related Exercise and the encouragement of lifelong participation, The Bulletin of Physical Education, 30(3), 27-34.

Green, K. (2009) Exploring the everyday 'philosophies' of physical education teachers from a sociological perspective, in: R. Bailey and D. Kirk (eds). The Routledge Physical Education Reader (pp. 183-206). London: Routledge Taylor and Francis.

Goodyear, V. & Armour, K.M. (2018) Social Media, Young People, Physical Activity and Health. Routledge.

Goodyear, V., Kerner, C. and Quennerstedt, M. (2017) Young people's uses of wearable healthy lifestyle technologies; surveillance, self-surveillance and resistance, Sport, Education and Society, DOI: 10.1080/13573322.2017.1375907.

Haerens, L., Kirk, D., Cardon, G. & De Bourdeaudhuij, I. (2011) Toward the development of a pedagogical model for health-based physical education, Quest, 63, 321-338.

Harris, J. (1993) Young people's perceptions of health, fitness and exercise, The British Journal of Physical Education Research Supplement, 13, 5-9.

Harris, J. (1994) Health related exercise in the National Curriculum: Results of a pilot study in secondary schools, The British Journal of Physical Education Research Supplement, 14, 6-11.

Harris, J. (1995) Physical education - a picture of health?, The British Journal of Physical Education, 26(4), 25-32.

Harris, J. (2000) Health-Related Exercise in the National Curriculum, Leeds: Human Kinetics.

Harris, J. (2010) Health-related physical education, in: R. Bailey (Ed), Physical Education for Learning: A Guide for Secondary Schools, London: Continuum.

Harris, J. & Almond, L. (1991) Learning to care, The Bulletin of Physical Education, 27(1), 5-11.

Harris, J. & Elbourn, J. (1992a) Highlighting health related exercise within the National Curriculum-Part 1, The British Journal of Physical Education, 23(1), 18-22.

Harris, J. & Elbourn, J. (1992b) Highlighting health related exercise within the National Curriculum-Part 2, The British Journal of Physical Education, 23(2), 5-9.

Harris, J. & Leggett, G. (2015) Influences on the expression of health within physical education curricula in secondary schools in England and Wales, Sport Education and Society, 20(7), 908-923.

Harris, J. & Cale, L. (2018) Promoting Active Lifestyles in Schools, Leeds: Human Kinetics.

Harris, J., Cale, L. & Hooper, O. (2017) Promoting active lifestyles in schools: From philosophical principles to inclusive pedagogies, The International Association for Physical Education in Higher Education (AIESEP) Conference, University of the Antilles, Guadeloupe.

Harris, J. Cale, L., Casey, A., Tyne, A. & Samaria, B. (2016). Promoting active lifestyles in schools. The PAL Project, Physical Education Matters, 11(3), 52-53.

Hastie, P. (2017) Revisiting the National Physical Education Content Standards: What do we really know about our achievement of the physically educated/literate person? Journal of Teaching in Physical Education, 36, 3-19.

Hastie, P. A., Chen, S. and Guarino, A. J. (2017) Health-related fitness knowledge development through project-based learning, Journal of Teaching in Physical Education, 36, 119-125.

Health Education Authority. (1993) Health and Physical Education Project Newsletter, 32, 1-2.

Hodges, M. G., Kulinna, P. H., van der Mars, H. & Lee, C. (2016) Knowledge in action; fitness lesson segments that teach health-related fitness in elementary physical education, Journal of Teaching in Physical Education, 35, 16-26.

Keating, X.D., Harrison, L., Chen, L., Xiang, P., Lambdin, D., Dauenhauer, B., Rotich, W. and Castro Pinero, J. (2009) An analysis of research on student health-related fitness knowledge in K-16 physical education programs, Journal of Teaching in Physical Education, 28, 333-349.

Kirk, D. (2010) Four Relational Issues and the Bigger Picture, in: D. Kirk. Physical Education Futures, (pp. 97-120). Abingdon Oxon: Routledge.

Kulinna, P.H., McCaughtry, N., Martin, J.J., Cothran, D. and Faust, R. (2008) The influence of professional development on teachers' psychosocial perceptions of teaching a health-related physical education curriculum, Journal of Teaching in Physical Education, 27: 292-307.

Lupton, D. (2016) The diverse domains of quantified selves: Self-tracking modes and dataveillance, Economy and Society, 45(1), 101–122.

McGeorge, S. (1993) The Exercise Challenge Teachers' Manual. Exercise and Health Group, Loughborough University.

McKenzie, T.L. (2007) The preparation of physical educators: a public health perspective, Quest, 59, 346-357.

Metzler, M., McKenzie, T., Van der Mars, H., Barrett-Williams, S. & Ellis, R. (2013) 'Health Optimizing Physical Education (HOPE): A new curriculum for school programs - Part 1: Establishing the need and describing the model', Journal of Physical Education, Recreation and Dance, 84(4), 41-47.

National Curriculum Council. (1990) Curriculum Guidance 5: Health Education. London: HMSO.

Oxley, J. (1994). HRE and the National Curriculum- an OFSTED inspector's view, The Bulletin of Physical Education, 30(2), 39.

Penney, D. & Evans, J. (1997) Naming the game. Discourse and domination in physical education and sport in England and Wales, European Physical Education Review, 3(1), 21-32.

Puhse, U., Barker, D., Brettschneider, W.D., Feldmeth, A.K. et al., (2011) International approaches to health-oriented physical education: local health debates and differing conceptions of health, International Journal of Physical Education, 3, 2-15.

Quennerstedt, M. (2008) Exploring the relation between physical activity and health – a salutogenic approach to physical education, Sport, Education and Society, 13(3), 276-283.

Rich, E. & Miah, A. (2017) Mobile, wearable and ingestible health technologies: Towards a critical research agenda, Health Sociology Review, 26(1), 84-97.

Sleap, M. (1990) Promoting health in primary school physical education. In N. Armstrong (ed). New Directions in Physical Education (pp 17-36.). Champaign, IL: Human Kinetics.

Tinning, R. (2010) Pedagogy and human movement: Theory, practice, research. Oxon: Routledge.

Trost, S. (2006) Public health and physical education, in: D. Kirk, M. O'Sullivan and D. Macdonald (eds), Handbook of Physical Education, (pp. 163-187). London, Sage.

Williamson, B. (2015) Algorithmic skin: Health-tracking technologies, personal analytics and the biopedagogies of digitized health and physical education, Sport, Education and Society, 20(1), 133–151.

8

Teaching Games for Understanding: From conception to Special Interest Group

Alan Ovens, David Gutierrez & Joy Butler

Our focus in this chapter is both substantive and obeisant. By substantive, we mean our aim is to document the history of Teaching Games for Understanding (TGfU) from its initial conception to its institutionalization. We note that little attention has been paid in the research literature to how an idea like TGfU evolves into a transnational community like the TGfU-Special Interest Group (Provan & Kenis, 2008; Ball, 2012). In this sense, we believe it is important to document and study this development in a way that acknowledges the complexity, collectivity and leadership involved. By obeisant, we mean our approach is to acknowledge and respect the central role of Joy Butler in the creation and evolution of this process. Specifically, the aim is to focus attention on the formative role that key actors like Joy played in the formation and success of TGfU as a curriculum model well known in the physical education community. Much of this chapter is based on an article written by Joy Butler herself, together with Alan Ovens (Butler & Ovens, 2015) and has been reproduced, revised and expanded with permission from the original publishers.

TGfU and network governance

Movements, like those advocating for TGfU, represent evolving and decentralized social networks made up of individuals who form a virtual community but are not members of the same formal institution or even country (Howard, 2002). For the purposes of this chapter, we use the concept of network governance (Ball & Junemann,

2012) as a lens to examine the evolution of the TGfU movement, with a particular focus on the interactions between actors and groups and their influence on the process of network formation (Sorenson and Torfing, 2005). The notion of network governance draws attention to the dense fabric of ties, expertise, reputation, and legitimation that work as governing mechanisms to network activity and how such patterns of relations become institutionalized and stabilized through the work of various nodal actors.

Using network governance in this way, we suggest the history of TGfU can be conceptualized as a networked community that has evolved through different configurations based on the leadership and energy contributed by key people. Leadership in such communities emerges in different ways. There is distributed leadership, with many people providing a range of leadership functions such as advocating in policy committees, validating key ideas, leading events (such as workshops), connecting to new members, and sharing their knowledge with others. At the same time, there are often who take on more formal leadership roles and provide leadership by encouraging and motivating others, setting and monitoring the agenda, sharing leadership, providing support, and building capacity. In the following discussion we focus on key people and events that have brought about a critical change within the TGfU community.

A concept born from concern

The genesis of TGfU can be traced back to social and educational transformations occurring as early as the 1950s and 1960s. While sport had always been popular, it was around this time that there was a rapid growth in the sport sciences and a corresponding focus on how to improve sports performance through the systematization of coaching and training (Tinning, 2010). Kirk (2010) identifies this as a period of time when physical education went through a significant paradigm shift from being broadly oriented around gymnastics to being broadly oriented around the teaching of sports techniques. This paradigm shift saw an increased attention given to sport and was dominated by what Tinning (2010) calls the "Demonstration, Explanation and Practice" approach to teaching, or what Rovegno (1995) identified as a molecular approach to teaching and learning.

As this molecular approach became popular, focused as it was on mastering the technical aspects of sports skills, there was a corresponding growing level of concern about this way of teaching and coaching. It was in Loughborough University that the people key to the TGfU model came into contact and struck up a useful and productive collaboration (Werner & Almond, 1990). Len Almond, who was newly appointed to Loughborough University in the 1970s, recalls a pivotal moment when he had the opportunity to watch Rod Thorpe teach net games to a group of postgraduate students and was fascinated by his approach (Video interview, 2012). This led to a series of meetings along with others like David Bunker, who had been developing their own approach through their work with students, teachers, advisors and colleagues. Through these meetings, the key principles of what would become TGfU were debated, distilled, and refined.

According to Kirk (2010), what was fundamentally different was the way this group challenged the molecular approach to teaching oriented around practicing technique prior to and isolated from game play. Instead, they promoted participation in games modified to suit the level and experience of the players and developed this in a way that made its organization and application coherent.

Expansion and proliferation

The publication of the model in the Bulletin of Physical Education in 1982 (Bunker & Thorpe, 1982) was a key historical moment in the evolution of the TGfU community. Prior to this, the network was centralized at Loughborough University and sustained through the workshops and discussions the Loughborough team had with students and teachers. Publication provided the means for both normalizing the principles involved and generating immense interest from pedagogy researchers and sports organizations (Kirk, 2010). In effect, the article enabled TGfU to become a concept around which a broad range of people could align as the basis of their own teaching and research. From a governance perspective, we can see that publication of the model also acted as a catalyst for a loose network of people to form who had an affinity with the model's principles and learner-centered pedagogy. Governance of this network essentially became decentralized with control exercised through a common language and concepts provided by the model.

The period between the 1980s and 2000s is interesting not so much for the ability of TGfU to change PE practice in schools, laudable as that might be, but in the degree to which the model became theorized, replicated, popularized and legitimized. In recognizing it as a significant form of pedagogy, researchers sought to better understand it using information processing and schema theory, situated learning, ecological psychology, dynamical systems theory, constructivism(s) and, more latterly, complexity theory. In addition, reflecting the affinity that many have with its underpinning educational principles, the model has spurred many interpretations and iterations of the original model as well as the promotion of models based on very similar ideas such as Tactical Games (Griffin et al., 1997; Mitchell et al., 2003, 2006, 2013), Games Sense (Thorpe, 1996; Light, 2013), Play Practice (Launder, 2001; Launder and Piltz, 2013), Invasion Games Competency model (Tallir et al., 2003, 2005; Mesquita et al., 2012), Tactical decision learning model, (Grehaigne and Godbout 1997, 1998; Grehaigne et al., 2005, 2012), Games Concept Approach (Rossi et al., 2006), the Clinic-Game Day approach (Alexander and Penny, 2005) and the Inventing Games model (Butler, 2016).

In many ways, this proliferation represents the forms of distributed leadership discussed earlier. The affinity that many researchers had in the PE pedagogy field with the potential of TGfU to contribute to a renewal and transformation in physical education drove much activity around advocacy for the model and establishing a research base for its legitimacy. However, at the same time this growing interest in TGfU led to the concern that there needed to be better coordination and communication between those involved. Joy Butler emerged as someone who could initiate this and do so with a sense of authority that would affect change. Interviews with others involved at this time identify her leadership qualities as including excellent communication and networking skills, tenacity, and a strong sense of vision for what could and should be accomplished.

Is also worth pointing out that another key attribute Butler possessed was her academic standing in the TGfU community that provided both legitimacy and influence. Although prolific in quantity and diversity, her work is undoubtedly linked to games teaching, and especially to TGfU. To show, although in a very brief way, the remarkable quantum of her work, we have compiled her publications. Based on Baker's (2016) review of literature on Canadian pedagogical models, table 1 lists all of Joy's numerous TGfU papers, chapters and books. We have categorized them according to the type of work (theoretical, practical or empirical) and to the contribution made to the original approach. In this sense, much of Joy's work contains one or several of the following ingredients to TGfU: complexity thinking, inventing games, and ethical aspects in games teaching.

Table 1: Butler's TGfU publications.

Theoretical	Practical	Empirical
Butler (2017) Griffin, Butler, & Sheppard (2017) *Butler (2016a)** *Butler (2016b)* *Butler (2016c)* **Butler (2016d)** **Ovens, & Butler (2016)** Butler & Ovens (2015) Memmert, Almond, Bunker, **Butler, Fasold, Griffin… Nopp (2015)** ***Butler, Storey, & Robson (2014)*** **Butler & Robson (2013)** **Storey, & Butler (2013)** Butler & Robson (2012) Butler & Griffin (2010)** Butler, Oslin, Mitchell & Griffin (2008) Mandigo, Butler, & Hopper (2007) Butler (2006) Butler (2005) Butler & McCahan (2005) Griffin & Butler (2005)**	*Butler (2016a)** Butler & Hopper (2016) Butler (2013b) Butler, Sullivan, McGinley, Vranjes (2007)	Slater & Butler (2015) Butler (2014) Butler (2013a) **Storey & Butler (2013)** Butler & Griffin (2010)** Griffin & Butler (2005)**

*Coordinated book that includes both theory and practical chapters.
** Coordinated books that include both Theory and empirical chapters.
Complexity thinking (in bold)
Inventing games (on italic)
Ethical aspects in games teaching (underlined)

Her mix of both personal qualities and academic depth ensured she was had a significant influence on how the loose and informal TGfU network would become stabilized into a formal group. While the early conceptualization of the model can be attributed to founders such as Rod Thorpe, David Bunker and Len Almond, the consolidation of a collective interest in the model into an organised special interest group, as the second half of this chapter describes, must be attributed to Joy Butler.

Institutionalization and consolidation

Following the rapid expansion and proliferation of the TGfU model through the 1980s and 90s, Butler felt there was a need to extend the model theoretically and better support practitioners using the model. She believed that the best way forward was to convene a conference and in 2001, along with Linda Griffin (University of Massachussetts, Amherst), Ben Lombardo (University of Rhode Island) and Rich Nastasi (Endicott College, MA), she ran the first TGfU conference at Plymouth State University in New Hampshire, US. While the conference was enthusiastically supported, with 150+ delegates from twenty-one different countries, the conference also provided an opportunity to discuss future possibilities. To discuss options, the conference organisers convened a town meeting (August 4th, 2001), which was attended by 70 delegates (almost half of those in attendance). As Butler and Griffin (2010) recall,

> "At a crowded town meeting, the conference organizers asked the international delegates where they thought they wanted to go from that point. The response was a resounding endorsement of Butler's proposal that an international committee be established to harness the groundswell of energy evident at the conference"
> (Butler & Griffin, 2010, p. 5).

It was in that moment that the TGfU Task Force was born, representing another transitional moment in the reconfiguration of the TGfU network governance. Collectively, there was recognition that there needed to be a coordinated approach to leadership of the network and a way of coordinating the diversity of activity occurring around the TGfU model. Perhaps most importantly, and very much part of Butler's political skillfulness, there was also a recognition that any centralization of governance needed a sense of legitimacy in the form of a partnership that would help sustain international interest and ensure the maintenance of quality research. AIESEP (Association Internationale des Ecoles Superieures d'Education Physique or International Association for Physical Education in Higher Education) was seen as a likely partner in establishing the conditions and networks necessary to theorize and research TGfU. AIESEP was, and is, a well-established and respected international organization immersed in teacher education in Higher Education. The AIESEP president Ron Feingold was present at the 2001 conference and endorsed the proposed application for a TGfU task force.

Figure 2: Inaugural meeting for the TGfU Task force at October 2002 AIESEP World Congress in La Coruna, Spain.

Front Row: Michael Darmody (Ireland), Doune McDonald, John Halbert (Ireland) David Kirk, Joy Butler
Second Row: Natalie Wallian (France), Jean-Francis Greghaigne (France), Robert Martin (US), John Cheffers (US),
Third Row: Keh Nuit Chin (Taiwan), Raymond Liu (HK), Ming Chow (HK) Stephen Tan (Singapore), Minna Blomqvist (Finland), Lauri Laakso (Finland)
Fourth Row: Luis Miguel García-López (Spain), Richard Light (AU), Richard Nastasi (US).
Fifth Row: Mary O'Sullivan (Ireland), Darryl Siedentop (US), Deborah Tannehill (US)

With Joy Butler being the key organizer, the first official meeting of the task force (October, 2002) set out to establish a mission statement and list a number of objectives. This proved to be a lengthy, but necessary, process. One of the substantial outcomes of the meeting was to establish a TGfU seminar conference series, to be held every two years. It should be noted that Butler has played a significant role in each of the subsequent conferences that have been held, including being a keynote at each event and always being a strong advocate for practices around equity, inclusion, and diversity.

Almost four years later, at the 2006 AIESEP World Congress in Finland, the TGfU Task force decided that the movement had become large enough to propose yet another change to its configuration. In effect, the proposal was to become a special interest group of AIESEP (which would be their first) and be governed by an executive committee established through the membership for the exclusive purpose of coordinating and sustaining the network. The policies and procedures, including election processes that had been inaugurated (somewhat on the fly) at the initial meeting in Finland (July 2006) were developed and strengthened. The transition of Task Force to SIG was ratified at the TGfU conference in Vancouver in 2008.

The TGfU Special Interest Group (SIG) initially provided for members to vote an Executive committee to provide centralized leadership. Consequently, Joy Butler became the first chair of the executive committee and she led the process of formalizing the policies and activities of the group. At the same time, executive members interviewed for this chapter remember her strong commitment to democracy and desire to find ways to expand participation in the group. She began to actively seek out teachers, coaches, and academics who were engaged in new TGfU projects and initiatives, encouraging them to become involved in the SIG. It is important not to forget the other members of the executive committee who were also important in contributing to the development of the SIG or their contribution to key activities at this time. Rather, we want to highlight her desire to find a mechanism to more formally recognize the growing group of international members in some way. Her solution was the proposal to form an International Advisory Board (IAB) as part of the TGfU Special Interest Group. This proposal was ratified at the TGfU SIG General Meeting on 29th October 2010 at AIESEP Congress, La Coruna, Spain and she moved from the chair of the Executive Committee to become the first chair of the IAB.

The development of the IAB was significant because it reflected Butler's dual commitment to increasing the diversity of participating scholars and practitioners in order to become a globally representative group, as well as enacting democratic principles to better address global challenges such as language, terminology, practical interpretations, advocacy, as well as philosophical and theoretical differences. The current role of the IAB is to disseminate TGfU SIG policies to critical organizations within member's country, while at the same time informing the SIG of pertinent information regarding progress of TGfU in each member's country.

Exploring the work in 'network'

Mapping the institutionalisation of the network is one thing, but it is also important to see how such reconfigurations affect what outcomes the network can achieve. The initial goal, revised slightly with the formation of the TGfU SIG, was to broaden international cooperation and understanding among teachers, coaches, researchers, students and institutions of the world through best practice, critical educational and research collaborations and exchanges. While this outlines the broad aspirations for the Special Interest Group, a series of objectives were also developed around which the strategic actions of the group could focus. These were:

1. Disseminate scholarly information, proceedings and resources
2. Promote international dialogue around theory, research and pedagogy.
3. Establish teaching / coaching programs
4. Create international networks for collaborative research, eg. Projects.
5. Review / reflect upon philosophy, theory & research.
6. Explore and secure funding resources

While it is beyond the scope of this paper to reflect on how these objectives have been achieved, it is possible to focus on two areas in particular. Firstly, with respect to the promotion and dissemination of scholarly inquiry around ways of knowing, learning and teaching through games centered approaches, the ongoing conferences, seminars and workshops have proven to be effective. There have been six TGfU conferences to date. The first three conferences were offered every two years, but then at the 2006 AIESEP task force meeting it was agreed that these should be every four years with a one-day seminar before each AIESEP world congress. Since the AIESEP congresses are also offered every four years but fall between the four-year cycle of the TGfU seminar conferences, this arrangement ensures that an international TGfU event takes place every two years. Table two lists the events, their location, theme, director and number of participants.

Table 2: History of TGfU Seminar conferences and One-day Symposia

Date	Location	Theme	Director & Participants
2001	**Seminar Conference 1** Waterville Valley, New Hampshire, USA Sponsored by Plymouth State University	Teaching Games for Understanding in Physical Education and Sport	Joy Butler 150 attendees 17 countries
2003	**Seminar Conference 2** Melbourne, AU Sponsored by Melbourne University	Teaching Sport and Physical Education for understanding	Richard Light 250 attendees 21 countries
2005	**Seminar Conference 3** Hong Kong Sponsored by the Hong Kong Institute of Education	A Global Perspective of Physical Education and Sports	Raymond Liu 90 attendees 15 countries
2006	**One-day symposia** Jyvaskyla, Finland Sponsored by AIESEP	The Role of Physical Education and Sport in Promoting Physical Activity and Health	Joy Butler and Richard Light
2008	**Seminar Conference 4** Vancouver, BC. Canada. Sponsored by University of British Columbia	Understanding Games: Enhancing Learning in Teaching and Coaching	Joy Butler 355 attendees 26 countries 5 continents
2010	**One-day symposia** La Coruna, Spain Sponsored by AIESEP	Exploring Personal and Social Responsibility in TGfU: From the Gymnasium to the Stadium	James Mandigo and Stephen Harvey
2012	**Seminar Conference 5** Loughborough, Leicester, UK Sponsored by University of Loughborough	Celebrating 30 years of TGfU	Mary Healy and Lorraine Cale 40 attendees 15 countries 4 continents
2014	**One-day symposia** Auckland, New Zealand Sponsored by AIESEP	Creating smart players through games centered learning	Dennis Slade
2016	**Seminar Conference 6** Cologne, Germany Sponsored by German Sport University	Just Play It – "Innovative, international approaches to games"	Daniel Memmert 450 attendees 23 countries 5 continents
2018	**One-day symposia** Edinburgh, United Kingdom Sponsored by AIESEP	Theory and Practice in TGfU	Linda Griffin 75 attendees 19 countries

Date	Location	Theme	Director & Participants
2022	**Seminar Conference 7** Worcester, United Kingdom Sponsored by Worcester University	TGfU: Inclusivity, Integration and Implementation	Don Vinson
2024	**Seminar Conference 8**	Advances in TGfU Innovation: Inspirtation and Inclusion	Alan Ovens University of Auckland

The effect of these conferences and one-day symposia has been to enable the sharing of ideas and expertise between coaches and teachers within regions, nationally, and internationally. In such contexts, the philosophical and sociological interpretations of TGfU can influence and be influenced by the input of participants from a broad international base

Secondly, with respect to creating a community capable of connecting to a broadly distributed membership, the development of a website has been essential. The first website, www.tgfu.org was developed initially by Task Force member Bob Martin and hosted on a site linked to a US University. Unfortunately, the Executive lost the rights to that particular URL. The second rendition of the website was professionally managed and easily navigable site. Executive members Tim Hopper and Stephen Harvey took on the time-consuming task of finding website designers who would oversee maintenance. Though the site looked excellent, it proved difficult to update and edit. The third and current website (https://tgfuinfo.weebly.com/) built on the excellent work established in the second, but moved it to a site that gives complete access and control to the Executive. Kelly Parry, who joined the team in 2012 and completed this work, in 2018 set up a 'communications team' (Ellen Gambles, Jesse Rhoades and Roberto Sánchez) in recognition of the growing evolution of platforms like twitter and blogs to connecting and informing SIG members.

Conclusion - final thoughts

TGfU has become a significant movement in physical education and gained global momentum as a viable approach to teaching physical education. Over three decades after the Bunker and Thorpe article (1982) outlined a model for the teaching of games in secondary schools, teachers and coaches are now embracing the notion that TGfU aligns closely with the humanistic, child-centered, and inquiry-oriented teaching advocated in contemporary schooling. As we have documented in this chapter, the fact that TGfU is highly relevant and popular can be attributed to the evolution of an enthusiastic community who align with and continue to develop the TGfU model (and its associated Game-Centred approaches). From a network governance perspective, this socially networked community has been configured and run in different forms, the most significant of which has been the development of the TGfU SIG. The development of the TGfU SIG was enabled by the leadership of Joy Butler, whose vision, drive and networking skills, enabled the SIG to become a globally representative group. Perhaps the true test of Butler's success will be to see if the TGfU SIG and its IAB can continue to thrive without her.

References

Alexander, K., & Penney, D. (2005). Teaching under the influence: feeding Games for Understanding into the Sport Education development-refinement cycle, *Physical Education and Sport Pedagogy*, 10:3, 287-301, DOI: 10.1080/17408980500340901

Baker, K. (2016). Models-Based Practice: Learning From and Questioning the Existing Canadian Physical Education Literature. Canadian Journal for New Scholars in Education/Revue canadienne des jeunes chercheures et chercheurs en éducation, 7(2).

Ball, S. (2012). *Global Education Inc.: New policy networks and the neoliberal imaginary*. London: Routledge.

Ball, S., & Junemann, C. (2012). *Networks, new governance and education*. Bristol, UK: The Policy Press.

Butler J. I. (2006). Curriculum constructions of ability: Enhancing learning through Teaching Games for Understanding (TGfU) as a curriculum model. *Sport, Education and Society*, 11(3), 243-258.

Butler, J. & Hopper, T. (2016). Inventing net and wall games. In J. Butler, *Playing Fair* (pp. 157-178). Champaign, IL: Human Kinetics.

Butler, J. (2013a). Situating ethics in games education. *Canadian Journal of Education*, 36(4), 93-114.

Butler, J. (2013b). Stages for children inventing games. Journal of Physical Education, Recreation & Dance, 84(4), 48-53.

Butler, J. (2014). TGfU–Would you know it if you saw it? Benchmarks from the tacit knowledge of the founders. European Physical Education Review, 20(4), 465-488.

Butler, J. (2016a). Playing Fair. Champaign, IL: Human Kinetics.

Butler, J. (2016b). Introduction to the Symposium Democracy in Action Through Inventing Games. Research Quarterly for Exercise and Sport, 87(S1), S37.

Butler, J. (2016c). Inventing Games Through Democracy in Action and Adaptation. Research Quarterly for Exercise and Sport, 87(S1), S117.

Butler, J. (2016d). We Are What We Teach: TGfU as a Complex Ecological Situation. *Research quarterly for exercise and sport*, 87(S1), S2.

Butler, J. (2017). Feminist directions for Teaching Games for Understanding (TGfU) Movement. *Cultura_Ciencia_Deporte*, 12(35), 87-88.

Butler, J. I. (2005). TGfU pet-agogy: Old dogs, new tricks and puppy school. *Physical Education and Sport Pedagogy*, 10(3), 225-240.

Butler, J. I., & McCahan, B. J. (2005). Teaching games for understanding as a curriculum model. In L.L. Griffin and J.L. Butler (Eds.), *Teaching Games for Understanding: Theory, research, and practice*. Human Kinetics (pp. 33-53). Champaign, IL.

Butler, J. I., Storey, B., & Robson, C. (2014). Emergent learning focused teachers and their ecological complexity worldview. *Sport, Education and Society*, 19(4), 451-471.

Butler, J., & Griffin, L. L. (Eds.). (2010). *More teaching games for understanding: Moving globally*. Champaign, IL: Human Kinetics.

Butler, J., & Ovens, A. (2015). TGfU and its governance: from conception to special interest group. *Agora para la educación física y el deporte*, 17(1), 77-92.

Butler, J., & Robson, C. (2012). If curriculum is a race (curerre) can TGfU put us back in? In E. Singleton and A. Varpalotai (Eds.), *Pedagogy in Motion: A Community of Inquiry for Studies in Human Movement* (pp. 147-168). Ontario, Canada. Althouse Press.

Butler, J., & Robson, C. (2013). Enabling constraints: Co-creating situated learning in inventing games. In A. Ovens, T. Hopper, & J. Butler (Eds.), *Complexity Thinking in Physical Education: Reframing Curriculum, Pedagogy, and -Research*, (pp. 107-120). New York: Routledge.

Butler, J., Oslin, J., Mitchell, S., & Griffin, L. (2008). The way forward for TGfU: Filling the chasm between theory and practice. *Physical & Health Education Journal*, 74(1), 6-12.

Butler, J., Sullivan, S., McGinley, S., & Vranjes, M. (2007). Danish longball: A novel game to introduce the batting/fielding games category. *Physical & Health Education Journal*, 73(3), 29-33.

Grehaigne J., & Godbout, P. (1998). Formative assessment in team sports in a tactical approach context. *Journal of Physical Education, Recreation & Dance 69*(1): 46–51.

Grehaigne, J. F., Richard, J. F, & Griffin, L. (2005). Teaching and learning team sports and games. New York, NY: Routledge Falmer.

Grehaigne, J., & Godbout, P (1997). Performance assessment in team sports. *Journal of Teaching in Physical Education 16*: 500–516.

Grehaigne, J.F.; Richard, J. F., & Griffin, L. L. (2012). *Teaching and learning team sports and games.* New York: Routledge.

Griffin, L. L., & Butler, J. (2005). *Teaching games for understanding: Theory, research, and practice. Champaign*, IL: Human Kinetics.

Griffin, L., Mitchell, S., & Oslin, J. (1997). *Teaching sport concepts and skills: A tactical games approach.* Champaign IL: Human Kinetics.

Griffin, L.L., Butler, J., & Sheppard, J. (2017). Athlete-centred coaching. Extending the possibilities of a holistic and process-oriented model to athlete development. In S. Phill (Ed), *Perspectives on athlete-centred coaching.* New York: Routledge.

Harvey, S., & Jarrett, K. (2014). A review of the game-centred approaches to teaching and coaching literature since 2006. *Physical Education and Sport Pedagogy, 19(3)*, 278-300.

Howard, P. (2002). Network ethnography and the hypermedia organization: New media, new organizations, new methods. *New media and society, 4*(4) 550-574.

Kirk, D. (2010). *Physical education futures.* London: Routledge.

Launder A (2001) *Play Practice: The games approach to teaching and coaching sport.* Adelaide: Human Kinetics.

Launder, A., & Piltz, W. (2013). *Play practice: Engaging and developing skilled players from beginner to elite.* Champaign IL: Human Kinetics.

Light, R. (2013). *Game sense: Pedagogy for performance participation and enjoyment.* Routledge Studies in Physical Education and Youth Sport. Oxen Abingdon: Routledge.

Mandigo, J., Butler, J., & Hopper, T. (2007). What is teaching games for understanding? A Canadian perspective. *Physical and Health Education Journal, 73(2)*, 14-20.

Memmert, D., Almond, L., Bunker, D., Butler, J., Fasold, F., Griffin, L., ... & Nopp, S. (2015). Top 10 Research Questions Related to Teaching Games for Understanding. *Research quarterly for exercise and sport, 86(4)*, 347-359.

Mesquita I, Farias C and Hastie P (2012) The impact of a hybrid sport-education-invasion games competence model soccer unit on students decision making skill execution and overall game performance, *European Physical Education Review 18(2)*: 205-219.

Mitchell, S., Griffin, L., & Oslin, J. (2006). *Teaching sport concepts and skills: A tactical games approach*. Champaign, IL: Human Kinetics.

Mitchell, S., Oslin, J., & Griffin, L. (2013). *Teaching sport concepts and skills: A tactical games approach for ages 7 to 18* (3rd edn). Champaign, IL: Human Kinetics.

Mitchell, S., Oslin. J., & Griffin, L. (2003). *Sport foundations for elementary physical education. A tactical games approach.* Champaign, IL: Human Kinetics.

Oslin, J., and Mitchell, S. (2006). Game-centred approaches to teaching physical education. In: Kirk D, MacDonald D and O'Sullivan M (eds) *The Handbook of Physical Education.* London: SAGE, pp. 627–651.

Ovens, A., & Butler, J. (2016). Complexity, curriculum, and the design of learning system. In C.D. Ennis (Ed.), *Routledge handbook of physical education pedagogies.* New York: Routledge.

Provan, K. & Kenis, P. (2008). Modes of network governance: Structure, management and effectiveness. *Journal of Public Administration Research and Theory, 18: 229–252.* doi:10.1093/jopart/mum015

Rossi, T, Fry, JM, McNeill, M, Tan, CWK (2006). The games concept approach (GCA) as a mandated practice: views of Singaporean teachers *Sport Education and Society, 12*(1): 93-111.

Rovegno, I. (1995). Theoretical perspectives on knowledge and learning and a student teacher's pedagogical content knowledge of dividing and sequencing subject matter, *Journal of Teaching in Physical Education, 14*: 283–304.

Slater, T., & Butler, J. I. (2015). Examining connections between the physical and the mental in education: A linguistic analysis of PE teaching and learning. Linguistics and Education, *30*, 12-25.

Sorensen, E. and Torfing, J. (2005). The democratic anchorage of governance networks, *Scandinavian Political Studies. 28*(3): 195-218.

Stolz, S., & Pill, S. (2014). Teaching games and sport for understanding: Exploring and reconsidering its relevance in physical education. *European Physical Education Review, 20*(1), 36-71.

Storey, B., & Butler J. L. (2010). Ecological thinking and TGfU: Understanding games as complex adaptive systems. In L. Griffin and J. Butler (Eds.), *More Teaching Games for Understanding: Moving globally* (pp. 69-87). Champaign, IL: Human Kinetics.

Storey, B., & Butler, J. (2013). Complexity thinking in PE: Game-centred approaches, games as complex adaptive systems, and ecological values. *Physical Education and Sport Pedagogy, 18*(2), 133-149.

Tallir, I. B., Musch, E., & Lenoir, M. (2003). Assessment of game play in basketball.

Paper presented at: *The 2nd International TGfU Conference: Teaching Sport and Physical Education*, Melbourne, University of Melbourne.

Tallir, I. B., Musch, E., & Valcke M. (2005). Effects of two instructional approaches for basketball on decision making and recognition ability. *International Journal of Sport Psychology 36*: 107–126.

Thorpe, R. & Bunker, D. (1997). A changing focus in games teaching. In Almond, L. (ed). *Physical Education in Schools (pp. 52-80)*. London, UK: Kogan Page.

Thorpe, R. (1996). Physical Education: Beyond the curriculum. In: Armstrong N (ed) *New Directions in Physical Education: Change and Innovation*, London: Cassell, pp.144–156.

Tinning, R. (2010). *Pedagogy and human movement: Theory, practice, research*. Oxon, UK: Routledge.

Werner, P. & Almond, L. (1990). Models of games education. *Journal of Physical Education, Recreation and Dance, 61*(4), 23-27.

Werner, P., Thorpe, R., & Bunker, D. (1996). Teaching games for understanding: Evolution of a model. *Journal of Physical Education, Recreation and Dance, 67*(1), 28-33.

9

Top 10 Research Questions Related to Teaching Games for Understanding

Daniel Memmert, Len Almond, David Bunker, Joy Butler, Frowin Fasold, Linda Griffin, Wolfgang Hillmann, Stefanie Hüttermann, Timo Klein- Soetebier, Stefan König, Stephan Nopp, Marco Rathschlag, Karsten Schul, Sebastian Schwab, Rod Thorpe & Philip Furley

This work has been republished with kind permission from Taylor & Francis, taken from Research Quarterly for Exercise and Sport, 86, 347–359, 2015. ISSN 0270-1367 (https://www.tandfonline.com/loi/urqe20), print/ISSN 2168-3824. DOI: https://doi.org/10.1080/02701367.2015.1087294.

Abstract

In this article, we elaborate on 10 current research questions related to the "teaching games for understanding" (TGfU) approach with the objective of both developing the model itself and fostering game understanding, tactical decision making, and game-playing ability in invasion and net/wall games: (1) How can existing scientific approaches from different disciplines be used to enhance game play for beginners and proficient players? (2) How can state-of-the-art technology be integrated to game-play evaluations of beginners and proficient players by employing corresponding assessments? (3) Can Complexity Thinking Be Considered a Suitable Theoretical Background for Teaching and Learning in Sports-Related Games? (4) How can complexity thinking be utilized to shape day-to-day physical education (PE) and coaching practices? (5) How can game making/designing be helpfully utilized for emergent learning? (6) How could purposeful game design create constraints that enable tactical understanding and skill development through adaptive learning and distributed cognition? (7) How can teacher/coach development programs benefit from game-centered approaches? (8) How can TGfU-related approaches be implemented in teacher or coach education with the goal of facilitating preservice and in-service teachers/coaches' learning to teach and thereby foster their professional development from novices to experienced practitioners? (9) Can the TGfU approach be considered a helpful model across different cultures? (10) Can physical/psychomotor, cognitive, affective/social, and cultural development be fostered via TGfU approaches? The answers to these questions are critical not only for the advancement of teaching and coaching in PE and sport-based clubs, but also for an in-depth discussion on new scientific avenues and technological tools.

Keywords: culture, physical education, sport psychology, technology

All across the world, people engage in, compete, and watch various types of sports. Since the institutionalization of sport in the late 19th century, an important question in sport sciences, sport psychology, human movement science, and sport pedagogy has been how children can be taught most effectively how to play. To generate tactical decision-making possibilities (Griffin & Butler, 2005) and to look for novel, creative solutions (Memmert, 2015), it is important for children to perceive what is relevant information in their environment and to consider this information in their behavior plan. Training of general game ability to carry out invasion, net/wall games, striking/fielding, or target games comes along with the development of useful, tactical, partially exceptional solutions as a base for sports like soccer, ice hockey, team handball, basketball, field hockey, softball, volleyball, beach volleyball, tennis, table tennis, American football, rugby, badminton, cricket, baseball, squash, curling, or golf (Mitchell, Oslin, & Griffin, 2013). Generally speaking, the conceptual approaches of teaching sport-related games in schools and clubs are always about the questions of "what to do" and "how to do" it in complex game situations. The "what" type questions allow for exploration of complex tactics and easily trainable (basic) tactics (Griffin, Mitchell, & Oslin, 1997; Memmert & Harvey, 2010); the "how" type questions embrace discussions of methodological principles for teaching tactical competencies and the attempt to empirically validate them—that is, to guarantee effectiveness and sustainability in physical education (PE) and club training, an issue that seems to be critical especially in PE (cf. König & Singrün, 2013). Additionally, more general principles of play, like space, depth, and width, are important for the development of understanding "what to do" and "when to do it" and, consequently, for the development of tactical skills.

For more than 35 years, different models have been developed in different countries to introduce team and racket sports in schools or sport clubs. Probably the most influential model worldwide has been the "teaching games for understanding" (TGfU) model, introduced by Bunker and Thorpe in 1982 (for a recent review, see Harvey & Jarrett, 2014, and Stolz & Pill, 2014b). The TGfU model succeeded in entering the curriculum plans of North America, Japan, Australia, New Zealand, and the United Kingdom. Further, the importance of TGfU becomes apparent in the regularly held and well-attended TGfU international conferences in partnership with the Association Internationale des Ecoles Superieures d'Education Physique or International Association for Physical Education in Higher Education (AIESEP). The TGfU model became the basis for a special interest group in AIESEP in 2002. Previous TGfU conferences have been held in New Hampshire (2001), Melbourne, Australia (2003), Hong Kong, China (2005), Vancouver, British Columbia, Canada (2008), and Loughborough, United Kingdom (2012), and the conference will be held in Cologne, Germany next year (2016). One-day symposia were held prior to the AIESEP World Congresses in Jyvaskyla, Finland, in 2006; La Coruna, Spain, in 2010; and Auckland, New Zealand, in 2014. The next symposium will be held in Istanbul, Turkey. In addition, the TGfU science community has published extensively in prestigious peer-review journals (e.g., Journal of Teaching in Physical Education; Sport, Education and Society; Physical Education and Sport Pedagogy; and European Physical Education Review. Finally, the impact of the TGfU model has become evident through the publication of more than 30 textbooks and conference books (Table 1) and 1,113 peer-reviewed articles (based on a Google Scholar search completed in December 2014) since 1989 (Butler & Ovens, 2015).

Table 1 Selected Overview Textbooks, Conference Books, and Significant Events in the Area of Teaching Games for Understanding (TGfU) and Subsequent Games Concept Approaches

Year	Authors	Content
1982	Bunker & Thorpe	Landmark article: a model for the teaching of games in secondary schools.
1986	Thorpe, Bunker, & Almond	Launches the TGfU approach into the physical education community with this book as the first TGfU resource.
1997	den Duyn	Emphasizes game sense and initial sport-specific movement skill development through the context of game play.
1997	Mitchell, Oslin, & Griffin	Teaches with the tactics of the tactical games model, skills, and off-the-ball movements to achieve greater flexibility for the teacher.
1999	Curriculum Planning and Development Division	The games concept approach became part of the National Curriculum. Revised physical education syllabus for primary, secondary, and preservice levels. Longitudinal study by researchers at Nanyang University followed.
2000	Metzler	Describes a variety of instructional models appropriate for TGfU and other physical education curriculum models.
2001	Launder	Uses the play practice approach to teaching and coaching sports to focus on teaching game play first instead of technique and skill.
2003	Butler, Griffin, Lombardo, & Nastasi	Presents selected quality representative papers from the First International TGfU Conference 2001.
2003	Mitchell, Oslin, & Griffin	Covers the elementary level as well as middle and secondary levels to show teachers how to move from a traditional approach to a tactical games teaching approach.
2003	Thorpe	Rod Thorpe presented TGfU to the Australian National Conference of Coaches and Officials. He subsequently worked with the Australian Sports Commission and the Australian Coaching Council to adapt TGfU for a broader range of sports deliverers (beyond teachers). The group decided Games Sense is a more attractive term for the modified approach, particularly for coaches.

2004	Light	Introduces Games Sense as an exciting and innovative approach to coaching and physical education that places the game at the heart of the session and explores key concepts as well as essential pedagogical theory.
2005	Griffin & Butler	Represents theory, research, and practice of TGfU through a comprehensive perspective, the latest research, the TGfU model, and tips to apply the TGfU approach.
2005	Grehaigne, Wallian, & Godbout	Focuses on the foundations and applications of constructivism for the teaching and learning of invasion sports and games with the tactical-decision learning model.
2006	Liu, Li, & Cruz	Proceedings for the Third TGfU International Conference: A Global Perspective of Physical Education and Sport, Hong Kong.
2006	Light, Webb, Piltz, Georgakis, & Brooker	Proceedings for the Asia Pacific Conference on Teaching Sport and Physical Education for Understanding.
2006	Mitchell, Oslin, & Griffin	Using the tactical games model, helps students to expand their ability to perform specific skills through modified game play in which they apply specific tactics.
2007	Rossi, Fry, McNeill, & Tan	Reports on the views of Singaporean teachers of a mandated curriculum innovation aimed at changing the nature of games pedagogy within the physical education curriculum framework in Singapore.
2007	Tallir, Lenoir, Valcke, & Musch	Introduction of the invasion games competence model.
2009	Hopper, Butler & Storey	Combines the ideas and perspectives of the Fourth International TGfU Conference in 2008 and highlights the current research and practice around the world in TGfU.
2010	Butler & Griffin	Brings the TGfU approach to life. This book is not a rehash or a revision of the 2005 book; it presents all-new material on TGfU.
2010	Hastie	Introduction of the student-designed games—making games for learning.

2010	Slade	Presents how to use games to keep kids active and involved and how to teach them fundamental movement skills and game sense that will help them develop a lifelong love of activity.
2012	Butler	A collection of research studies written by practicing physical educators with a focus on reconceptualizing physical education through TGfU.
2012	Pill	Focuses on Australian football sport teaching and how to bridge the gap between the game sense theory and practical application of game-centered skill teaching.
2013	Mitchell, Oslin, & Griffin	An integrative comprehensive textbook covering early grades to secondary grades for a tactical model that helps students to expand their ability to perform specific skills through modified game play in which they apply specific tactics.
2013	Ovens, Hopper, & Butler	Focuses on complexity thinking in the context of physical education and enables fresh ways of thinking about research, teaching, curriculum, and learning.
2013	Pill	Introduces ideas and activities of working with a game-centered Game Sense and sport education approach to physical education games and sport teaching.
2014	Light, Quay, Harvey, & Mooney	Examines new approaches in games teaching and team sport coaching that are player/student-centered and inquiry-based.
2014	Pill	With the game sense theory, develops a teaching guide for early-years and primary school educators for physical education.
2015	Memmert	Introduces tactical creativity in the field of TGfU and discusses on the basis of a new theoretical framework (tactical creativity approach) new rules for training conditions for teaching and coaching tactical creativity to children and young people.

As highlighted in Figure 1, the conferences and symposia have provided a fertile means for supporting and stimulating research activity around TGfU. In the last two decades, several suggestions for rethinking, theorizing, and exploring the basic TGfU model by Bunker and Thorpe (1982) have been published (e.g., Chow et al., 2007; Dodds, Griffin, & Placek, 2001; Kirk & MacPhail, 2002, 2009; Oslin & Mitchell, 2006; Stolz & Pill, 2014a; also see Table 1).

Figure 1 "Teaching games for understanding" (TGfU) Conferences impact on scholarly output: Articles (Butler & Ovens, 2015). © Agora for Physical Education and Sport. Reproduced by permission of Agora for Physical Education and Sport. Permission to reuse must be obtained from the rightsholder.

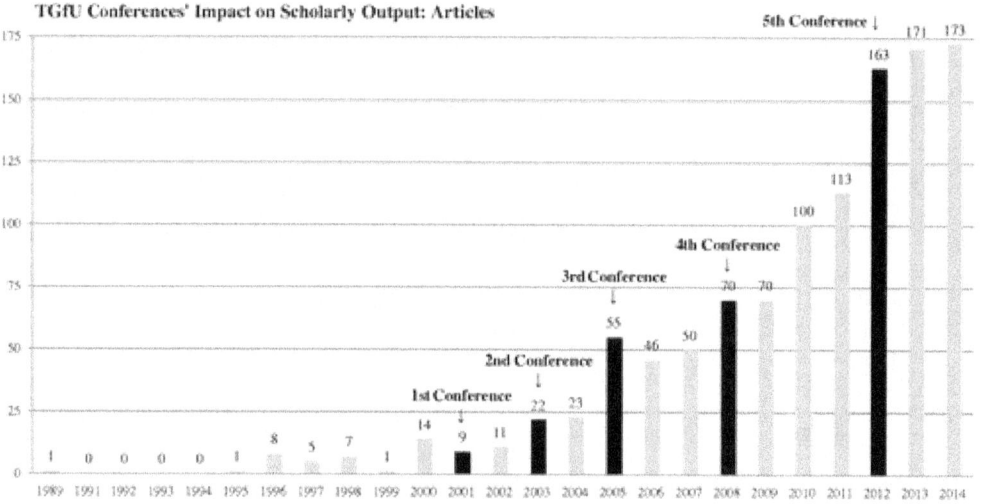

In summary, the TGfU framework has stimulated a bulk of research activity and has applied implications for teaching and coaching of both tactical and technical skills in different sport-related games. The emerging game-centered approaches place the learner in problem-solving situations, in which decision making is of central importance and coincides with skill and movement development within this game-centered context. In the following section, we will discuss the top 10 prevailing research questions related to TGfU to enhance and develop this concept in the area of invasion and net/wall sports. A central aim is to introduce recent frameworks and models from other kinds of disciplines like psychology, pedagogics, and ecological psychology to test the value of adding them to TGfU and—if appropriate—try to combine them with the TGfU approach.

Top 10 Research Questions Related to Teaching Games for Understanding

In this section, the proposed top 10 research questions relating to the TGfU model are presented. These research questions were derived when establishing the conference themes for the upcoming TGfU conference in Cologne in 2016. Forty-two scientific board members from 16 different countries developed and finalized the conference themes (see http://www.tgfu2016.info). In this collaborative endeavor, six overarching themes emerged and have been published on the conference homepage:

- Using scientific approaches from different disciplines (e.g., pedagogy, psychology) to enhance game play for beginners and proficient players. This theme encompasses approaches associated with TGfU and other related approaches (e.g., small-sided games) for promoting decision making, anticipation, attention, and perception within games-based learning to develop creative and intelligent performers.
- Using technology to evaluate game play for beginners and proficient players that encompasses game-play evaluation/assessment.
- Complexity thinking in learning through games to consider the broad movement to understanding game learning as dynamic and nonlinear and as part of forming a complex learning system. The recognition of games as complex adaptive learning systems raises questions about how best to utilize complexity thinking to shape day-to-day PE and coaching practices.
- Game making/designing for emergent learning to enable young people to design, create, or invent their own games. How can purposeful game designing create constraints that enable tactical understanding and skill development through adaptive learning and distributed cognition?
- Teacher/coach development in game-centered approaches—preservice and in-service teachers/coaches learning to teach by using TGfU-related approaches as well as professional development of novice to experienced practitioners. This topic can also link to pedagogical strategies associated with TGfU such as facilitation, observation, and analysis as well as questioning.
- Understanding games for learning and cultural development. This theme encompasses physical/psychomotor, cognitive, affective/social, and cultural development via TGfU approaches, which include indigenous cultural perspectives.

From these six overarching themes, the lead author derived 10 research questions in collaboration with the co-authors that are critical to the field of TGfU (see

Table 2). In the following sections, we provide a brief overview and rationale for the top 10 research questions. Our central aim is to highlight why these questions are of central importance to the field, rather than providing a comprehensive review of the literature for the individual questions.

Table 2 Top 10 Research Questions Related to Teaching Games for Understanding (TGfU)

1	How can existing scientific approaches from different disciplines (e.g., pedagogy, psychology) be used to enhance game play for beginners and proficient players?
2	How can state-of-the-art technology be integrated to game-play evaluations of beginners and proficient players by employing corresponding assessments?
3	Can complexity thinking be considered a suitable theoretical background for teaching and learning in sports-related games?
4	How can complexity thinking be utilized to shape day-to-day physical education and coaching practices?
5	How can game making/designing be helpfully utilized for emergent learning (i.e., enabling young people to design, create, or invent their own games)?
6	How could purposeful game design create the constraints that enable tactical understanding and skill development through adaptive learning and distributed cognition?
7	How can teacher/coach development programs benefit from game-centered approaches?
8	How can TGfU-related approaches be implemented in teacher or coach education with the goal of facilitating preservice and in-service teachers/coaches' learning to teach and thereby foster their professional development from novices to experienced practitioners?
9	Can the TGfU approach be considered a helpful model across different cultures?
10	Can physical/psychomotor, cognitive, affective/social, and cultural development be fostered via TGfU approaches?

1. How Can Existing Scientific Approaches From Different Disciplines (e.g., Pedagogy, Psychology) Be Used to Enhance Game Play for Beginners and Proficient Players?

The first question asks how approaches related to TGfU can benefit from established findings in neighboring disciplines in promoting decision making, anticipation, attention, and perception within game-based learning to develop creative and intelligent performers. One of the notions of recent research endeavors is to add further knowledge to the originally pedagogical-directed game-centered model of TGfU. This knowledge may come from other scientific communities such as psychology or sport psychology and can be exemplified by the research field of creativity (Guilford, 1967; Sternberg & Lubart, 1995). The primary aim of the current games-centered approaches (see Table 1) is to teach/coach tactical problem solving through small-sided games (Hill-Haas, Dawson, Impellizzeri, & Coutts, 2011) in different types of invasion games (e.g., basketball, netball, soccer), thereby enabling learners to find the best tactical solutions. In addition to teaching tactical abilities concerned with finding the ideal solution to a given situation, tactical creativity refers to the production of varying, rare, and flexible decisions in different invasion, striking, target, and net/wall game situations (Memmert & Roth, 2007). Thus, new options and possibilities to foster tactical creativity could be incorporated in the TGfU approach (for a comprehensive discussion, see Memmert, 2015).

The TGfU approach would benefit from further research areas in psychology or exercise psychology. Among others, these areas include motivation research (Friedman & Förster, 2001; Higgins, 1997), attention research (Goldstein, 2011; Kasof, 1997), memory research (Baddeley, 2007; Soto & Humphreys, 2007), as well as general learning research (Cleeremans, Destrebecqz, & Boyer, 1998; Reber, 1993) or exercise research (Hoff, Wisløff, Engen, Kemi, & Helgerud, 2002). All of these paradigms have already been transferred to sport sciences and have elucidated how people undertake fast and effective training to understand and store new content in more effective ways. For example, the significant influence of motivation on decision-making performance was demonstrated experimentally (Memmert, Hüttermann, & Orliczek, 2013). A longitudinal study by Memmert (2007) showed the effects of an attention-broadening training program on the development of creative performance in the area of sports. Recent empirical evidence has indicated that working memory can be considered a core concept in understanding performance processes in invasion and net/wall games (Furley & Memmert, 2013). Research studies have verified that implicit and analogy learning is a powerful learning mechanism for technical and tactical skills in a complex environment (for a review, see Jackson & Farrow, 2005). Transferring core ideas from the science of training showed the necessity of learning game ability during longer periods of time (König & Singrün, 2013; Roth & Kröger, 2011).

2. How Can State-of-the-Art Technology Be Integrated to Game-Play Evaluations of Beginners and Proficient Players by Employing Corresponding Assessments?

The assessment of game play or game performance continues to be and will be one of the most difficult assignments in PE (Chen & Rovegno, 2000; Gréhaigne, Godbout, & Bouthier, 1997; Gréhaigne, Richard, & Griffin, 2005; Griffin & Richard, 2003; Mitchell et al., 2013; Oslin, Mitchell, & Griffin, 1998; Richard, Godbout, Tousignant, & Gréhaigne, 1999). Individual game performance is a complex construct that is influenced by a number of different parameters (Hohmann & Brack, 1983; Wagner, Finkenzeller, Würth, & von Duvillard, 2014) and should not be confused with game success (Lames, 1998). The evaluator needs to differentiate individual performances in the context of team performance from innumerable different game situations and has to consider the complexity of the interactions (Carling, Reilly, & Williams, 2009; Drust, Atkinson, & Reilly, 2007). Key performance indicators of tactical behavior are also predominantly accessible as qualitative data, which are subject to reliability and validity issues (e.g., Memmert & Harvey, 2008; Nadeau, Richard, & Godbout, 2008). The most frequently used instrument to measure individual tactical behavior following the TGfU approach in invasion games is the Game Performance Assessment Instrument (GPAI; Arias & Castejón, 2012; Arias-Estero & Castejón, 2014; Mitchell et al., 2013; Oslin et al., 1998). Another accepted instrument to measure game ability is the team sport assessment procedure (TSAP; Arias & Castejón, 2012; Gréhaigne et al., 1997; Nadeau et al., 2008).

In 2002, the International Society for Technology in Education developed the National Educational Technology Standards for Teachers to define useful technologies to facilitate a variety of assessments and evaluation strategies (see Willis, 2012). Some studies have examined the purpose and usefulness of technologies, especially video recording, by using the GPAI and TSAP to evaluate game-play performance and complex tactical behavior (Arias-Estero & Castejón, 2014; Harvey, Cushion, Wegis, & Massa-Gonzales, 2010; Pritchard, Hawkins, & Wiegand, 2008; Tallir, Lenoir, Valcke, & Musch, 2007). One approach to analyze multiple players in a sporting environment is to use manual (Perš & KovaČiČ, 2000) and, more recently, automated tracking systems (Baca, 2008; Baca, Dabnichki, Heller, & Kornfeind, 2009; Barris & Button, 2008) to examine the interaction among teammates and opponents during competition (Grunz, Memmert, & Perl, 2012). In many of the cases, tracking systems are only useful for indoor settings like a gymnasium or sports hall (e.g., basketball, netball, badminton, table tennis). Several systems, however, have recently been used successfully for outdoor games (e.g., Randers et al., 2010; Sarmento et al., 2014). As an example, tracking techniques have revealed that skilled players cover less distance than less-skilled players in netball. However, the underlying tactical mechanisms are still unclear. For example, it is not clear if this finding is because expert players make better decisions and execute only the necessary runs to receive a pass or to be in an effective offensive position (Ng & Chow, 2012; Perl, Grunz, & Memmert, 2013). Assessments (e.g., Perl & Memmert, 2011) in combination with (tracking) technology measure performances in authentic match situations. Tracking techniques can support a student-centered approach to teaching game performance and skills execution in PE, but it seems to be necessary to develop more advanced key game-related indicators (e.g., finding space, marking opponents, optimal locations of shots; Chow, Tan, Lee, & Button, 2014) to fully exploit the potential benefit.

In summary, using technology to evaluate game play can help teachers link what is taught to what is assessed. But, of course, there are a number of difficulties that have been identified including cost and accessibility of technology (Woods, Karp, & Miao, 2008) and the necessary training time for teachers to develop the relevant skills and understand the technology's use (Silverman, 1997; Thomas & Stratton, 2006).

3. Can Complexity Thinking Be Considered a Suitable Theoretical Background for Teaching and Learning in Sports-Related Games?

Recently, the notion of complexity thinking has emerged as a theoretical orientation in response to the ostensible limitations of the traditional ways of understanding PE. Complexity thinking in learning through games considers the broad movement to understanding game learning as dynamic and nonlinear and as part of forming a complex learning system. According to Ovens, Hopper, and Butler (2013, p. l), "complexity provides ways of understanding that embrace uncertainty, non-linearity and the inevitable 'messiness' that is inherent in educational settings, paying attention to the ways in which the whole is greater than the sum of its parts."

In this respect, it is important to note that complexity does not reflect a single body of thought or unified theory as there is little consensus and no solid, agreed-upon body of knowledge (Alhadeff-Jones, 2008; Richardson & Cilliers, 2001). Originally, the ideas about complexity stem from disciplinary fields as diverse as physics, biology, economics, sociology, and law (Mason, 2008). As the definition of complexity is elusive and the task of understanding complexity is itself complex (Ovens et al., 2013), complexity is often characterized in terms of the objects of study (Davis & Sumara, 2006), which are usually modeled as systems of interacting entities. Importantly, it is assumed that the system is self-organizing and is continually constructing its own future as continuity and transformation (Stacey, 2001). Critically, the focus is not on the system itself but instead on the process of interaction among the entities of the system, which enables the emergent properties and forms that are the focus of inquiry (Byrne, 2005).

While acknowledging that complexity is difficult to define, researchers within this field of inquiry share a set of concepts and ideas as a theoretical starting point (Ovens et al., 2013):

- *Complex systems* are assumed to exist in situations in which a large number of agents (in sports, e.g., athletes, coaches, and teachers) are interacting with each other in dynamic ways and are changed as a consequence of this dynamic interaction. Constraints (e.g., rules of a game) on a system influence the pattern of interaction and the consequentially occurring changes among the agents. Such constraints allow, for example, teachers and coaches to create certain games to shape a system for an athlete's emergent learning (e.g., Davids, Button, & Bennett, 2008; Ennis, 1992).
- *Emergence* refers to the central idea of complexity that certain properties or features appear that were not previously present as a functional characteristic of a system (Mason, 2008; Richardson & Cilliers, 2001). Therefore, the concept of emergence and complex systems becomes more than the sum of their parts—for example, when teamwork or tactics emerge from the activities and interactions of players.
- *Adaptation and learning* can be defined as the ability of complex systems to continuously reorient their structures to maintain coherence with the environment—for example, when athletes develop new tactics to enhance game play (Ovens et al., 2013).

4. How Can Complexity Thinking Be Utilized to Shape Day-to-Day PE and Coaching Practices?

In a general sense, the theoretical orientation of complexity thinking should encourage teachers, educators, and researchers to conceptualize learning in sport and PE as more organic and emergent (Butler, Storey, & Robson, 2014). With regard to teaching and learning through games, the potential of complexity is not a superior explanatory system or metadiscourse providing a more complete or superior set of explanations, but rather, it provides a new approach that has the potential to generate new, creative, and innovative ways of understanding and teaching sport games. Complexity thinking in the field of teaching and learning in games is still evolving, and future research and practical work are needed to establish the optimistic claims of complexity thinking within games. For example, one critical question to explore is how coaches and teachers can implement and shape evidence-based constraints in games to achieve the most beneficial emergence of learning and adaption among players (see Davids et al., 2008).

5. How Can Game Making/Designing Be Helpfully Utilized for Emergent Learning (i.e., Enabling Young People to Design, Create, or Invent Their Own Games)?

With the help of simple games, students and athletes should be encouraged to develop game understanding and tactical consciousness by reflecting on games in a permanent process in group discussions. Teachers and coaches ask questions about "what," "where," and "why," and not just "how." In this way, a verbal and bodily interaction in games is tightly interrelated. Thus, the concept has changed over the last decades to a more student-centered, problem-based approach and away from a teacher-centered approach (Tan, Chow, & Davids, 2012). In addition, Light and Fawns (2003, p. 161) argued "that games taught in PE using TGfU as a form of educational conversation in which the mind, expressed in speech, and the body, expressed in action, embody the ideal holistic learning experience that simultaneously provides for cognitive, affective, social, and physical learning."

Practical sessions have to be developed that particularly highlight the possibility of modifying and designing games to enable tactical understanding and skill development through adaptive learning. Teachers and coaches are encouraged to expand their interventions and approaches from motor and cognitive domains to social domains (Butler et al., 2014). As Butler (2013) explains, the inventing-games approach has three educational purposes: (a) to bring play back into games, (b) to help players learn about game structure, and (c) to help players learn about "democracy in action." With a similar intention, Greve (2013) analyzed the idea of learning by reflecting using the example of team handball, and Loibl (2001) transferred the concept of generic learning to basketball.

6. How Could Purposeful Game Design Create the Constraints That Enable Tactical Understanding and Skill Development Through Adaptive Learning and Distributed Cognition?

The TGfU concept enables young people to design, create, or invent their own games. TGfU is an instructional model focused on developing learners' abilities to play games (Kirk & MacPhail, 2002). One of the ways in which TGfU has been implemented has been through game invention, which enables learners to design games as a way of learning about game complexity. Learning begins within games that are modified to reduce skill demands and free players to engage cognitively in game play and learn physical skills as they are needed to enable play (Light & Fawns, 2003). By laying down simplified rules, altering the playing fields, and altering the play equipment, it is possible to modify and adjust game forms to the respective performance level of learners, or rather, the appropriate level of challenge (Hastie, 2010; Light & Fawns, 2003)—a strategy that has, for example, been adopted in net and wall games (Bohler, 2006). Rather than breaking a game into parts (e.g., rules, tactics), the learning process is seen as a system of interaction and adapting subsystems (Rovegno & Kirk, 1995). Game techniques are not explicitly altered before learners have reached a certain performance level requiring particular new techniques. Game forms are designed as a challenge to the players for an integrative development of their game understanding, tactical consciousness, decision-making processes, and technique execution. Therefore, learning is viewed as a self-organizing process that is emergent and adaptive with respect to different conditions.

7. How Can Teacher/Coach Development Programs Benefit From Game-Centered Approaches?

For teachers or coaches, it is not easy to implement game-centered approaches like TGfU in their units. This is because there is limited consensus regarding best practices with regard to how teachers and coaches can be supported by incorporating the respective education and training approaches within their own teaching or preparation programs. Beyond that, there is limited research that focuses on evaluating the most suitable use of pedagogy based on game-centered approaches to achieve the best outcome for students' learning results (Parry, 2014). In the lines of traditional pedagogies, performance-based teaching methods applying skill drills and technique practice still dominate PE (Pill, 2013). In comparison to traditional skill-based approaches, however, game-centered approaches such as TGfU, demand a more constructivist and student-centered pedagogy (Fisette, 2006). In this context, Memmert and König (2007) analyzed the impact of students' acceptance and the general feasibility of game-centered approaches in PE. Teachers have to accommodate a different focus of learning within which they have to act as an information instructor and facilitator by placing the learner in the center of the learning process (Butler, 1997; Dyson, Griffin, & Hastie, 2004). In this regard, pedagogical strategies associated with TGfU such as facilitation, observation, analysis, and questioning have been advocated to be beneficial for developing effective teaching and coaching strategies.

In the past, relatively short instruction periods for implementing game-centered approaches provided only limited support for teachers or coaches and therefore failed to foster a pedagogical knowledge base to employ game-centered pedagogy (Harvey & Jarrett, 2014). Short instructional periods (i.e., workshops) tend to lead to an epistemological gap between game-centered approaches in theory and teaching practice. This gap, however, might be bridged through more professional learning communities by further examining professional development and teacher learning within game-centered approaches (Light, 2008) and by integrating more empirical research into teacher education—an idea that may help teachers-to-be understand and compare learning concepts on the basis of empirical evidence (König, 2014b).

However, there is another side to this discussion that is often reported by teachers and coaches and has not been adequately addressed so far. The problem is that TGfU has flourished with researchers in universities and institutes of higher education, yet the TGfU influence on teachers/coaches appears to have failed to reach them and become part of normal practice. This issue may be due to the fact that researchers publish their work in journals that are not accessible to most teachers/coaches. However, insufficient attention has been paid to (a) the ways in which ideas are absorbed into professional practice; (b) recognition of teachers' concerns, their school culture, and professional practice; and (c) how teachers can incorporate the ideas of TGfU into their practice.

Currently, researchers speak of "translational research," but it tends to be directed through the eyes of researchers who may have insufficient understanding of the problems of practice and overlook its internal complexity. This issue needs to be addressed and can be regarded as a research priority for the whole profession.

8. How Can TGfU-Related Approaches Be Implemented in Teacher or Coach Education With the Goal of Facilitating Preservice and In-Service Teachers/Coaches' Learning to Teach and Thereby Foster Their Professional Development From Novices to Experienced Practitioners?

To effectively implement TGfU in school or club units, teachers and coaches have to be supported with effective professional endorsement that provides them with knowledge and skills they can implement in their teaching routines. Such a professional development has to focus on both the content and profound knowledge of how children learn most effectively (Corcoran, 1995). Dealing with new ideas is a difficult task and requires a solid theoretical framework that supports this process of change (Guskey, 2002). In her detailed overview, Parry (2014) proposed a professional-development model that supports teachers in implementing game-centered approaches like TGfU. The model consists of four key phases: (a) introductory workshop, (b) planning/designing, (c) implementation, and (d) evaluation. In Phase 1, an introductory game-centered approach workshop is conducted by one of the "experts" for the teacher participants to identify what preexisting knowledge the participating teachers have and what professional learning they need. The concept of Phase 2 is that teachers elaborate on their units of work and subsequent lesson plans together. Units and lessons are further analyzed using a benchmark observational system for game-centered approaches. During Phase 3 implementation, teacher participants are asked to teach the planned units and lessons in school. Teachers are required to submit their lesson reflections for analysis, and then teacher interviews are conducted in Phase 4. Additionally, we might learn from Borggrefe and Cachay's (2015) analysis of athlete–coach communication exploring how information can be imparted more effectively.

At present, there is no conceptual framework that provides a comprehensive guide to developing informed practice. If researchers cannot provide a comprehensive up-to-date picture of how their work can inform practice, how can we expect practitioners on their own to develop informed practice and improve learning? This relates to another big issue. We need to build a collaborative venture to ensure that new research (in all of the diverse fields) is made accessible in forms that can be "turned" into guides that become a significant and sustainable part of everyday professional practice. Surely, this issue is of major concern and therefore needs to be highlighted as a research priority. In summary, implementing a game-centered approach like TGfU demands complex professional learning that considers a wide range of contextual factors within the educational setting.

9. Can the TGfU Approach Be Considered a Helpful Model Across Different Cultures?

Generally, learning has been shown to be influenced by sociocultural experiences of learners in specific contexts (e.g., Davis & Sumara, 2003). Therefore, a major topic in the development and implementation of pedagogical and methodological models or theories must be the consideration of cultural differences in physical, cognitive, and/or social learning. Based on Pinar's (2012) extensive considerations in the curricula of teaching, teaching concepts or models should not be understood as a fixed frame, but as a malleable one, which should be adapted to cultural and social characteristics of a specific peer group.

Stolz and Pill (2014b) as well as Harvey and Jarrett (2014) reviewed the TGfU literature and reported that the approaches in the practical implementation of TGfU in various countries and cultures differ more or less from each other. Thus, particularly, the different revisions of the TGfU approach in the worldwide PE literature seem to be underdeveloped for the understanding and the implication of their contents in practice (Stolz & Pill, 2014b). Comparing teaching in Singapore to teaching in Australia, Light and Tan (2006) stated that social and cultural differences in these two countries have a significant impact on the interpretation and the implementation of the TGfU teaching method. Nevertheless, further empirical studies are needed to further elucidate the TGfU concept in different cultural and social environments.

Butler (2014) stated that the development of the TGfU concept is based on a Western-oriented social-cultural background, as three important founders of TGfU are from Western countries. Thus, a major challenge of future research will be the identification of the precise global-cultural characteristics that influence the implementation and success of TGfU in learner development. A culture-orientated research perspective should not only focus on pedagogical and social approaches. In addition, further research from physical/psychomotor and/or psychological/cognitive (e.g., creativity) perspectives with a cultural background could help improve the way of teaching games all over the world.

10. Can Physical/Psychomotor, Cognitive, Affective/Social, and Cultural Development Be Fostered Via TGfU Approaches?

The TGfU-approach seems to be an appropriate way to develop physical literacy (Mandigo & Corlett, 2010), and research has shown that cognitive abilities could significantly be fostered by this approach (e.g., decision-making skills in soccer; Harvey et al., 2010). That physical and psychomotor skills can be developed in high-intensity movement situations that occur in games seems hardly surprising. Therefore, future research might want to extend the TGfU approach to health-related topics. For example, as Western populations are affected by inactivity and obesity, future research could address how game-centered approaches might be implemented to foster strength and endurance purposefully, an approach that has been successfully realized for individual sports (König, 2014a).

Whereas Mandigo and Corlett (2010) reported evidence in their review that TGfU can promote social skills like fairness, democratic behavior, or social responsibility, further questions on social perspective could highlight ways in which this approach should be adjusted to support inclusive behavior and the integration of disabled people in games and sports citizenship.

Conclusion

In the past, in the present, and surely in the future, the original TGfU model of Bunker and Thorpe (1982) has gained, is gaining, and will gain growing significance in research, teaching, and coaching in invasion and net/wall games around the world. Kirk and MacPhail (2002) originally stated:

> *In particular, we suggest that explicit attention to the learner's perspective, game concept, thinking strategically, cue recognition, technique selection, and skill development as the clustering of strategies and techniques, and situated performance as legitimate peripheral participation in games, elaborate upon the already existing but implied learning principles of the Bunker-Thorpe model.*
> (pp. 280–281)

This statement delivers a number of major challenges for research in game-centered approaches, like more manipulation checks, improved assessment tools, longitudinal research designs, which might require specific approaches for data analyses (Snijders & Bosker, 1999), and longer intervention programs (Harvey & Jarrett, 2014). Hence, the content of the original Bunker and Thorpe model will be enhanced and thus gain in growing significance.

In summary, our top 10 research questions related to TGfU recommend more integration of other scientific disciplines with specific frameworks as well as contextual and ecological research of game-centered approaches. In this regard, special attention should be paid to technological tools, complex and emergent learning systems, and teacher/coach and learner/cultural development. Challenging our TGfU community to embrace these research foci could lead to a reorientation of the general research content and methodology in the context of TGfU research.

References

1. Alhadeff-Jones, M. (2008). Three generations of complexity theories: Nuances and ambiguities. In M. Mason (Ed.), Complexity theory and the philosophy of education (pp. 62–78). Chichester, UK: Wiley-Blackwell.
2. Arias, J. L., & Castejón, F. J. (2012). Review of the instruments most frequently employed to assess tactics in physical education and youth sports. Journal of Teaching in Physical Education, 31, 381–391.
3. Arias-Estero, J., & Castejón, F. (2014). Using instruments for tactical assessment in physical education and extra-curricular sports. European Physical Education Review, 20, 525–535.
4. Baca, A. (2008). Tracking motion in sport—trends and limitations. In J. Hammond (Ed.), Proceedings of the 9th Australasian Conference on Mathematics and Computers in Sport, MathSport (pp. 1–7). Tweed Heads, NSW, Australia: The Australian & New Zealand Industrial and Applied Mathematics Journal (formerly, The Journal of the Australian Mathematical Society).
5. Baca, A., Dabnichki, P., Heller, M., & Kornfeind, P. (2009). Ubiquitous computing in sports: A review and analysis. Journal of Sports Sciences, 27, 1335–1346.
6. Baddeley, A. (2007). Working memory, thought, and action. Oxford, UK: Oxford University Press.
7. Barris, S., & Button, C. (2008). A review of vision-based motion analysis in sport. Sports Medicine, 38, 1025–1043.
8. Bohler, H. R. (2006). Spielen lernen durch Taktik lernen—Beispiel Netz- und Wandspiele. [Learning how to play through tactics]. Sportunterricht, 55, 260–266.
9. Borggrefe, C., & Cachay, K. (2015). Kommunikation als Herausforderung. Eine theoretisch-empirische Studie zur Trainer-Athlet-Kommunikation im Spitzensport [Communication as challenge. A theoretic-empirical study on coach–athlete

communication in high-performance sports]. Schorndorf, Germany: Hofmann.
10. Bunker, D., & Thorpe, R. (1982). A model for the teaching of games in secondary schools. Bulletin of Physical Education, 18, 5–8.
11. Butler, J. (1997). How would Socrates teach games? A constructivist approach to teaching games. Journal of Physical Education, Recreation & Dance, 68(9), 42–47.
12. Butler, J. (2012). Reconceptualizing physical education through teaching games for understanding. Morrisville, NC: Lulu.
13. Butler, J. (2013). Stages for children inventing games. Journal of Physical Education, Recreation & Dance, 84(4), 48–53.
14. Butler, J. (2014). TGfU—would you know it if you saw it? Benchmarks from the tacit knowledge of the founders. European Physical Education Review, 20, 465–488.
15. Butler, J., & Griffin, L. L. (2010). More teaching games for understanding: Moving globally. Champaign, IL: Human Kinetics.
16. Butler, J. I., Griffin, L. L., Lombardo, B., & Nastasi, R. (2003). Teaching games for understanding in physical education and sport: An international perspective. Oxon Hill, MD: American Alliance for Health, Physical Education, Recreation and Dance Publication.
17. Butler, J., & Ovens, A. (2015). The TGfU governance networks: From conception to special interest group. Agora for Physical Education and Sport, 17, 77–92.
18. Butler, J., Storey, B., & Robson, C. (2014). Emergent learning focused teachers and their ecological complexity worldview. Sport, Education and Society, 19, 451–471.
19. Byrne, D. (2005). Complexity, configurations and cases. Theory, Culture & Society, 22, 95–111.
20. Carling, C., Reilly, T., & Williams, A. (Eds.). (2009). Performance assessment for field sports. London, UK: Routledge.
21. Chen, W., & Rovegno, I. (2000). Examination of expert and novice teachers' constructivist-oriented teaching practices using a movement approach to elementary physical education. Research Quarterly for Exercise and Sport, 71, 357–372.
22. Chow, J. Y., Davids, K., Button, C., Shuttleworth, R., Renshaw, I., & Araújo, D. (2007). The role of nonlinear pedagogy in physical education. Review of Educational Research, 77, 251–278.
23. Chow, J. Y., Tan, C. W. K., Lee, M. C. Y., & Button, C. (2014). Possibilities and implications of using a motion-tracking system in physical education. European Physical Education Review, 20, 444–464.
24. Cleeremans, A., Destrebecqz, A., & Boyer, M. (1998). Implicit learning: News from the front. Trends in Cognitive Sciences, 2, 406–416.

25. Corcoran, T. C. (1995). Transforming professional development for teachers: A guide for state policymakers. Washington, DC: National Governors' Association.
26. Curriculum Planning and Development Division. (1999). physical education syllabus for primary, secondary, pre-university levels. Singapore: Ministry of Education.
27. Davids, K., Button, C., & Bennett, S. J. (2008). Dynamics of skill acquisition: A constraints-led approach. Champaign, IL: Human Kinetics.
28. Davis, B., & Sumara, D. (2003). Why aren't they getting this? Working through the regressive myths of constructivist pedagogy. Teaching Education, 14, 123–140.
29. Davis, B., & Sumara, D. J. (2006). Complexity and education: Inquiries into learning, teaching, and research. Mahwah, NJ: Lawrence Erlbaum.
30. den Duyn, N. (1997). Game sense: Developing thinking players. Belconnen, ACT, Australia: Australian Sports Commission.
31. Dodds, P., Griffin, L. L., & Placek, J. H. (2001). A selected review of the literature on development of learners' domain-specific knowledge. Journal of Teaching in Physical Education, 20, 301–313.
32. Drust, B., Atkinson, G., & Reilly, T. (2007). Future perspectives in the evaluation of the physiological demands of soccer. Sports Medicine, 37, 783–805.
33. Dyson, B., Griffin, L. L., & Hastie, P. (2004). Sport education, tactical games, and cooperative learning: Theoretical and pedagogical considerations. Quest, 56, 226–240.
34. Ennis, C. D. (1992). Reconceptualising learning as a dynamical system. Journal of Curriculum and Supervision, 7, 115–130.
35. Fisette, J. L. (2006). Spielverständnis lehren durch das 'Taktik-Spiel_Modell'—Beispiel basketball [Learning understanding of the game through the 'tactic-game-model'—example basketball]. Sportunterricht, 55, 267–273.
36. Friedman, R. S., & Förster, J. (2001). The effects of promotion and prevention cues on creativity. Journal of Personality and Social Psychology, 81, 1001–1013.
37. Furley, P., & Memmert, D. (2013). 'To whom should I pass?' The more options the more attentional guidance from working. PLoS One, 8, e62278. 10.1371/journal.pone.0062278.
38. Goldstein, B. (2011). Cognitive psychology: Connecting mind, research and everyday experience. Independence, KY: Cengage Learning.
39. Gréhaigne, J. F., Godbout, P., & Bouthier, D. (1997). Performance assessment in team sports. Journal of Teaching in Physical Education, 16, 500–516.
40. Gréhaigne, J. F., Richard, J.-F., & Griffin, L. L. (2005). Teaching and learning team sports and games. New York, NY: Routledge.
41. Grehaigne, J. F., Wallian, N., & Godbout, P. (2005). Tactical-decision learning

model and students' practices. Physical Education & Sport Pedagogy, 10, 255–269.

42. Greve, S. (2013). Lernen durch Reflektieren im Sportspiel. Möglichkeiten im Vermittlungsprozess im Rahmen des Sportunterrichts am Beispiel Handball. [Learning by reflecting in sports game. Possibilities in the mediation process within physical education at the example of handball]. Berlin, Germany: Logos.

43. Griffin, L., & Butler, J. (2005). Teaching games for understanding: Theory, research, and practice. Champaign, IL: Human Kinetics.

44. Griffin, L. L., Mitchell, S. A., & Oslin, J. L. (1997). Teaching sport concepts and skills: A tactical games approach. Champaign, IL: Human Kinetics.

45. Griffin, L. L., & Richard, J. -F. (2003). Using authentic assessment to improve students' net/wall game play. Teaching Elementary Physical Education, 3, 23–27.

46. Grunz, A., Memmert, D., & Perl, J. (2012). Tactical pattern recognition in soccer games by means of special self-organizing maps. Human Movement Science, 31, 334–343.

47. Guilford, J. P. (1967). The nature of human intelligence. New York, NY: McGraw Hill.

48. Guskey, T. R. (2002). Professional development and teacher change. Teachers and Teaching: Theory and Practice, 8, 381–391.

49. Harvey, S., Cushion, C. J., Wegis, H. M., & Massa-Gonzales, A. N. (2010). Teaching games for understanding in American high-school soccer: A quantitative data analysis using the Game Performance Assessment Instrument. Physical Education and Sport Pedagogy, 15, 29–54. 10.1080/17408980902729354.

50. Harvey, S., & Jarrett, K. (2014). A review of the game-centered approaches to teaching and coaching literature since 2006. Physical Education and Sport Pedagogy, 19, 278–300.

51. Hastie, P. (2010). Student-designed games: Strategies for promoting creativity, cooperation, and skill development. Champaign, IL: Human Kinetics.

52. Higgins, E. T. (1997). Beyond pleasure and pain. American Psychologist, 52, 1280–1300.

53. Hill-Haas, S. V., Dawson, B., Impellizzeri, F. M., & Coutts, A. J. (2011). Physiology of small-sided games training in football: A systematic review. Sports Medicine, 41, 199–220.

54. Hoff, J., Wisløff, U., Engen, L. C., Kemi, O. J., & Helgerud, J. (2002). Soccer specific aerobic endurance training. British Journal of Sports Medicine, 36, 218–221.

55. Hohmann, A., & Brack, R. (1983). Theoretische Aspekte der Leistungsdiagnostik im Sportspiel [Theoretical aspects of performance analysis in team and racket

sports]. Leistungssport, 13, 5–10.
56. Hopper, T., Butler, J., & Storey, B. (Eds.). (2009). TGfU—Simply good pedagogy: Understanding a complex challenge. Ottawa, Ontario: Physical & Health Education, Canada.
57. Jackson, R. C., & Farrow, D. (2005). Implicit perceptual training: How, when and why? Human Movement Science, 24, 308–325.
58. Kasof, J. (1997). Creativity and breadth of attention. Creativity Research Journal, 10, 303–315.
59. Kirk, D., & MacPhail, A. (2002). Teaching games for understanding and situated learning: Rethinking the Bunker-Thorpe model. Journal of Teaching in Physical Education, 21, 177–192.
60. Kirk, D., & MacPhail, A. (2009). Teaching games for understanding and situated learning: Rethinking the Bunker-Thorpe model. In R. Bailey & D. Kirk (Eds.), The Routledge physical education reader (pp. 269–283). Oxford, UK: Routledge.
61. König, S. (2014a). 'Killing two birds with one stone'—on the effectiveness of implicit training processes in physical education. International Journal of Physical Education, 15, 15–28.
62. König, S. (2014b). Physical education: Implementation of empirical research into teacher education. In P.-M. Rabensteiner & G. Rabensteiner (Eds.), Education: Vol. 3. Internationalization in teacher education (pp. 154–166). Baltmannsweiler, Germany: Schneider Verlag Hohengehren.
63. König, S., & Singrün, P. (2013). Wirkungen und Festigkeit von motorischen Lern- und Trainingsprozessen im Sportunterricht [Effect and consistency of motor learning and training processes in physical education]. Spectrum der Sportwissenschaften, 25, 4–31.
64. Lames, M. (1998). Leistungsfähigkeit, Leistung und Erfolg—ein Beitrag zur Theorie der Sportspiele [Ability to perform, performance and success—A contribution to the theory of sport games]. Sportwissenschaft, 28, 137–152.
65. Launder, A. G. (2001). Play practice: The games approach to teaching and coaching sports. Champaign, IL: Human Kinetics.
66. Light, R. (2004). Coaches' experiences of games sense: Opportunities and challenges. Physical Education & Sport Pedagogy, 9, 115–131.
67. Light, R. (2008). Complex learning theory—Its epistemology and its assumptions about learning: Implications for physical education. Journal of Teaching in Physical Education, 27, 21–37.
68. Light, R., & Fawns, R. (2003). Knowing the game: Integrating speech and action in games teaching through TGfU. Quest, 55, 161–176.

69. Light, R., Quay, J., Harvey, S., & Mooney, A. (2014). Contemporary developments in games teaching. Abingdon, UK: Routledge.
70. Light, R., & Tan, S. (2006). Culture, embodied experience and teachers' development of TGfU in Australia and Singapore. European Physical Education Review, 12, 99–117.
71. Light, R., Webb, P., Piltz, W., Georgakis, A., & Brooker, R. (Eds.). (2006). Proceedings for the Asia Pacific Conference on Teaching Sport and Physical Education for Understanding. Sydney, Australia: University Press.
72. Liu, R., Li, C., & Cruz, A. (Eds.). (2006). Teaching games for understanding in the Asia-Pacific region. Hong Kong: Department of Creative Arts and Physical Education, The Hong Kong Institute of Education.
73. Loibl, J. (2001). Basketball. Genetisches Lehren und Lernen. Spielen—erfinden—erleben—verstehen [Basketball. Genetic teaching and learning. Playing—inventing—experiencing—understanding]. Schorndorf, Germany: Hofmann.
74. Mandigo, J., & Corlett, J. (2010). Teaching games for understanding of what? TGfU's role in the development of physical literacy. In J. I. Butler & L. L. Griffin (Eds.), More teaching games for understanding. Moving globally (pp. 69–78). Champaign, IL: Human Kinetics.
75. Mason, M. (2008). What is complexity theory and what are its implications for educational change? Educational Philosophy and Theory, 40, 35–47.
76. Memmert, D. (2007). Can creativity be improved by an attention-broadening training program? An exploratory study focusing on team sports. Creativity Research Journal, 19, 281–291.
77. Memmert, D. (2015). Teaching tactical creativity in team and racket sports: Research and practice. Abingdon, UK: Routledge.
78. Memmert, D., & Harvey, S. (2008). The Game Performance Assessment Instrument (GPAI): Some concerns and solutions for further development. Journal of Teaching in Physical Education, 27, 220–240.
79. Memmert, D., & Harvey, S. (2010). Identification of non-specific tactical problems in invasion games. Physical Education and Sport Pedagogy, 15, 287–305.
80. Memmert, D., Hüttermann, S., & Orliczek, J. (2013). Decide like Lionel Messi! The impact of regulatory focus on divergent thinking in sports. Journal of Applied Social Psychology, 43, 2163–2167.
81. Memmert, D., & König, S. (2007). Teaching games at elementary schools. International Journal of Physical Education, 44, 54–67.
82. Memmert, D., & Roth, K. (2007). The effects of non-specific and specific concepts on tactical creativity in team ball sports. Journal of Sport Science, 25, 1423–1432.

83. Metzler, M. W. (2000). Instructional models for physical education. Boston, MA: Allyn & Bacon.
84. Mitchell, S. A., Oslin, J. L., & Griffin, L. L. (1997). Teaching sport concepts and skills: A tactical games approach (Vol. 1). Champaign, IL: Human Kinetics.
85. Mitchell, S. A., Oslin, J. L., & Griffin, L. L. (2003). Sport foundations for elementary physical education: A tactical games approach. Champaign, IL: Human Kinetics.
86. Mitchell, S. A., Oslin, J. L., & Griffin, L. L. (2006). Teaching sport concepts and skills: A tactical games approach (2nd ed.). Champaign, IL: Human Kinetics.
87. Mitchell, S. A., Oslin, J. L., & Griffin, L. L. (2013). Teaching sport concepts and skills: A tactical games approach (3rd ed.). Champaign, IL: Human Kinetics.
88. Nadeau, L., Richard, J. -F., & Godbout, P. (2008). The validity and reliability of a performance assessment procedure in ice hockey. Physical Education and Sport Pedagogy, 13, 65–83.
89. Ng, W. X., & Chow, J. Y. (2012, June). Performance analysis of netball players as a function of position and skill: Sports technology in action. Paper presented at the second Association of Southeast Asian Nations Universities Conference on Physical Education and Sport Science, Kuala Lumpur, Malaysia.
90. Oslin, J. L., & Mitchell, S. A. (2006). Game-centred approaches to teaching physical education. In D. Kirk, D. MacDonald, & M. O'Sullivan (Eds.), The handbook of physical education (pp. 627–651). London, UK: Sage.
91. Oslin, J. L., Mitchell, S. A., & Griffin, L. L. (1998). The Game Performance Assessment Instrument (GPAI): Development and preliminary validation. Journal of Teaching in Physical Education, 17, 231–243.
92. Ovens, A., Hopper, T., & Butler, J. (2013). Complexity thinking in physical education. Reframing curriculum, pedagogy and research. London, UK: Routledge.
93. Parry, K. A. (2014). Supporting teachers to implement TGfU: A needs based approach to professional learning. In University of Sydney Papers in HMHCE: Special Games Sense Edition (pp. 127–149). Retrieved from http://sydney.edu.au/education_social_work/research/centres_and_networks/ADPN/HMHCE-papers/resources/HMHCE_GS_Ed_Article_08_2014.pdf. [Google Scholar]
94. Perl, J., Grunz, A. & Memmert, D. (2013). Tactics in soccer: an advanced approach. International Journal of Computer Science in Sport, 12, 33–44.
95. Perl, J., & Memmert, D. (2011). Net-based game analysis by means of the software tool SOCCER. International Journal of Computer Science in Sport, 10, 77–84.
96. Perš, S., & Kovačič, S. (2000). A system for tracking players in sports games by computer vision. Electrotechnical Review, 67, 281–288.
97. Pill, S. A. (2012). Play with Purpose: Developing game sense in AFL footballers.

Hindmarsh SA, Australia: Australian Council for Health, Physical Education and Recreation.

98. Pill, S. A. (2013). Play with Purpose for fundamental movement skill teaching. Kent Town, SA, Australia: Australian Council for Health, Physical Education and Recreation.

99. Pill, S. A. (2014). Play with Purpose: Developing netball game sense. Hindmarsh, SA, Australia: Australian Council for Health, Physical Education and Recreation.

100. Pinar, W. (2012). What is curriculum theory? New York, NY: Routledge.

101. Pritchard, T., Hawkins, A., & Wiegand, R. (2008). Effects of two instructional approaches on skill development, knowledge, and game performance. Measurement in Physical Education and Exercise Science, 12, 219–236.

102. Randers, M. B., Mujika, I., Hewitt, A., Santisteban, J., Bischoff, R., Solano, R., ... Mohr, M. (2010). Application of four different football match analysis systems: A comparative study. Journal of Sports Sciences, 28, 171–182.

103. Reber, A. S. (1993). Implicit learning and tacit knowledge: An essay on the cognitive unconscious. Oxford, UK: Oxford University Press.

104. Richard, J.-F., Godbout, P., Tousignant, M., & Gréhaigne, J. F. (1999). The try-out of a team sport assessment procedure in elementary and junior high school physical education classes. Journal of Teaching in Physical Education, 18, 336–356.

105. Richardson, K., & Cilliers, P. (2001). What is complexity science? A view from different directions. Emergence, 3, 5–23.

106. Rossi, T., Fry, J. M., McNeill, M., & Tan, C. W. K. (2007). The games concept approach (GCA) as a mandated practice: Views of Singaporean teachers. Sport, Education and Society, 12, 93–111.

107. Roth, K., & Kröger, C. (2011). Ballschule. Ein ABC für Spielanfänger [Ballschool—An ABC for beginners]. Schorndorf, Germany: Hofmann.

108. Rovegno, I., & Kirk, D. (1995). Articulations and silences in socially critical work on physical education: Towards a broader agenda. Quest, 47, 447–474.

109. Sarmento, H., Marcelino, R., Anguera, M. T., Campaniço, J., Matos, N., & Leitão, J. C. (2014). Match analysis in football: A systematic review. Journal of Sports Sciences, 32, 1831–1843.

110. Silverman, S. (1997). Technology and physical education: Present, possibilities, and potential problems. Quest, 49, 306–314.

111. Slade, D. (2010). Transforming play: Teaching tactics and game sense. Champaign, IL: Human Kinetics.

112. Snijders, T. A., & Bosker, R. J. (1999). Multilevel analysis: An introduction to basic

and advanced multilevel modeling. London, UK: Sage.

113. Soto, D., & Humphreys, G. W. (2007). Automatic guidance of visual attention from verbal working memory. Journal of Experimental Psychology: Human Perception & Performance, 33, 730–737.

114. Stacey, R. (2001). Complex responsive processes in organisations: Learning and knowledge creation. London, UK: Routledge.

115. Sternberg, R. J., & Lubart, T. I. (1995). Defying the crowd. New York, NY: Free Press.

116. Stolz, S. A., & Pill, S. (2014a). A narrative approach to exploring TGfU-GS. Sport, Education and Society. Advance online publication. 10.1080/13573322.2014.890930.

117. Stolz, S., & Pill, S. (2014b). Teaching games and sport for understanding: Exploring and reconsidering its relevance in physical education. European Physical Education Review, 20, 36–71.

118. Tallir, I. B., Lenoir, M., Valcke, M., & Musch, E. (2007). Do alternative instructional approaches result in different game performance learning outcomes? Authentic assessment in varying game conditions. International Journal of Sport Psychology, 38, 263–282.

119. Tan, C. W. K., Chow, J. Y., & Davids, K. (2012). 'How does TGfU work?': Examining the relationship between learning design in TGfU and a nonlinear pedagogy. Physical Education and Sport Pedagogy, 17, 331–348.

120. Thomas, A., & Stratton, G. (2006). What we are really doing with ICT in physical education: A national audit of equipment, use, teacher attitudes, support, and training. British Journal of Educational Technology, 37, 617–632.

121. Thorpe, R. Teaching games for understanding: Does it meet your needs? Paper presented at the Second International Conference: Teaching Sport and Education for Understanding, Melbourne, Australia (2003, December)

122. Thorpe, R., Bunker, D., & Almond, L. (1986). Rethinking games teaching. Loughborough, England: Department of Physical Education and Sports Science, University of Technology.

123. Wagner, H., Finkenzeller, T., Würth, S., & von Duvillard, S. P. (2014). Individual and team performance in team-handball: A review. Journal of Sports Science and Medicine, 13, 808–816.

124. Willis, J. (2012). Adapting the 2008 NETS-T Standards for use in teacher education: Part II. International Journal of Technology in Teaching and Learning, 8, 78–97.

125. Woods, M. L., Karp, G. G., & Miao, H. (2008). Physical educators' technology competencies and usage. Physical Educator, 65, 82–99.

10

The Way Forward for TGfU: Filling the Chasm between Theory and Practice

Joy Butler, Judy Oslin, Stephen Mitchell & Linda Griffin

In the discipline of physical education, we are all affected by the chasm that exists between theory and practice and by our current joint failure to translate TGfU into a reality in classrooms and sports clubs. Paradoxically, some individuals and institutions find their interests are served by such a gap, since silence and denial have long helped society to default to the status quo. Some educators help to widen the chasm, and some work to bridge it, depending upon their position. The purpose of this article is to search for ways to make the essential work of narrowing, filling or bridging the chasm between theory and practice go forward most rapidly and effectively TGfU stands ready to bring physical education into line with all other subject areas, as they pursue educational goals in critical thinking, problem solving, and decision making.

We will describe how TGfU, as a curriculum approach implemented in quality physical education programs, can integrate the overall goals of schooling. The approach is becoming broadly accepted in many countries as an effective method of teaching games, and it is time for more Canadian physical educators to get on board and help move it forward. In this article we will (a) describe how teachers can get involved in teaching TGfU, using tried and tested means for implementing curricular innovations and (b) identify the cautions that teachers have, the pedagogical strategies for dealing with these, and the successes of students, as more of them become better games players and experience greater enjoyment through engagement with TGfU.

Partnerships Required to Fill the Chasm

If indeed silence and denial do help society default to the status quo, how does this contribute to the growing chasm between theory and practice, when it comes to TGfU? Educators who are not reflective, and are therefore silent about their practice, are likely to teach what they know in the way that they were taught, rather than examining the reasons why they teach particular activities. These practitioners will default to positions such as "it's the way it's always been done" rather than considering the bigger picture issues (e.g. what should be the emphasis in our teaching and learning, how is this reflected in the way we assess?). Some teachers are aware that different teaching approaches are critical for the range of learning styles in the class but remain in denial as they continue to use only a didactic, teacher-centered and technique-based approach in teaching games. Other teachers are simply unaware of TGfU's existence as a new curriculum model, or have not had the opportunity to find out about it because of the paucity of district workshops. Some teachers have examined the approach and are skeptical. They await more concrete evidence from researchers before incorporating the model in their teaching repertoire. Some teachers have encountered TGfU and struggle with trying to implement it with students and to justify it to colleagues who are not familiar with the new approach and may offer some resistance.

The struggle and effort required to implement new curriculum models is often enough to dissuade teachers from the initial attempt. Teachers have enough to deal with in the current climate without adding this to the pile! But it is here that the rubber meets the road - researchers cannot work in a vacuum or in isolation, especially when it comes to TGfU as a 'hands-on' approach is integral to researching this model. As Kirk and Tinning (1992) suggest, "Theory and practice cannot be separated, but will continue to refine and redefine each other in a continuous process of organic change" (p.4). The evolution of TGfU needs to evolve in this interactive process (called praxis).

To research praxis, theorists need to understand teachers and work with and alongside practitioners. Such discourse, however, designed to help "bolster some of the conceptual and practical obstacles they were intended to critique… seems to mitigate against meaningful communication between theorists and practitioners (Davis &C Sumara, 2003, p. 137)." Each group stares across the chasm pointing fingers at the other. On one hand, practitioners accuse the theorists/researchers of being unrealistic and out of touch with the rigors and demands of the mechanical and apparent linear structures of schooling. The theorists, on the other hand, accuse practitioners of being bogged down by daily routines that they forget the purpose of their work.

Is there one group that is not getting it? The metaphor of the bridge is limited; filling in the space seems much more productive with both sides working on filling in the void from each end. Perhaps it is not just researchers and teachers that cause the chasm. Administrators are frequently unwilling or unable to provide the necessary infrastructure to sustain change in curricular design or implement a curricular innovation. Unless administrators provide the necessary infrastructure, it is hard to sustain any change in curricular design or implement any curricular innovation. However, most administrators are too busy to find out what is going on in each and every subject area. It is the practitioner who must make the need known to this group and who must be clear about the need for in-service work, collaboration amongst colleagues in various schools, and the importance of connection to professional organizations.

Why TGfU?

One of the benefits of alternative curricular models is that they are different from usual practice. Examining different models forces us to become cognizant of the differences, and examine them in order to make judgments. This process, in turn, can help us to revisit and understand our beliefs and values about education. It is here we would like to start - by examining what we believe to be the benefits of the TGfU model.
(see table 1)

TGfU's natural alliance with other disciplines comes via constructivism. TGfU stands ready to bring physical education into line with all other subject areas as they pursue educational goals such as critical thinking, problem solving and decision making. Since TGfU is based on constructivist learning theory, PE teachers can converse with other subject areas thereby serving to unite rather than divide. As we all work to create democratically informed and responsible citizens who have a sense of balance in their lives, the PE teacher is seen to be pulling in the same direction as other members of staff. The benefits of using TGfU to provide a more holistic games education experience for children in physical education include the following:

- increased motivation to play games in and outside physical education
- increased competence; better acquisition of skills
- on-the-ball as well as off-the-ball
- better development of decision-making skills

Through questioning, the teacher helps students to explore possible solutions to problems, which then become the focus of a situated practice. The teacher also

Table 1. The Benefits behind the TGfU Model

- The TGfU focus moves from how to what, when, where and then leads to a better understanding of why. Students need to critically think and problem solve.
- Students often have to make decisions in small groups and concepts such as negotiating, compromising and listening are developed.
- Students are continuously placed in decision-making situations, which build on their creativity and willingness to question.
- Students learn to appreciate fairness, equity and the need to cooperate to compete (i.e. good sporting behaviors).
- Students are encouraged to self-regulate and learn to share various roles and responsibilities. They develop empathy and consideration for each position and officials.
- Students are able to challenge themselves at their own level - similar to children at play.
- Students are encouraged to construct their own cognitive maps regarding the similarities and differences among games through the classification system, thus fostering transfer.
- Students often achieve increased competence / perceived competence which promotes continued participation.

(Butler, 2005)

facilitates practice, by either simplifying the game, or introducing more challenging game conditions, based on the students' abilities. In this way, the teacher is working with the students' prior knowledge to develop new knowledge. Some of the problem solving skills in games can be organized into three domains, namely, psychomotor, cognitive and affective (as defined in Table 2).

Table 2. Domains of problem solving

Psychomotor (i.e., moving) domain	• On-the-ball skills • Off-the-bell movements
Cognitive (i.e., thinking) domain	• Tactical awareness • Game knowledge
Affective (i.e., feeling) domain	• Game appreciation • Sport citizenship

Constructivist Learning Theory, TGfU and Games Education

Many educators believe that TGfU is grounded in constructivist learning theory since this model is predicated on the belief that learning consists of individuals' constructed meanings. Perkins (1999) emphasized three tenets of constructivists' learning theory: the active learner, the social learner, and the creative learner. As active learners, students are not passive recipients of knowledge, but are involved in tasks that stimulate decision making, critical thinking and problem solving. As social learners, students construct knowledge through social interaction with their peers, facilitated by the teachers. As creative learners, students are guided to discover knowledge themselves and to create their own understanding of the subject matter.

The following are a set of guiding principles to bring both TGfU and the constructivist learning theory to life in your classroom.

1. Learning is an active process

The learner uses sensory input and constructs meaning from his or her experiences. The learner needs to do something, i.e., learning is not the passive acceptance of knowledge that exists "out there" but that learning involves the learner's engagement with the world (e.g. a problem is posed, such as, "How does your team stop the opponent from scoring?" The group can base their answer on what they already know as a group, and then, through further examination, build their schema of understanding).

2. Students learn-to-learn as they learn

Learning consists both of constructing meaning and constructing systems of meaning. Each meaning the student constructs makes him or her better able to give meaning to other experiences which can fit a similar pattern (e.g. leading a pass in basketball is essential to learning a fast break and these can be both transferred to other invasion games such as soccer and hockey).

3. The critical action of constructing meaning is mental

Physical actions, hands-on experiences (e.g., games) may be necessary for learning; however, it is not sufficient. Teachers need to provide activities which engage the mind (e.g. how will students learn to make good selection of technique in the game situation?).

4. Learning involves language
The language we use influences learning. There is a collection of arguments, presented most forcefully by Vygotsky, that language and learning are inextricably intertwined (e.g. discussing how to solve a problem with team mates generates understanding of key concepts).

5. Learning is a social activity
(Wertsch, 1985) Learning is intimately associated with the connections students have with their teacher and their peers, and these connections need to be purposefully planned. As teachers we need to recognize the social aspect of learning and use interaction with others, the debate of ideas (Wallion, 2005) and the application of knowledge as integral aspects of learning (e.g. games are socially constructed).

6. Learning is contextual
Students do not learn isolated facts and theories in some abstract place of the mind separate from the rest of their lives. Students learn in relationship to what else they know and what they believe, which also includes their biases and
fears (e.g. games provide the context).

7. Students need knowledge to learn
It is not possible to assimilate new knowledge without having some structure developed from previous knowledge to build on. Teachers need to connect to the state of the learner, and must provide a path into the game for the learner based on that learner's previous knowledge ie,g. playing games at the start of the unit).

8. Learning takes time
It is not instantaneous. Thus, for learning to occur, students need to revisit ideas, think about them, play with them and use them (e.g. continuous use of games and games forms).

9. Motivation is a critical component in learning
Motivation includes an understanding of ways in which the knowledge can be used (e.g. decision-making in play).

The Way Forward for Teachers and Administrators

We believe that in the best interests of schools and schooling, innovative approaches to teaching should be implemented, particularly in an educational climate in which critical thinking, problem solving and decision-making are valued. As previously mentioned, these are the cornerstone of constructivist approaches to teaching and learning, currently valued so highly in education. Yet in physical education, we have not been wholly successful at implementing innovation and this is the responsibility of both teachers and administrators. For many teachers, TGfU represents a different way of thinking, a challenge to previously held beliefs, and potentially, an implied criticism of previous practice. Open mindedness on the part of these teachers is critical, as is a willingness to think openly when confronted with opinions such as, "Kids can't play a game until they have learned the skills!" Proponents of TGfU argue that young learners can play a game if teachers take the time to modify it. If students are unable to play the game a teacher wants them to, the question to ask might be, "How can I modify the game so they can play it?" Let us bear in mind that the number one question asked (by students) during a games lesson is "When can we play a game?" Yet game modification is not easy, and we encourage teachers to consider available resources such as the books by Mitchell, Oslin & Griffin (2003, 2006) and Griffin & Butler (2005) as good places to start in making a transition to TGfU.

The Way Forward for Researchers

In 1986, Thorpe and Bunker challenged researchers to answer the question, "Does TGfU work?" and urged us to undertake studies that involved questionnaire design, attitude measurement and the collection of performance data. Today, this question remains largely unanswered. The following suggestions are offered in the context of multiple theoretical perspectives that will hopefully lead to broad and profound improvements in physical education:

1. Establish strong empirical data that would support our intuitive sense that this approach works for students (e.g. Kretchmar, Rink, Thorpe & Bunker). Many TGfU advocates have made this request.
2. Continue to explore and examine subjective outcomes (e.g. to play well and to enjoy playing) as well as objective outcomes (e.g. skill acquisition) and to value both, regardless of how difficult they are to assess and measure.
3. Focus on all aspects of the child - examine the outcomes of the affective domain as well as the increasingly well-documented cognitive and psychomotor domains (Holt, Strean & Bengoechea, 2002).

4. Continue to consider the nature of understanding, and to consider its place in the learning environment (Rink, 2001; Kirk & MacPhail, 2002; Kretchmar, 2003).
5. Continue to ask relevant and probing questions and to involve all major players in finding answers - practitioners, curriculum designers, researchers, administrators and students (Macdonald, Kirk, Mealer, Nilges, Schempp, & Wright, 2002).
6. Examine student learning outcomes of different putative methodologies to determine if what we think we are teaching is actually what we teach.
7. Develop research studies that examine the four fundamental pedagogical principles:
    a) Sampling
    b) Modification-representation,
    c) Modification-exaggeration
    d) Tactical complexity in order to guide the practice of planning the games curriculum
8. Continue to make connections with the coaching community, e.g. Games Sense (Kidman, 2005; Australian Sports Commission, 1995).
9. Continue to develop and validate authentic assessment instruments such as TSAP and GPAI (Buder, Griffin, Lombardo & Nastasi, 2003).

Diversity within the TGfU Movement

One of the key concerns expressed at the 2001 TGfU conference was confusion with regard to the different terms used to describe what is essentially one model. Macdonald et. al. (2002), advise us to "avoid theoretical fads" and it is true that many teachers are wary of these and are reluctant to jump on the next new bandwagon with a snappy name. Instead of creating confusion and suspicion with different terms, however, it might be wise to consider the benefit in adopting one name which could be universally recognized (Buder, Griffin, Lombardo & Nastasi, 2003).

Since its inception, the TGfU model has been the product of collaboration and diverse influences. To minimize confusion and to understand the different names that have influenced the TGfU model, we offer the following 'glossary' of terms:

1. **Teaching Game for Understanding - *England and Wales***
   This approach was developed at Loughborough University in the late 70s (Bunker & Thorpe, 1982).
2. **Games Sense and Play Practice - *Australia.***
   Games Sense has been used in application to the coaching environment, and Play

Practice when specifically aimed to encourage beginners (Launder, 2001).
3. **Tactical Approach - *USA***
   The original 6-stage model was collapsed into three to provide easier access for practitioners (Mitchell, Oslin & Griffm, 1997, 2006).
4. **Games-Concept Approach - *Singapore***
   Research at Nanyang Technological Institute has centered around sociological study of PETE students and the impact TGfU has had on their understanding of educating students through the physical (McNeil, Fry, Wright, Tan, Tan & Schempp, 2004).
5. **Invasion Games Competence Model -**
   Europe (Belgium, Portugal, Netherlands, Czech Republic)
   This model examines: 1) the competence of players in modified invasion games, 2) players' competence as supportive participants, (Musch et. al., 1998).

Of the above interpretations, arguably the name 'TGfU' carries the highest recognition, and, certainly, it has the right of seniority. Regardless of the terminology used, there are common threads that run through these interpretations leading to the perception that there are more similarities than differences. Mitchell (2005) identified some of these similarities and suggested the various interpretations are really "different paths up the same mountain", the common goal (at the mountain's summit) being better understanding, appreciation and performance during game play. Mitchell argued that the various interpretations of TGfU are game-based instructional approaches to games learning, motivational for students in their emphasis on games playing, and that each places the learning of skilled performance within the context of games playing. Further, Mitchell emphasized the problem solving nature of all interpretations of TGfU and, in particular, the use of the what, why, when, where, and how questions as a means of challenging and stimulating student cognition. Mitchell concluded that while time and energy could be spent debating differences in nomenclature and interpretation of the original TGfU model, perhaps that time and energy might be better directed at focusing on these common elements inherent in the various interpretations.

How affiliation to larger groups can help move TGfU forward

After the first TGfU conference in New Hampshire, USA, in 2001, a forum emerged that aimed to provide a place for curriculum exploration. The International TGfU Task Force was established in 2002 under the umbrella organization of AIESEP (Association des écoles supérieures d'éducation physique). Its goals were to harness the groundswell of energy created at the conference, and to funnel this energy into the promotion of research and good practice in TGfU through active communication and the recruitment of teachers and coaches. An international group such as the task force allows for a more organic development of the movement, combining forces from the theorists/researchers and practitioners from each country.

The mission of the task force, "A global representative group of institutions and individuals committed to the promotion and dissemination of scholarly inquiry", was to help close the chasm. Its goals were to organize regular conferences, to publish proceedings after conferences, to establish a registry of interested members (listserv), to establish a web site (tgfu.org), to publish proceedings and resource materials, to disseminate relevant information, and finally, to establish teaching squads comprised of educators grouped geographically and organized by national professional organizations.

Conclusion

The desire is to combine theory and practice in what Kirk and Tinning (1992) describe as a continuous process of "organic change" (p.4). We believe this structure prevents ownership of the approach by any one group and thereby emancipates the movement. Our challenge is that there is no certain way forward, but what we do know is that we need to move forward tentatively with clear communication by all who participate: researchers, teacher educators, practitioners, administrators, and students. We close this discussion about the way forward for TGfU with a quotation from Pinar, (1994).

> *"The production of curriculum knowledge is important to the advancement of the field. However, if this production does not originate in an emancipatory intention but in a static one - such as an essentially atheoretical accumulation of a 'body of knowledge' or the application of theory (i.e. comprehension) to practice {i.e. improvement) then no fundamental movement in the historical situation can occur. The state of the field is arrest. For movement to occur, we must shift our attention from the technical and the practical, and dwell on the emancipation. Not until we are in emancipatory relation to our work will we devise theory and formulate strategic action which will in Walkers term "improve" the nation's schools" (p.95).*

N.B. Please see the tgfu.org website for information about membership to AiESEP, the TGfU Special Interest Group (SIG).

References

Australian Sports Commission (1995). Game Sense, Retrieved November 5, 2006, from http://www.ausport.gov.au/coach/scnse.asp.

Bunker. D. & Thorpe. R. (1982). A model for the teaching of games in the secondary school. Bulletin of Physical Education, 10, 9-16.

Butler, J., Griffin, L., Lombardo, B., & Nastasi, R. (Eds.) (2003). Teaching games for understanding in physical education and sport. Reston. VA. AAHPERD publications.

Butler, J. (2005. December). Democracy in action using inventing games. Paper presented at the meeting of the Teaching Games for Understanding Conference, Hong Kong.

Davis. B. & Sumara. D. (2003). Why aren't they getting this? Working through regressive myths of constructivist pedagogy. Teaching Education, 14(2). 123-140.

Griffin, L L & Butler. J. (Eds.), (2005), Teaching games for understanding: Theory, research and practice, Champagne. II: Human Kinetics.

Holt, N. L, Strean. W.B., & Bengoechea. E.G. (2002). Expanding the reaching games for understanding model: New avenues for future research and practice. Journal of Teaching Physical Education, 21, 162-176.

Kidman. L (2005). Athlete-Centered Coaching: Developing inspired and inspiring people. New Zealand, Human Kinetics.

Kirk, D. & Tinning, R. (1992). Physical education pedagogical work as praxis. Paper presented at the annual meeting of the American Educational Research association, San Francisco. CA.

Kirk, D. & McPhail. A. (2002). Teaching games for understanding and situated learning: Rethinking the Bunker-Thorpe model. Journal of Teaching Physical Education, 21(2), 177-192.

Kretchmar, S. (2005). Teaching games for understanding and the delights of human activity. In L. Grifiin. & J. Butler (Eds.), Teaching games for understanding: Theory. research and practice (pp. 199-212), Champagne, II: Human Kinetics.

Launder. A. (2001). Play practice: The games approach to teaching and coaching sport. United Kingdom, Human Kinetics.

Macdonald, D, Kirk, D., Metzler, M., Nilges. L., Schempp. P, & Wright, J. (2002). Its all very , in theory; Theoretical perspectives and their application in contemporary pedagogical research. Quest, $4, 133-156.

McNeill, M.C. Fry, J.M.. Wright, S.G,, Tati. W.K.C.Tan. K.S.S., Schempp P.G. (2004). In the local context; Singaporean challenges to teaching games on practicum, Sport. Education and Society 9 (1), 3-32.

Mitchell, S.A., Oslin, J.L.. & Griffin. LL. (2003). Sport foundations for elementary physical education: A tactical games approach. Champaign. IL. Human Kinetics.

Mitchell, S. A., (2005. December). Different paths up the same mountain: Global perspectives on TGfU, Paper presented at the meeting of the Teaching Games for Understanding Conference. Hong Kong.

Mitchell. S.A., Osiin, J.L, & Griffin, LL. (2006). Teaching sport concepts and skills: A tactical games approach. Champaign. IL. Human Kinetics.

Musch, E. Mertens, B. Graça. A, Tinuncrs, E, Meertens, T. Taborsky, E Remy. C. Multael, M. Vonderlynck. V. & De Clercq, D. (1998). "The Invasion Games Competence Model: an alternative approach to games instruction and learning, presented on CD-ROM. Retrieved December 7th 2006 from http://scholar.google.com/scholar

Perkins. D. (1999), The many faces of constructivism. Educational Leadership, 57(3), 6-11.

Pinar, W. E (1994). Autobiography, politics and sexuality. Essays in curriculum theory 1972-1992. New York, NY. Peter Ung.

Rink, J. (2001). Investigating the assumptions of pedagogy, journal of Teaching Physical Education, 20, 112-128.

Thorpe, R., & Bunker, D. (1986). Is there a need to reflect on our games teaching? In R.Thorpe, D. Bunker and L. Almond (Eds.) Rethinking games teaching, (pp, 25-34). England, University of Technology. Loughborough, Dept of PE and Sports Science.

Wallion, N. (2005, December). Assessing learning as an understanding: towards a semi-constructivist approach in ball games. Paper presented at the meeting of the Teaching Games for Understanding Conference. Hong Kong.

Wertsch, J. V. (1985). Vygotsky and the Social formation of mind, Cambridge, MA. Harvard University Press.

11

Stages for Children Inventing Games

Joy Butler

This work has been republished with kind permission from Taylor & Francis, taken from the Journal of Physical Education, Recreation & Dance, Volume 84, 2013 - Issue 4.

Introduction

Children have always made up their own games. During recess and out in the yard or street, all they need to be up and running are a ball and a few friends. Building on this natural instinct to play, students often invent games that are usually fun, fair, and inclusive. Inventing Games (IG) is an offshoot of teaching games for understanding (TGFU), which was constructed by educators in the United Kingdom (Thorpe, Bunker, & Almond, 1986). It structures educational outcomes to help students learn about game structures, rules, and the principles of fair play, principles outlined in National Association for Sport and Physical Education (NASPE) Standard 2. These principles are applied not only to game play, but to students' lives as members of a democratically organized society who might be expected to exhibit the responsible social behaviors referenced in Standard 5. This article offers practical advice for teachers who want to experiment with Inventing Games in their schools.

Inventing Games is organized around the TGFU classification system developed by Thorpe, Bunker, and Almond building on the work of Margaret Ellis (1983). This organizes games by intent or primary rule into four classifications: target games, striking games, net/wall games, and invasion games (Table 1).

Table 1. TGFU Categories and Intent

TGFU Category	Main Intent of the Game (Primary Rule)
Target Games (e.g., archery, bowling, curling)	To send away an object and make contact with a specific, stationary target in fewer attempts than opponent
Striking Games (e.g., baseball, cricket, rounders)	To place the ball away from fielders in order to run the bases and score more runs than the opponents
Net/Wall Games (e.g., badminton, pickleball, tennis, volleyball)	To send ball back to opponent so that they are unable to return it or are forced to make an error. Serving is the only time the object is held
Invasion Games (e.g., basketball, hockey, soccer)	To invade the opponent's defending area and to shoot or to take the object of play into a defined goal area

The IG approach has three educational purposes:
1. To bring play back into games (Standards 3, 4, and 6)
2. To help players learn about game structure (standard 2)
3. To help players learn about "democracy in action" (Butler, 2005; Standards 5 and 6)

This article focuses on one of the game categories—invasion games—which is most often used in schools and so probably the most familiar. It offers a process that the author has developed over the last 15 years or so and builds on the "games making" work of Almond (1983) and "games shaping" notions of Ellis (1986). The process has 10 stages, which can be organized into a unit over varying numbers of classes, depending on desired outcomes, grade level, experience, and student ability. The outline offered here is not specific for any grade level, but Table 2 offers a guide to necessary stages for various grade levels.

Inventing Games workbooks can be developed that are specific for the grade level being taught. The workbooks would need to delineate all the stages of the IG process relevant to the grade level suggested in Table 2. Individual workbooks can track, structure, and record individual progress, and group scribes can use group workbooks to structure and record collective processes. Sets of IG cards can also be developed that serve as reminders and prompts for inventing games processes. These will be referred to in the course of this article.

LIFETIME CONTRIBUTIONS IN PHYSICAL EDUCATION

Table 2. Recommended Stages for Grade Levels

No	Stages	3-4	5-6	7-8	9-10	11-12
1A	Intentions and expectations: Establish group system, roles, and a policy for making decisions	X	X	X	X	X
1B	Define invasion games	X	X	X	X	X
2	Establish the game through democratic process	X	X	X	X	X
3	Play the game	X	X	X	X	X
4	Refine the game	X	X	X	X	X
5	Identify the role of coach		X	X	X	X
6	Establish the official's role		X	X	X	X
7	Showcase all the games	X	X	X	X	X
8A	Identify defensive strategies			X	X	X
8B	Refine defensive skills			X	X	X
8C	Identify defensive transpositional strategies (defense to offense)				X	X	X
9A	Identify defensive strategies			X	X	X
9B	Refine defensive skills				X	X
9C	Identify offensive transpositional strategies (offense to defense)				X	X
10	Connect students' invented games to established national invasion games			X	X	X

Stage 1:
Creating Democracy in Action and Defining the Game Category

1A. Democracy in Action. Intentions and expectations: Establishing group system, roles, and a policy for making decisions (Standards 2, 5, and 6).

It is important for each group (of four to six students) to design simple, fair processes that will help them to work together cohesively and make ethical decisions (Standard 5) that will later transfer into sound decision-making in game play. The construction of this decision-making process depends on the following structures:

 a. Consensus building (not every decision may be unanimous)
 b. Group decision-making processes (Must everyone speak? Should a hand be put up to speak? Should they have a talking stick?)
 c. Majority rules voting (How will decisions be made? By vote? What if there is a tie?)
 d. Conflict resolution (How will conflicts be resolved? By the group? By the teacher?)
 e. Inclusion (How can everyone be involved? What if they don't speak up?)

The following reminders about group process might be included in the workbook or on an IG card, depending on the group's abilities:

- Contribute to your group discussion; you have the right to do so.
- Listen to your peer until she or he has finished speaking.
- Be respectful of your peers' ideas, even if you don't agree.
- Be responsible for contributing to the decision-making process in the group.
- Consider alternative ideas as the game unfolds.
- Use your vote wisely.

Students establish their own system of making group decisions based on these five principles.

Teachers need to resist the temptation to "help" students to easy answers, remembering that process is just as important as outcomes in this stage. On a similar note, students may wish to rush this stage of the process in order to get on with game invention. The teacher will need to listen carefully to what is being done and said to ensure that everyone's opinion is heard and respected and that matters are not being rushed through.

Debrief: The teacher will invite each group to summarize its processes and may draw attention to differences and similarities in the ways that these have been constructed.

Roles: Two roles that need to be quickly established are that of scribe and that of equipment manager. These are summarized on the IG cards as follows:
  1. Scribe
  The scribe records decisions your group has made about game set up (playing area, equipment size, ball type, goal dimensions, and rules)
  2. Equipment manager
  The equipment manager makes a list of the equipment you will need and hands it in to the teacher. After the teacher hands out your game equipment, the equipment manager delivers it to the group and sees that it is properly returned at the end of class.

1B. Game Constructs: Invasion Games (Standards 2, 5, and 6)

In this stage, the groups identify some invasion games and discuss and define their basic constructs, regulations, and rules. They go on to identify three differences and three commonalities among them, and they consider the differences between regulations and rules. These are noted in the workbook by the group scribe.

The teacher serves as both the facilitator and monitor of the discussions and, as a resource, provides information about invasion games. The teacher also makes sure, in the lesson debrief, that the groups' summaries of invasion games and their characteristics are comprehensive and accurate.

Students are usually quick to suggest that invasion games have a goal at each end and that the main intention of those playing them is to invade the opponent's defending area to score while protecting their own goal. As the teacher tests students' hypotheses, it helps them to articulate ideas about the classification and to become more conscious of game constructs. For example, if someone suggests that baseball is an invasion game, the rest of the class can point out that since invasion games have goals at each end, baseball does not fit.

Debrief: The characteristics or structures of invasion games can be summarized as follows:
- A goal at each end
- Clear boundaries

- Scoring areas
- Attack opponents' goal while defending own
- Offense: maintain possession and score goals
- Defense: regain possession
- Transposition: quick moves to and from offense and defense

Stage 2:
Inventing the Game (Standards 1, 2, 4, 5, and 6)

Each group creates a rough outline of its game. These might include the basic boundaries, the type of goal and ball, the scoring system, a name for the game, and (most important) a short list of about five rules, including a safety rule. These can be refined as the game develops and are recorded in the group workbook. The functions of rules are summarized on the following IG card and/or included in the workbook:

Rules:
a. Allow the game to flow
b. Provide a structure to which all players can relate
c. Provide a safe environment
d. Establish fairness
e. Envolve everyone
f. Make the game fun

Students help the scribe to fill in the workbook as they work through their game design. Blank spaces can be left for students to enter their own drawings of the equipment and playing areas. Older students can add more detail in terms of measurements and size.

The teacher can observe and monitor the way the groups work together but should allow considerable freedom in this stage as students exercise their imagination. Part of the process is that even the most impractical ideas can be rethought and redesigned. Since students work at different rates, some groups will be active much more quickly than others; this allows the teacher to focus on groups that need more help. As one or two groups get moving, the others tend to catch up quite quickly.

Debrief: This might be a good time to highlight group processes that are working well.

Stage 3:
Playing the Game (Standards 1, 2, 3, 4, 5, and 6)

Once the group has decided on its game, the equipment manager shows the teacher the completed workbook (signed by all the members of the group), collects equipment, and directs the group to their assigned playing area.

Through quick observations of each group's game play, the teacher determines whether the games flow and whether they are fair and accessible. Quick interventions may be appropriate. If, for instance, a player is stuck in a restrictive role, the teacher might ask the group's reasoning before weighing in. Will positions rotate, for instance? Questions such as, "How can the group introduce a rule that results in more movement for everyone?" or follow-up questions such as, "Why do we want everyone involved?" may help.

Debrief: At the end of the class, the teacher invites each group to decide how well they worked together to set up the game, analyze the game to see if it is working (and why or why not), and define what makes it fun. Answers are recorded in the workbooks.

Stage 4:
Refining the Game (Standards 2, 5, and 6)

As the games are played, the teacher can encourage the students to use game time-outs as needed to refine their games. The teacher may call these timeouts personally or allow students to do so, depending on their age and abilities. Time-out topics might include the following:

  a. Does the game flow?
  b. Is it structured?
  c. Is it safe for everyone?
  d. Is it fair?
  e. Is everyone involved?
  f. Is it fun?

These questions might be introduced as a package with older students or one at a time with younger ones. As students work through these questions, they consider changes and improvements to their game. Changes in regulations would change court dimensions, ball size or type, goal size, and the scoring system. These can be manipulated to make the game more accessible or more challenging. Changes in rules usually influence the flow, fairness, and accessibility of games. For example, a rule created by a fourth-grade group demarked the centerline as a boundary for offense players, stopping traffic at the goalmouth, allowing and providing defensive players with more time to strategize. Reversing this rule (by preventing defensive players from crossing the mid-line) set up offensive players with more time to take shots on goal. Rules can be defined as prescriptive (must do) and proscriptive (must not do). The balance of these two can be appreciated by older students, as they consider what restricts and what increases game flow.

With receptive groups, the idea of a "Committee Box" can be introduced. This allows any student to take one of the following cards to make proposals during timeouts:
   a. Change existing rule card
   b. Add rule card
   c. Drop existing rule card
   d. Restate rule card

The group discusses the cards, putting ideas to a vote or consensus. This promotes understanding of committee work and offers a glimpse into how national bodies modify rules. (The teacher can offer examples.) The teacher's role here is to facilitate game modifications that render the game easier or more challenging.

Debrief: The end of this stage offers a useful opportunity for the teacher to ask groups what they have learned about the value and role of rules.

Stage 5:
Identifying the Role of Coach (Standards 5 and 6)

With the games underway after rule or regulation changes, the next step is to share them with the class—but first, each group elects and records the name of a coach (nominating self or others) after they have discussed what this role involves. The teacher guides the discussion of criteria and responsibilities, using the following IG card:

a. What is the role of a leader?
b. How can leaders help groups make decisions?
c. What is clear communication?
d. What is respectful communication?
e. Why is it important to listen?

Debrief: The end of this stage invites some teacher-facilitated discussion of coaching. Why do we need coaches? Do we always need coaches? How did the game change after a coach was appointed?

Stage 6:
Establishing the Role of the Official (Standards 5 and 6)

It is important for students to serve as officials, since it helps them understand the rules (and thus play better) and develop empathy and respect for people in this role. This is also a good time for students to draw up a list of penalties and signals for rule violations and add these to their workbooks. The next phase of game playing has all groups working with these player coaches (except when they are serving as officials) and all players taking a turn as official. The teacher's role in this lesson is to "coach" to students in these two roles.

Debrief: Once again, this session might conclude with some discussion on the differences in the experience of playing with the inclusion of the coach and official.

Stage 7:
Showcasing the Games (Standards 1, 2, 3, 4, and 6)

In large classes, groups can be paired up, as one group demonstrates to the other and several games are showcased simultaneously. In smaller classes, groups can first demonstrate their game to another group before being invited to show their game to the whole class. The following sequence can be used:

1. Each coach explains the game to the audience (another group or the whole class).
2. All members of the group then showcases the game.
3. After a few minutes of play, the audience comments or suggests improvements.
4. Pair up groups.
5. Have each group play the other group's game, with the coach explaining and guiding the process.
6. Students choose which game they wish to play.
7. If all students prefer one game—then both groups can play it (in my experience, students always pick the game they have invented).
8. If the groups haven't found a name for the game, others in the class could be invited to help out.

Debrief: What did the students learn from watching other groups' games? What suggestions did they accept? What do they think of their games now?

Stage 8:
Defense (in 3 Parts): Strategies, Skills, and Transposition)
(Standards 1, 2, 3, 4, and 6)

8A. Identifying Defensive Strategies.

With the game established and somewhat developed, the teacher can move into the most interesting part of the process: developing game play through organized tactics.

Many teachers prefer to start with offensive tactics to capture student interest. Though it is true that many students are more excited by scoring than preventing goals, a good offense takes the opponents' defense into consideration. How better to understand what opponents are trying to do than by considering their defensive systems first?

The basic questions of defense are as follows:
1. "How can your team try to stop the other team from scoring?"
2. What are your opponents' defensive tactics? Why do you need to know?

Possible solutions:
- Covering/marking a player (full court, half court, sagging)
- Covering/marking an area
- Double-teaming

In their teams (not groups), students brainstorm answers to these questions. The coach lists ideas in the workbook and decides which one to try first during game play. During time-outs, players evaluate their success and consider further improvements, using the following IG card or section in the workbook.
1. Try ideas out and modify during time-outs.
2. How did your chosen defensive strategy work?
3. How did the offense manage to score against your team?

During this problem-solving stage, it is important for teachers to encourage students to work through trial and error, noting why something worked and why it didn't. This helps players construct a schema for situational strategy planning.

Debrief: Discuss what was learned in planning one strategy. Define the difference between strategies and tactics.

8B. Defining Defensive Skills (Standards 1, 2, 3, 4, and 6).
This sophisticated stage is best reserved for more experienced students. The teacher can suggest it for some groups and not others. It helps players identify the skills needed for implementing strategies, such as observational skills, movement analysis, appreciation of progressive skills practice, and the forging of connections between practice and game play. First, players are invited to list defensive skills in their workbooks.

Possible solutions:
- Staying with the player
- Keeping goal side of player
- Tackling
- Anticipation – interception – reading

Debrief: How has the skill practice helped the strategy and game play?

8C. Identifying Defensive Transpositional Strategies (Defense to Offense).
Again, this stage is best reserved for more experienced players. Often, players win the ball on defense but move into offense slowly, thus losing it again. Changing from defense into offense requires team organization.

Problem-solving questions on this IG card include the following:
1. How does your team gain possession from the team with the ball/object?
2. What have you noticed about your opponents' defense that would allow your team to penetrate their defense?
3. Once in possession, what system/organization helps you to move quickly into offense?

Possible solutions:
- Interception
- Intuition
- Reading the game
- Considering offense options
- Closing down passing lanes
- Forcing an error with defensive pressure

Stage 9:
Offense (in 3 Parts): **Strategies, Skills, and Transposition** (Standards 1–6)

9A. Identifying Offensive Strategies.

As with the defensive stage, this begins with the identification of problem questions.
- How do you keep possession of the ball/puck to set up scoring opportunities?
- How can your team score more points/goals than your opponents?

Possible solutions:
- Keep ball moving, short, safe controlled passing
- Focus on the player with the ball
    - What to do with the ball?
- Focus on the players without the ball
    - Where to go to be available for a pass?
    - Creating space for the player with the ball
- Division of roles to cover goal
- Transpositional awareness
    - Risk in losing possession
    - Creating space for opportunity
    - Thinking two or three moves ahead

The same method of trial and error is used with offensive and defensive strategies. The teacher might digitally record game play so that students can more easily analyze what is going to work, what isn't, and why. Time-outs are used at the teams' discretion as strategies become refined and adaptive.

A coaching session may be appropriate for distinguishing between on-the-ball and off-the-ball play. Possible foci for follow-up might include player support and assistance for the player with the ball.

9B. Refining Offensive Skills.
1. Identify and list skills that are required to use offensive strategies effectively.
2. Ask students to design a practice that isolates these skills. Start slow and build up to full speed.
3. Ask the coach to watch the drill and ask him/her for ideas for improvement.
4. Develop the skill until it is almost game like.
5. Go back to the game and try the refined skills within the game context. Do they help?

Possible solutions:
- Moving to receive pass
- Passing to open players
- Supporting role
- Creating open spaces
- Carrying, passing, receiving, shooting skills
- Combining locomotor and manipulative skills

9C. Identifying Offensive Transpositional Strategies.
Problem question: If your team loses possession, how will the team switch quickly to defensive mode?

Possible outcomes:
- Interception
- Intuition
- Reading the game
- Considering offense options
- Closing down passing lanes
- Forcing an error with defensive pressure

Stage 10: Connecting Students' Invented Games to Established National Invasion Games (Standards 1–6)

For one or two lessons, allow students to play an invasion game of their choice, using a completely different means of propelling the ball/puck. For example, if students chose a throwing IG game, they might choose a kicking or implement game, such as soccer or hockey. Identify transferable concepts. These might include the need for rules and officials, modifying behavior, keeping possession, obtaining possession, passing the ball ahead of teammates, or player-to-player defense.

Assessment

Rubrics based on the outcomes sought can be made up for each stage. The use of Game Performance Assessment Instruments work really well with this approach - particularly at the end of the game-making stage and then after each of the three stages in either defense or offense.

Conclusion

If learning is to be sustainable and transferable, experiences need to be meaningful and thus memorable. Chalking up a blueprint game for each of the categories, or including these in the workbooks will help students fully understand and appreciate the game structures of subsequent games.

References

Almond, L. 1986. "Games making.". In Rethinking games teaching Edited by: Thorpe, R., Bunker, D. and Almond, L. 67–70. Loughborough, , UK: Loughborough University of Technology.

Butler, J. Democracy in action using an inventing games unit. Paper presented at 3rd International Conference of Teaching Games for Understanding (TGFU) in Physical Education and Sport. Hong Kong, China. December.

Castle, K. 1990. Children's invented games. Childhood Education, 67(2): 82–85.

Ellis, M. A games classification system. Paper presented at AIESEP International Conference on Team Games. Rome, Italy.

Ellis, M. 1986. "Making and shaping the game.". In Rethinking games Edited by: Thorpe, R., Bunker, D. and Almond, L. 61–65. Loughborough, , UK: University of Technology, Department of PE and Sports Sciences.

Rovegno, L. and Bandhauer, D. 1994. Child designed games: Experience teachers' concerns. Journal of Physical Education, Recreation & Dance, 65(6): 60–64.

Thorpe, R., Bunker, D. and Almond, L. 1986. Rethinking games teaching. Loughborough, UK: Loughborough University of Technology, Department of Physical Education and Sports Science.

12

Teaching & Learning Social Jusice through Inventing Games

Joy Butler

Editors note: With grateful thanks to Human Kinetics Publishing, the chapter is reprinted with minor edits from Joy's book Playing Fair.

The sixth-grade class is inventing games, within the category of invasion games. The students have discussed and decided on the basic structures of their game (boundaries, goals, ball) and agreed on five rules. Now it is time to try it out. They race off to set up their equipment, and as Mr. Uppal scans them quickly, he notices that one group is already playing. He moves toward them to praise their initiative, but is confused when he sees that they are throwing the ball at each other. His heart sinks. His first instinct is to put a stop to this game; dodgeball is not allowed in many North American schools for good reasons. Instead, he bites his tongue and pulls the group together.

Mr. Uppal: Hey! Well done! You are the first group to get playing! Can someone explain the game?
Sophie, the biggest girl in the group, shoots up her hand.
Sophie: Well. It's based on dodgeball, but we changed it up, 'cause in real dodgeball you can get hurt. We're using these soft, squishy balls, and the rule is that you have to aim below the waist and we have a rescuer that brings people back to life.
She smiles happily at her teacher.
Mr. Uppal: You explained that very concisely, and I understood it!
Sophie and the group laugh.
Mr. Uppal: So where did the ideas come from?

Sophie glances at the other kids in the group.
Sophie: I remembered it from summer camp.
Mr. Uppal: The whole thing?
Sophie nods. She knows she's on shaky ground here. Mr. Uppal looks around the group.
Mr. Uppal: So did you all agree on this?
One of the boys speaks up—a little too quickly and loudly.
John: Yeah. We all really, really like dodgeball, but we know you don't, so we made it really safe and everything.
Mr. Uppal watches the others carefully.
Mr. Uppal: How about the rest of you?
A couple of the students keep their faces expressionless. They don't nod, but they don't disagree either. Mr. Uppal knows better than to put them on the spot.

The charter of the International Olympic Committee (IOC) articulates a high regard for human rights (Seaman, 2010), including the right to practice sport. The Olympic spirit depends on fair play and mutual understandings that preclude discrimination of any kind. This notion that all people have equal power—to live freely, to vote, and to speak—is central to democracy. Without social justice, there can be no equality. Yet rights imply civic responsibilities in that they must be actively taken up through involvement in the community, and teachers can help students buy in to such engagement.

The inventing games process offers teachers an opportunity to teach consciously to promote ethical awareness and active, engaged citizenship, which Freire (1989) called dialogic education. Varela (1999) stated that ethical awareness is developed through actions carried out in context; a helpful term for this is democracy in action. As students negotiate, debate, overcome conflict, and navigate through problems together while inventing games, they enter a microcosm of community life, encountering the challenges and joys of civic responsibility.

The inventing games process helps teachers do the following:
- Promote democratic and emancipatory processes in teaching and learning.
- Equip students for democratic collective learning by helping them discuss and actively listen to new ideas, perspectives, and experiences.
- Provide students with opportunities to make decisions that are fair, equitable, and sound, while helping them develop the aptitudes they need to do so.

- Plan for student learning about social issues by having students work authentically and equitably while inventing games.
- Address moments of aporia (i.e., stuck places) by considering democracy in action.

The vignette at the beginning of this chapter illustrates these premises. The teacher, Mr. Uppal, resists his urge to resolve the situation, and instead opts to engage the students in discussion. Following is a continuation of his dialogue with the students:

Mr. Uppal: Can anyone remind us what this unit is called?
Sophie: Inventing games.
Mr. Uppal: Yes, OK, but in which category of games?
Sophie: Invasion games.
Mr. Uppal: Yes, good. So remind me what some of the characteristics are for invasion games.
Tamson: There is a goal at each end.
Mr. Uppal: Yes, good. And what's the purpose of the goals?
Tamson: To send the ball into the goals to score and beat the other team.
Mr. Uppal: Right! So where are the goals in this game?
Sophie: Mmm, we don't have any.
Mr. Uppal: Well you kind of do . . . .
There is a little pause.
Sophie: Oh right. We use each other as the goals!
Mr. Uppal chooses not to address this, but notes it for later discussion.
Mr. Uppal: OK. So can you quickly regroup and redesign your game to include goals—one at each end?

About 15 minutes later, the group is fully engaged in the newly adapted game complete with two goals (mini soccer nets). Throwing at human targets is still part of the game, and most of the students are flushed and beaming with joy.

Mr. Uppal: I see you've included the goals at each end. So how have you included these in your game?
Sophie: We used—
Mr. Uppal: Thanks, Sophie, but let's have someone else explain this time.
Tamson: I can explain! If we manage to get the ball past all the opponents and it lands in the goal, we score 5 points. If we hit one of the opponents, we get 1 point. They still have to sit down and they can still be rescued.

Mr. Uppal: That sounds pretty good! Thank you, Tamson. The next step now is for you all to ask yourselves six questions. These are all listed in your games sheet. I'm going to invite the whole class to do the same task.

What Mr. Uppal does first is draw the students' focus to their own game constructs. They are able to see that their original dodgeball game simply does not meet the constraints of the invasion game, and they are willing and able to adapt it to fit these constraints. However, the issue of human targets has still not been addressed. Rather than tackling this head on, Mr. Uppal poses six questions to help all the students in his class (not just the most vocal) engage in dialogue about the educational value of the games they have designed.

Mr. Uppal: (*addressing the whole class and passing around a handout that he now reads*): Here are your six questions:
Is this game fair?
Is it safe?
Is everyone involved?
Is it challenging?
Does it flow?
Is it fun?
He keeps a sharp eye on Sophie, who seems reluctant to spend time on this task.
Sophie: Yes to all of them! Let's get on with the game!
Mr. Uppal: Perhaps that's true for you at the moment, Sophie, but I want each group to discuss this point by point. Remind me, now—how did your group make decisions?
Sophie: We agreed that after a discussion we would vote.
Mr. Uppal: Well great! So let's have the recorder write down the number of votes for each of the questions on the sheet. That'll help you keep track. You have three minutes to finish this.

When the class reassembles, Mr. Uppal asks if the answers were unanimous, and most students nod. Mr. Uppal turns to the dodgeball group.
Mr. Uppal: How about you, group 1? Who was the recorder?
John: We had 6s on most questions, but we had only a 3 on if it was safe and only a 4 if it flowed.
Mr. Uppal: (*turning to the rest of the class*) What do you think this group needs to do now to get their scores up to 6?
Several students: (*raising their hands*) They should change their rules!

Mr. Uppal: I agree. Not everyone's happy with the way things are working, group 1. See if you can fix it. I'll be over in a few minutes to help. The rest of you can get back to your games and consider tweaking them to make them even better!

We can see how the inventing games structure reinforces the democratic process by flushing out the views and opinions of all members of the group. Rather than making this process personal by isolating and emphasizing individual opinions and objections, Mr. Uppal keeps it objective by pointing out that consensus has not been achieved. Students can see that the game does not follow the guidelines and is thus an anomaly in the class. By supporting those in the minority, Mr. Uppal makes it easier for students to disagree with the way things are.

When Mr. Uppal returns to group 1, a discussion about human targets is in full swing:
John: I think Mr. Uppal wants us to take out the human targets rule.
Sophie: But that would change the whole game!
Tamson: Yeah! I like it!
Amy: I don't. I always get hit.
There is a brief silence.
Sophie: Well, move out of the way!
Amy: You think I don't try? You think I'm useless!
Mr. Uppal: What have you decided—any rule changes?
Sophie: We can't agree.
Mr. Uppal: Who can summarize the discussion so far?
Sophie: Well, some of us still want to keep the human target rule in, and some want it out. They say you don't like it.
Mr. Uppal: Well, it's true. I don't. But if all six of you decide to keep it, then that's your decision. No one forced you to play this.
Tamson: Why don't you like it?
Mr. Uppal: Well, it's complicated, but there's no game I know of where players deliberately aim to hit a player. I think the reason for that is that it encourages people to throw balls at someone else, and it can hurt them, not necessarily physically either. I've seen kids use this game as an excuse to bully others. And that's pretty unpleasant.
Mr. Uppal quietly leaves as the students continue the discussion.
Tamson: What about if we tagged someone with the ball instead, rather than throwing it at someone?
John: The loose balls take up a lot of time to collect, and that's why we lose the flow of the game.

Sophie: OK. Let's try that!

Mr. Uppal deliberately refrains from telling his students what is right early in the process, preferring that they figure it out for themselves and take ownership of their decisions. First, he engages the students in a little deconstruction of the games construct; then he reinforces the democratic decision-making process they have agreed to follow. This allows dissenting opinions to be heard and respected. In turn, students can think more broadly about the social issues involved. Only at this point does Mr. Uppal offer his own ideas and experience, which the students are more ready to hear and understand. This example provides a good illustration of democracy in action. Nieto (2000) and Freire (1989) pointed out that reflection is not the result of intellectual effort alone. It occurs through praxis, or the union of action and reflection on the world in order to transform it (Freire, 1989, p. 51). Bringing these insights into the educational realm, we can offer students opportunities to examine, discuss, and reflect on content; grapple with ethical responsibility; analyze critically; and enact the democratic ideals of equality, freedom, and justice. The learning process must not be just practical (e.g., how to vote and offer opinions), but also, as Mathews (1996) suggested, cognitive and affective (e.g., how to keep an open mind, stand in another's shoes, and make decisions with others).

Revisiting the True Meaning of Competition

Without competition, there is no game. However, the various interpretations of the word competition have led to some confusion. Critics of new approaches to sport education often fear that innovators are against any form of competition. However, it is truer to say that most are reacting to a narrow interpretation of the term. Adages such as "Winning isn't the best thing—it's the only thing" and "Win at all cost" reveal a zero-sum view of competition (i.e., whatever is won by one opponent is directly lost by the other). However, other interpretations exist, and as Stoll and Beller (2000) suggested, it is in the interests of our students that we explore them. Nastasi (1992) and Siedentop, Hastie, and van der Mars (2011) offered alternative and more expansive definitions of competition.

Cooperation is a key concept inherent in competition. For a team to compete (i.e., meet, come together, or strive against others to attain a goal), they must work together. In inventing games, the decisions learners make in groups off the court or field when creating games can readily transfer to the game itself. The words *compete* and *competence* derive from the Latin word *competere*. Etymologically speaking, to compete means "to strive to achieve a goal." Competition provides a space where people strive to become competent (the best they can be), and opponents are a necessary part of this process. If this is understood, competitors can appreciate their opponents and thank them for their help at the end of the game. When it is not understood, the opponent is reduced to anonymity, and respect, fairness, equality, and honor are traded in for a victory. This leads to unfair practices such as stacking teams and cheating.

A second meaning of *competition* is "to come together." In competition, people come together to showcase their talents, meet like-minded people, and celebrate a shared culture.

Teaching Social Justice and Democracy in Action

To embrace human rights is to become aware that without social justice there can be no fairness or equality; consequently, democratic processes cannot function. Essential to the definition of democracy is the notion that all people have equal power to live freely, to vote, and to speak. With these rights comes the civic responsibility to exercise these rights through active interest and involvement in the community. Teachers play a crucial role in preparing students to do this. There are two key aspects of teaching for social justice through the practice of democracy in action. The first is addressing societal inequities through anti-oppression education. The second is using some of the pedagogical tools to teach social justice—in this case, democracy in action, situated ethics, and inventing games.

Understanding Societal Inequities

As Young pointed out (1990), the democratic process breaks down when unfairness and an imbalance of power occur. Let's consider the nature of power in relation to the games curriculum.

Power over, or coercive power. This is the power structure in hierarchies. The school administration, which controls the curriculum, is supported by the school board, local government, and the law. Sometimes the culture of the school reinforces practices that seem to go without saying. These might include the disciplinary mastery approach to teaching sport, or inequitable practices such as dodgeball.

Power from within, or empowerment. As educators, we seek to empower our students through active creative experiences such as singing, writing, solving problems, making art, and dancing. Through inventing games, we offer active creative experiences in the ethical domain, as we encourage students to speak up, listen, negotiate, and make decisions that will enhance the effectiveness of the group.

Collective power. Collective power is the power people gain when they act in concert. In the inventing games process, students begin to understand that they are part of a community they can trust. They come to accept that they sometimes need to set aside their own interests in favor of common goals. They learn when to take care of themselves and when to take care of others.

Power with, or social power (influence, rank, status, or authority). Social power determines how much weight an individual opinion carries, how much members are listened to in a group, and how much they are respected. As young people struggle to reach the expectations of adulthood, they rely heavily on their peers to establish self-esteem. Young people who see themselves as outsiders and not accepted by their peers are more likely to withdraw, become depressed, and become targets for bullying (Boyce, King, & Roche, 2008).

Earned and unearned social power. Unearned power is privilege, the power you get not from anything you are have done or created, but from who you happen to be—your gender, your race, your social class, the wealth you've inherited, the opportunities handed to you. With privilege often comes entitlement, a feature of hierarchy (Starhawk, 2011, p. 45). This often plays out along the lines of gender and race in physical education classes.

Teaching for Social Justice

Left unaided in group decision-making processes, students fall back on informal or culturally determined systems of interaction, ranging from the much-loved football huddle to a reliance on acknowledged leaders. These systems are products of cultural, generational, and gender norms. Although there is much to celebrate in all social institutions (church, family, state, school), the active and engaged citizen must always examine them for bias. The challenge for the teacher is to find ways to limit privilege while helping students find positive ways to be rewarded for their efforts.

Very often, we learn about what we believe when we confront real-life situations. In inventing games, these situations arise frequently and naturally as students encounter moments of aporia (rupture or stuckness). When we are faced with situations that challenge what we know, we struggle to make new sense of the universe and push beyond our current moral constructs. Varela (1999), who called this new, more conscious, sense of what is right ethical know-how, believes that it evolves over time through small decisions and actions, rather than being handed down as a set of a priori principles. As students invent and negotiate to create their games, they develop their capacity for personal and social responsibility, free inquiry, decision making, social justice, cooperation, and competition.

A key concept in teaching for social justice is *Aporia*. This term describes the moment of disruption caused by disagreement, or a place of stuckness caused by not knowing what to do next. This experience contributes to a greater understanding of how democracy works and how the absence of social justice may cause it not to work. Moments of aporia are signposts that indicate the opportunity to make connections between game structures and democratic principles.

Skills for Democracy in Action

Just as in Teaching Games for Understanding (TGfU), ethical understanding, tactics, skills, and effective game play develop through well-designed gamelike activities and structured group processes.

Students take responsibility by doing the following:
- Taking on roles such as recorder, equipment manager, and coach
- Paying attention to social relations
- Helping to resolve conflict

They learn good judgment by doing the following:
- Realizing that sometimes they must put the good of the group before their personal benefit
- Contributing ideas and actions for the greater good of the group

They become models and teachers for others by doing the following:
- Making mistakes and acknowledging them so that their realizations become part of the group's learning
- Modeling behaviors such as listening, respecting, understanding, and forgiving
- Demonstrating integrity

- Developing, discussing, and refining values
- Bringing practical experience, skills, and training to game play
- Bringing special talents and passing on newly developed skills
- Mentoring and accepting mentorship
- Making thanks and appreciation part of the experience of healthy competition

They learn that conflict can provide opportunities for learning by doing the following:
- Learning to trust each other and the group process
- Addressing conflict honestly, respectfully, and directly
- Resolving difficulties and moving on

The notion of situated ethics counteracts the common assumption that ethical behavior occurs when we apply a set of a priori principles, such as the Ten Commandments, to a given situation. Rather, it suggests that such principles emerge over time and in context. Some (although by no means all) ethical principles form the basis of democratic culture, along with certain skills and attributes that make democracy work.

Skills for Group Process

As they work together to invent their games, students also construct group structures that represent and serve the needs of all members. The teacher's role includes drawing attention to successes and challenges, and supporting students as they develop fair and effective ways of working, such as the following:

- Agreed-upon structures and processes for making decisions
- Clear and transparent agreements about how people gain decision-making power
- Clear ways for people to take on tasks and responsibilities
- Clear agreements about the scope of each member's authority
- Clear structures of accountability: Who do people report to? How, when, and in what form is an accounting given?
- A group culture of appreciation and thanks to those who make contributions and take on tasks
- A culture of tending to and mutually caring for those holding responsibility
- A fair and transparent systems of rewards
- Training and mentoring to help people take on new responsibilities

The teacher must also be vigilant in rewarding and encouraging the development of skills and strategies that support the process of the group, including the following:

- Doing what they say they'll do quickly and effectively
- Asking for help and guidance when needed
- Passing on tasks they cannot do
- Making sure others complete tasks
- Handling crises calmly when they arise
- Planning, strategizing, and looking ahead

Pedagogical Steps in the Inventing Games Process

There are often clear signals that the game has stopped being fair or that learners are stuck: the game falters, voices are raised, or someone has walked off with the ball. Rather than seeing these moments of aporia as an educational failure, teachers who are focused on emergent learning see them as opportunities for learning.

Teaching democracy in action makes many more demands on the teacher than running drills, refereeing dodgeball, or coaching. However, teachers can take certain steps when a group encounters a moment of aporia or difficulty, such as a group of sixth-grade girls confronting the boys on their team who had grabbed all the offensive positions and relegated the girls to defense. Following is an outline of the steps a teacher might take in this situation:

1. Assess the emotional state of the group. Are members able to debrief and negotiate in their heightened state? Might a cooling-off period be necessary?
2. Ask pertinent questions. Following are some examples:
    - How were the decisions made about who played?
    - Who took the most power in making these decisions?
    - Who benefited? Who did not?
    - What other ways of determining players' positions might be considered?
    - Why is it important to include everyone in decision making and take some time to hear all views? What other situations mirror this one?
3. Define the moment of breakdown in communication. In this instance, it might be when the boys imposed a ruling that did not involve the girls in a fair process or when the group decided that offense was more desirable than defense.
4. Identify the democratic principle that was violated, and remind the students that they had agreed to adhere to that principle. Why was it set aside? In this instance, the group had settled on a democratic decision-making process. The reasons the boys ignored it are complex; they reflect the socialization and enculturation of both boys and girls.

5. Identify a democratic attribute or value that might make the inventing games process work more smoothly. In this instance, possible responses are respect, empowerment, and fairness. Democracy does not work when power inequities exist among voters.
6. Consider how the situation might be resolved. Possible solutions are reestablishing and reinforcing the negotiated group decision-making process and applying it to decisions about player roles.
7. Consider policies or practices that might help prevent this situation from recurring. How might the group become of aware of players' grievances, and how might they be addressed?
8. Have students write about the experience to clarify what they learned and, in particular, to identify the principles, concepts, and structures they encountered. In this way, students can develop their own schemas of ethical situations and principles of democracy in action to guide their thinking and reactions. Individual writing can help less vocal students identify their thoughts and feelings, which may help them be more articulate and confident in future discussions.
9. Resolve to learn. Hopefully, the teacher will resolve to better educate the class about offensive and defensive roles. This is a good opportunity to discuss mutually supportive teamwork.

Figure 1 illustrates the rationale behind the preceding steps. The horizontal line provides the learning situation through the inventing games and democratic processes. The vertical line indicates issues regarding social justice and situated ethics. In the scenario of the indignant girls, the following concepts might emerge from a dialogue resulting from skillful teacher questioning:

- *Social justice issues:* Social power, fairness, gender inequity
- *Democratic principles:* Group process, decision making
- *Game constructs:* The assumption that offense positions are more important and more desirable than defense positions

Figure 1. Components of ethical situations

```
         Social
         justice
         issue

Inventing    Ethical    Democratic
games       situation    process
process

         Situated
         ethics
```

Other Topics for the Democracy-in-Action Classroom

Many of the topics teachers are exploring with students in our current research program focus on forms of power. These have included the following:

- Why do students stack teams to annihilate their opposition?
- What happens when students use each other as human targets—for example, in dodgeball?
- What happens when smaller students, students from minorities, or less skilled players are not selected for teams, or not equally included in game play?
- What happens when someone doesn't participate in decisions and then complains about them?
- What is cheating, exactly? Is it ever OK to keep quiet about an action that is unfair?
- Why do we need referees? How should they be treated?
- How can a group make fair decisions?
- Does everyone have the same rights, including the right to be heard?

Teacher-researchers found the worksheet in figure 2 to be useful for understanding how an ethical situation, the social justice issue it raises, and the democratic principles involved are related. This worksheet uses the example of students stacking teams (when students are left to choose their own teams) and offers possible responses and solutions.

Figure 2. Worksheet for understanding the relationship between social justice issues and democratic principles in an ethical situation.

Name: **Grade:**

Situated ethic
Summarize the moment
or situation of aporia
(impassable or euphoria)

Social justice issue
- What is happening
- What is wrong or right with this situation?
- Why is this happening?

Situation
Stacking of student
selected teams:
Designed to stack
the better players
onto one team thus
allowing an easy win

Possible responses
- Students intent on winning only
- The challenge and joy of playing the game is lost
- Association of winning with success with least effort
- Dog eat dog world
- Work ethic gone?

Principle(s)
- Fairness?
- Work ethic?

Democratic principle(s)
What is the underlying principle?

How can this situation be sustained or resolved?

Teacher-centered process	Student-centered process

187

Applying this kind of critical analysis to moments of aporia requires attentiveness and mental agility, but this should not discourage teachers from initiating these discussions. Although we may not always know the answers going in, this is perhaps the point. As with most learning, meaning is constructed in the process and through authentic engagement. I am continually surprised by the innate sense of fairness of most young learners, as well as by their aptitude for quite sophisticated ethical dialogue.

Summary

Most parents and teachers would agree that young people have strong ideas and feelings about what is fair and that they are able to voice these, given the right opportunities. It is these opportunities that are provided by the inventing games process. As students negotiate the structures and rules of their games, they learn to think more broadly about their own responsibilities and behaviors as their learning transfers into the situations they encounter in "real life." Democracy-in-action principles include group process, personal and social responsibility, free inquiry, decision making, and social justice. These principles represent a framework on which students can build ideas and organize information about social issues and democratic process. A key point underlies the arguments offered in this chapter: To embrace human rights is to become aware that without social justice there can be no fairness or equality and consequently, democratic processes cannot function.

References

Boyce, W. F., King, M. A. & Roche, J. (2008). *Healthy settings for young people in Canada.* Ottawa, ON: Public Health Agency of Canada.

Freire, P. (1989). *Pedagogy of the oppressed.* New York, Continuum.

Matthews, D. (1996). Reviewing and previewing civics. In W. C. Parker (ed.), *Educating the democratic mind* (pp. 265-286). Albany, NY: State University of New York Press

Nastasi, R. J. (1992). Distinguishing conflict and competition: A model for understanding some teaching interactions in athletics. *Educational Considerations*, 19(2), 45-48.

Nieto, S. (2000). Placing equity front and center: Some thoughts on transforming teacher education for a new century. *Journal of Teacher Education*, 51(3), 180-187.

Seaman, B. (2010). Redefining competition in sport: The "freedom of excess.) *Law Now*, 34(3), 1-5.

Siedentop, D., Hastie, P.A. & van der Mars, H. (2011). *Complete guide to sport education.* Champaign, IKL: Human Kinetics.

Starhawk. (2011). *The empowerment manual: a guide for collaborative groups.* Gabriola Island, BC: New Society Publishers.

Stoll, S., & Beller, J. (2000). Do sports build character? In J. R. Gerdy (Ed.), *Sports in school: The future of an institution* (pp 18-31). New York: Teachers College Press.

Varela, F.J. (1999). *Ethical know-how: Action, wisdom, and cognition.* Stanford, CA: Stanford University Press.

13

TGfU Pet-agogy: Old Dogs, New Tricks and Puppy School

Joy Butler
University of British Columbia, Vancouver, Canada

This work has been republished with kind permission from Taylor & Francis, taken from Physical Education and Sport Pedagogy, 10:3, 225-240, DOI: 10.1080/17408980500340752

Despite its manifest attractions, Teaching Games for Understanding, (TGfU) still has a long way to before it achieves acceptance. Though advocates would like to see it assume its rightful place in mainstream physical education and sports programs worldwide, the current reality is that TGfU is debated with more passion than it is practiced. As far as TGfU is concerned, theory has been slow to translate into reality. This paper examines the ways in which this disconnect plays out in schools and institutes of higher education through the key populations involved: teachers; administrators; researchers, professors and students in PETE programs. It also offers some suggestions as to how the chasm between theory and practice might best be crossed.

It is teachers who deliver the curriculum, interface directly with students, and have the most immediate control over their learning environment. While there are undoubtedly plenty of innovative, inspirational teachers in the profession, teachers are often conservative (Lortie, 1975) and thus treat new ideas and innovations with some skepticism.

Head teachers and administrators have a great deal of control over decisions both about the content of the curriculum and the way in which it is delivered. Since they appoint, reward and influence teachers on the basis of these decisions, they are in a powerful position. However, they are not always knowledgeable about current developments in Physical Education, nor effective in implementing the curricular innovation they do espouse (Butler, p.179, 1995).

PETE programs provide an environment within which young teachers are able to develop and refine their skills and beliefs. It is therefore, though perhaps arguably, the most fertile ground in which to plant the seeds of change. In addition, pre-service teachers in PETE programs seem, on the whole, to be likely prospects as curricular innovators and change agents. Though some do have preconceived ideas about teaching (based on their coaching experiences and also on the way in which they themselves were taught) many are willing and indeed eager to experiment. PETE students are usually energetic and idealistic. Yet it is also true to say that the philosophy of PETE Programs, as defined by researchers/professors, strongly influences the ability of these student physical educators to adopt new ideas. In the current climate, PETE programs are being asked to meet demands that are essentially in conflict. For example, on the one hand, there is popular and indeed governmental concern about obesity and health. This has translated into health and wellness components both in Basic Instructional Programs (BIP) and majors' programs. On the other hand, PETE Programs are still heavily influenced by the demands and paradigms of Professional Sports.

> "This blurring of issues has led to considerable confusion and some unacceptable consequences. It has made it easy, for example, for the anti-competition lobby to rationalize the case for excluding all competitive sports, and including more activities geared toward lifetime health and fitness. (Butler, p.178, 1995)

By excluding all competitive sports, we are in danger of throwing the baby out with the bath water. This is an unnecessary sacrifice, since programs can instead embrace lifetime activities which include games education based on constructivist learning theory. TGfU not only provides a sound educational philosophy that is consistent with the whole ethos of most K-12 schools, it can also provide a useful medium through which PETE programs can balance and examine the demands of physical education.

Let us now examine this argument, and these two contexts – schools and institutes of higher education - in more detail.

Schools

It will come as no surprise that a traditionally based view of learning prevails in our nation's schools, particularly when we consider that they have an aging work force. The largest sector of the K-12 teaching profession are teachers (35.3%) who have over 20 years of experience (NCES, 2000). The well-known cliché used in the title of this paper suggests that we cannot teach old dogs new tricks. We do tend to assume that older (or more established) teachers have become set in their ways, and also that they have adopted more conservative outlooks. Evans (1989) summarizes the stereotying of the older teacher:

> "At midcareer all professionals, including teachers, are prone to demotivation (boredom, loss of enthusiasm, diminished job interest) and a leveling off of performance. The growth curve flattens out, particularly those who do not move into new roles or change jobs; and energy flags (p.11).

Prawat (1992) suggested that many teachers prefer to adhere to outmoded forms of instruction that emphasize factual and procedural knowledge at the expense of deeper levels of understanding. Simply put, the change required for teachers to adopt a TGfU approach successfully is to switch their role from that of "coach" to that of "facilitator." This change is difficult for many teachers, who have the coaching model in their bones.

However, while Rusch and Perry (1993), found that many of the perceptions that younger teachers had of older teachers were stereotypical, they "…did not find older teachers to be less willing to invest in a school improvement effort (p.10)." They cited that, "older experienced teachers frequently engage in a learning experience with a new, younger teacher in order to understand new methods and current theories." These are obviously the teachers with whom we would hope to place our student teachers who were well versed in a TGfU approach, in the belief that each would benefit from the experience.

All learning is about change and all change is about learning. The rub is that change is not always comfortable. This is especially true for teachers, who often work with little support and in highly stressful circumstances. Teachers are also sharply aware that when they experiment with the latest 'new approach' (or 'fad') there's a risk that their students will lose out (Butler, 1996).

Teachers who do make the shift from a traditional approach to constructivist learning theory often do so through the understanding that their role needs to change to accommodate the changed focus of learning. My study about teacher change (Butler, 1993) showed that the central predictor of change for teachers was their core beliefs about why they teach, what they teach, and how they teach it. This was more important than age or length of service. Festinger (1957) suggested that when our actions are incongruent with our beliefs, cognitive dissonance is created. To restore equilibrium, we must either defend our existing actions or change them. This radical change can only happen when teachers have the time, space and tools to engage in reflection, discussion and consideration of their views and beliefs. Researchers (Brozo, 1994; Etchberger & Shaw, 1992) show that teachers who engage in constant reflection are more able to accept such change. Teachers need a place to process their discomfort, to discuss their core beliefs and align them with practice. In this sense, the key is affect. When teachers line up their beliefs, practice and passion the results are dynamic! In other words real change, long lasting change, happens when head, heart and physical activity are in synch.

How could we encourage more teachers to try TGfU? We could use top down innovation models like the national curriculums modeled in Singapore and the UK, or the national standards established by NASPE (2004). These have their place – but often practitioners have become adept at perverting or avoiding such dictums. My research on a school system in Boston suggests that teachers are adept at paying lip service to 'documents designed to please administrators' (Butler, 1995). The real change, I believe, comes from grass roots advocacy. This parallels the empowerment perspective of learners in the TGfU learning process, which is pioneered by enlightened classroom teachers. That said, national organizations such as NASPE can be highly influential in creating change – there are plans afoot to involve such organizations in helping to encourage teachers to try TGfU. This will be discussed at the end of this paper. It is perhaps sufficient to note here that successful school reform depends on changes in the classroom practices of individual teachers (Cuban 1986). As TGfU advocates, we need to find ways to support teachers as decision makers and change agents (Pace, 1992), and to offer them a forum for reflection and debate. The newly instituted TGfU Task Force, again discussed at the end of this paper, will hopefully go some way to providing this kind of support.

1) PETE Programs

TGfU advocates believe that learners in TGfU classes are empowered as they understand the game by playing it. Taking this one step further, I believe our PETE students are capable of understanding teaching through the process of teaching, and by considering all aspects of the child's context and experiences, rather than studying 'teaching skills' out of context and in isolation. Our traditional games classes focus on the teaching and acquisition of isolated skills that may have no connection to the game as it is played. In much the same way, our PETE programs often focus on effective teaching skills which are isolated from each other in the broader educational context. This causes PETE students to lose sight of the primary goal, which is to improve student learning. In both situations, the skills are an important part of the experience, but they need to be set in their larger context. If PETE students were taught in a more holistic way, which we might term 'teaching teaching for understanding,' they would surely focus more, and more quickly, on the learners' needs and learning process and then relate their teaching skills to these.

It is clearly important to examine the pedagogical research upon which a program is based, since this usually determines the philosophical context within which the program operates. This philosophical context influences instructors' decisions about what content to deliver their students and in what order to deliver its various components. Such decisions include whether or not to be receptive to student centered programs. This, in turn, impacts the way PETE students will themselves teach. Clear mission statements and conceptual frameworks go a long way to helping programs connect theory and practice. This is demonstrated by the positive impact the NCATE/NASPE accreditation process has had upon those programs that have used it to update and clarify their mission statements and conceptual frameworks.

> "The current document (initial PE program report manual) ... reflects consensus among experienced physical educators at all levels as to what a teacher needs to know, believe and be able to do. These 10 standards for beginning physical education teachers, and their associated performance-based outcomes, are based on knowledge of best practice from research in physical education and related fields" *(p.1, NASPE, 2001)*

The research paradigm employed by the department is also crucial. There are three dominant paradigms within North American physical education pedagogy - behaviorist research, socialization research, and research based on critical theory. Each paradigm differently defines research and its relationship to practice (Bain, 2000). A behaviorist might consider the cause and effect of the type of research upon which the PETE program practice is based, and examine the nature of PETE students it produces. Another way to examine the PETE program would be from the socialization perspective. Bain (2000, p.38) would have us believe that the question we should be asking is, "How well has pedagogical research served as a guide to thinking about practical problems in physical education?" For the critical theorist, the question becomes "Has this research empowered participants to act more effectively on their own behalf (Bain, 2000, p.39)?"

Table 1 below gives a brief glance at what the critics and advocates of each paradigm have to say about its perspective.

Research Paradigm	Advocates	Critics
Social (Teachers & Perceptions)	Developmentally appropriate activities offer a more powerful reward for learners	Separation exists between theory and practice
Critical (Issues of gender, race, class etc.)	Participants are empowered by process	Findings are distorted by researchers' political agenda
Behaviorist (Effective Teaching Focus)	Teaching skills are targeted for change. Contingencies in workplace used to control behavior of ST	Overemphasizes basic skills, neglects higher order learning. Beliefs & values are not studied

Social Theory Paradigm

The focus is on teachers (rather than research on teaching), their perceptions of the learning context and how these influence their actions. Advocates of this research paradigm suggest that it shows that learner enjoyment (which focuses on more than just having fun, and instead includes developmentally appropriate activities) is a more powerful reward than learner achievement, and that learning is often outside teacher control. Social researchers believe that their research provides insight and understanding that can serve to guide but not prescribe teaching and policy decisions. Research themes often involve teachers' perceptions of their work and the way in which these perceptions influence their actions. It is the view of social theorists that research can provide a guide to thinking but not a guide to action. Critics suggest that this has led to a separation between research and practice, in that there is little evidence to suggest that social theory research has changed the way in which physical education teachers view teaching.

Critical Theory Paradigm

The focus is on issues of gender, race or class – and the research is often grounded in feminist or neomarxist ideology. Advocates of this paradigm suggest that participants are empowered by the research process and will consequently act more effectively on their own behalf. Practitioners become part of the research process: they help frame questions, interpret data, and examine insights that might serve as a basis for action. Critics, however, suggest that findings are distorted by the researchers' political agenda.

Behaviorist Theory Paradigm

The focus is on effective teaching. Advocates suggest that teaching skills can be identified and selected behaviors can then be targeted for change. For example: advocates suggest that cues can help learners focus on the right way to perform the action and feedback statements can encourage them to continue to try to get it right. Interventions are often successful in producing changes in targeted behaviors.

Critics suggest that behaviorists falsely assume that behavior changes under the control of contingencies (such as the selection of the program, cooperating teacher, school context) will continue after the completion of the program, when contingencies may change. Critics also suggest that behaviorists have had very little influence on teacher education or public schools. Examining decisions about teacher education programs raises questions about the beliefs and values of the decision makers and the politics of universities and school systems. Behaviorists do not study beliefs and politics.

Aligning Program Research Base suitable for TGfU Inclusion

It seems clear that social theory or critical theory research provide a more congenial context for TGfU in PETE programs, rather than those influenced by a dominance of behaviorist rhetoric. Yet behaviorist research dominates our PETE programs. Within the confines of a behaviorist PETE program, it is assumed, for instance, that pedagogical questions are too confusing for PETE students. Departments and institutions thus make decisions for them (much as traditional games programs do). We assume that learners and students need a set of skills before they can play the game, or go into teaching. Yet finding viable answers to certain questions is central to the formation of a young teacher's philosophy and choice of methodologies. For example, some philosophical decisions fall within the areas of:

Planning
- When should learners receive information about how to execute a motor skill – before playing the game or after?
- What, and how much, information do learners need at one time?
- What should learners practice and when?

Teaching
- Which teaching approach should be used to achieve the desired learning outcome?
- What methodology will be most effective in achieving the desired learning outcome?
- Knowledge
- What should students know?
- Why should they know this?

Assessment
- How do we measure our effectiveness as teachers?
- How do we measure student learning?

Learning
- What environment is conducive to learning?
- How do we know that learning has taken place?

PETE students are ready and able to debate these pedagogical questions. Yet in the same way that critics of TGfU suggest that learners don't know enough about the game to play it before they learn the skills, behaviorists suggest that PETE students are incapable of pedagogical debate. In the same way that we can modify games in order to make them developmentally appropriate, so too can concepts be modified for our PETE students, in order that they may be introduced to the whole picture, pedagogically speaking. I believe that it is not only possible but essential for our young teachers to make decisions about the kinds of learner outcomes they are seeking. When PETE students compare TGfU with the model with which they are more familiar (see table 2), questions such as the following arise:

1. How much emphasis should we place on skill acquisition and how much on conceptual understanding, which helps learners make sense of information and experiences?
2. Should students know 'how to' before they know 'what to'?
3. Should tactics and strategies be taught before skills?
4. Is the role of the teacher to help students acquire knowledge or to help them construct meaning?
5. Is the role of the learner to demonstrate what they have learned by rote or to apply what is known (and discover what is unknown)?
6. Is the role of the learner to perform or to think and to make decisions?

At the heart of the constructivist approach to games education is the belief that it is important for players to make correct decisions in the light of tactical awareness. The child, not the teacher, becomes central. The pedagogical mindset changes from one that focuses on what is wrong with the learner's performance to one that focuses on how the teacher can help learners define and solve the problem being presented.

Table 2. Polarization of behaviorist and constructivist approaches

	Behaviorist / Transmission Model	Constructivist (TGfU) / Tranactional Model
Why is it taught (Philosophical & Historical Perspectives)		
Culture	Factory / product model	Village Green / progressive education
Belief System	Dualism	Integration of mind/ body / spirit
Context	Isolation, links with coaching and professional sport	Integration of school and community
Training	Efficiency / military influence	Movement Education
Experience	Specialism / sport	Integration and inclusiveness
What is it taught (Curriculum)		
Purpose	Acquisition of knowledge	Construction of meaning
Objective	To define what we know	To discover what is unknown and apply what is known
Outcome	Performance	Thinking and decision-making
Game frameworks	Seasonal activities	Classifications
How is it taught (Pedagogy)		
Instruction	Teacher - centered	Student – centered, developmental, progressive
Strategy	Part - Whole	Whole - Part - Whole
Content	Techniques based	Concept based
Context	Teacher - student interaction	Multi-dimensional interaction
Teacher Role	Transmission of information	Facilitation of problem - solving
Learner Role	Passive Learning	Active Learning
Evaluation	Mastery	Demonstration of understanding and contributions to process

Pre-Service Teachers

As I said earlier, it's tempting to hope that the energy of PETE students makes them ideal vehicles for change. Let's look a little more closely now at some of the issues they face in the light of the five teaching stages defined by Ryan (1989).

1. Fantasy
2. Euphoria
3. Survival
4. Apprenticeship
5. Rediscovery

These stages can be applied to three populations discussed in this paper:
pre-service teachers as they grapple with practica and student teaching
novice teachers as they become initiated into the profession
more experienced teachers as they make the paradigm shifts necessary to embrace innovations such as TGfU.

The first stage: Fantasy

Researchers such as Lortie (1975) and Bain (2000) have found that people who become PE teachers are often idealists. They cite reasons such as the following for joining the profession: "I love playing sports"; "I want to be active and not do a desk job"; "I love children"; "I want to pass on love of sports to all". This may cause some initial confusion for new teachers – often an inability to make a clear distinction between caring and friendship where learners are concerned. Nevertheless, while the novice teacher may struggle to draw a line in the sand, Tate (2000) points out in his work on excellence in teaching, that love of children is not just a trite notion. He believes that it makes teachers go the extra mile – it helps them teach children, not just their subject. It is this passion, the affect mentioned earlier in this paper, that takes teachers beyond the behaviorist insistence on teaching skills and makes them consider the whole child and the whole curriculum. It is the same motivation that encourages seasoned teachers to change their teaching style when they understand that it is incongruent with their core beliefs.

However, as McCreaty suggests, there is little emphasis in most PETE programs on emotional understanding. And yet, interestingly, my experience with PETE students lends me to believe that, for them, it is a high priority. Over the past 10 years, I have set the same task to sophomore students as they enter the PETE program. First they are invited to identify what makes a good sporting experience for them, and then to define the kind of experiences they wish to provide for students in their PE classes. They unfailingly cite affective experiences more than cognitive and psychomotor ones. After allowing them 10 minutes of free-writing, I spread their verbal responses across the 3 behavioral domain categories (without indicating what the columns represent). My original intent was to tease out the differences between their own experience and what they wish for their students, but what became clear was the length of the affective lists in each case. The following are representative entries: "work with others", "improve communications", "understand limitations and strengths of others", "enjoy the experience", "challenge oneself", "improve leadership skills", "develop character".

Second Stage: Euphoria

In the second stage of euphoria, young teachers feel like they've 'arrived.' It's the famous 'honeymoon period.' Charmed by the initial good behavior of their learners, young teachers can become overconfident. They see that learners will 'sit and stay on command' and don't realize that attentiveness must be earned on a daily basis. They often ignore the danger signs that a more experienced teacher would notice – such as lack of comprehension, small insurrections, and overfamiliarity. McCaughtry & Rovegno's (2003) findings in their recent study assume importance here. They found that as problems emerged, pre-service teachers often engaged in the following behaviors:

1. They blame learners for difficulties, without questioning their own inability to match tasks with the learners' skill levels.
2. They fail to transfer motor development learning from the classroom setting to actual teaching experiences.
3. They believe that their teaching is correct, even when confronted with disconfirming evidence.
4. They ignore or discredit the emotions of learners.

Third stage: Survival

The more problems that novice teachers experience, the more they tend to blame their learners, and the less comfortable they feel discussing the situation. The focus of senior teachers is often discipline – which leads them to ignore pedagogical issues in favor of a controlled learning environment. Additionally, some believe that the rites of passage should be endured alone, that they should be 'thrown into the deep end', as they were. This adds a second level to the novice and pre-service teacher's urge to cover up serious problems. Let's face it, their idealism may also be shattered by cynical teachers who load students with work, difficult classes, and problematic learners. Given that the student teacher's ability to cope is compromised by fatigue, and often a sense of failure, disappointment and depression, the conditions are ripe for a return to safe conservatism at this vulnerable stage in the novice teacher's career.

Student teachers may be enthusiastic about trying out TGfU, but find resistance from cooperating/ master teachers. They find themselves in a serious dilemma. Rather than put their grade on the line, many student teachers will elect to teach units that are viewed more favorably by their cooperating teachers (Butler, 2004). Even when cooperating teachers were willing to allow student teachers to 'try out' a TGfU unit, student teachers (Butler & Light, in print) described their fear of supervisors who had little or no familiarity with TGfU, and thus viewed such units with some skepticism.

Fourth stage: Apprenticeship

The student teacher who survives does so by creating a comfort zone. Hard work and careful organization reduce the possibility of surprises and unpredicted events in the classroom. The student teacher is organized, and probably has a filing cabinet stocked with fallback lessons, and other resources. The research on excellent teachers (Tate, 2000), shows that a consistent trait is a strong commitment to hard daily work.

This is the prime time when student teachers and novice teachers, who have achieved a certain level of confidence, are ready to introduce or be introduced to a new model such as TGfU. But it is important to remember that this change may be uncomfortable and difficult, since it necessarily involves a broadening of the comfort zone.

Fifth Stage: Rediscovery

The fifth stage is the rediscovery of the feelings and passion that made them choose the teaching profession. Teachers who enter this stage, and not all teachers do, have achieved a certain level of humility. Though they may use charm they are not necessarily charismatic. They prefer learners to be the ones on stage. The focus changes from the teacher to the learner, from 'I to Thou.' It is when teachers make this essential shift that they are ready to understand learners and what they need. For example, good teachers understand child development and what is appropriate for different age levels. 'Teacher of the Year' awards are not based on teachers' grasp of subject matter - although all good teachers know their content – but on their passion for student learning.

Again, this shift fits well with the introduction or reinforcement of the TGfU model, in which the focus is less on teacher direction than student learning.

Moving from the comfort zone into unfamiliar areas can be a challenge, but paradoxically, this very discomfort - the disconnect between avowed principle and actual practice, educational philosophy and teaching methodology - can be a wonderful incentive. Nevertheless, practicing teachers have indicated that they need careful, structured support through the process of change (Butler, 1996).

The essential ingredient for change is a core belief in empowering the student learner (Butler 1993). It is passion for adventure, creativity and exploration and, as Kretchmar (2004) would have it, the search for 'delight,' that drives us to rediscover the dream, to become the best we can be as educators, and dare to hope for the same for our learners.

Conclusion

There is no blueprint for change. TGfU advocates and researchers will continue to publish, disseminate research and work in the field to change hearts and minds. However, the following conditions seem central to providing an appropriate context in which change and experimentation may thrive:

1. Healthy dialogue in the exchange of diverse ideas (Hobbs et al 1998);
2. Practices that are empathetic, communicative and participatory (Lueddeke,1999);
3. Teacher toleration of uncertainty and a willingness to try things out;
4. Links between faculty from education programs and teachers and administrators (as with professional development schools, Hobbs, 1998);
5. Administrative support (Butler, 1996).

It seems that teachers at all stages of their careers, preservice, novice and seasoned, can benefit from the opportunity to discuss core beliefs, to examine ways in which they translate into practice, and to experiment with approaches that will bring the two into closer alignment. After the first TGfU conference in New Hampshire, USA, in 2001, a forum emerged that aims to provide a place for such exploration. The International TGfU Task Force was established in the hope that it would harness the groundswell of energy created at the conference, and funnel it into the promotion of research and good practice in TGfU through active communication and the recruitment of teachers and coaches. The AIESEP (Association des Ecoles Superieures D'Education Physique) board was eager to nurture the proposal, and the task force was launched in October 2002 at an AIESEP conference, La Coruna in Spain. The mission of the Task force was quickly defined as 'a global representative group of institutions and individuals committed to the promotion and dissemination of scholarly inquiry.' The Task Force will be able to centralize the many permutations of the initial approach practiced in England in the 60's, including Games Sense (Kidman, 2001) and Play Practice (Launder, 2001) in Australia, Concept Based Games (McNeil et al, 2004) in Singapore, Tactical games in US (Griffin, Oslin and Mitchell, 1997).

The objectives of the task force include the following:
- Review the philosophy behind the original TGfU conception and its subsequent development to provide for an accurate representation of its purpose
- Disseminate scholarly information and teaching resources through a variety of media
- Promote discussion and dialogue among membership by establishing a forum

on issues relating to both the TGfU theoretical and curriculum framework and instructional practices
- Establish teaching programs to assist institutions, schools and individuals in the implementation of the TGfU approach
- Coordinate collaborative research efforts and publication of information after each workshop, meeting or conference

It is to be hoped that the Task Force will be a catalyst for change, in that it will encourage those engaged in education through the physical to engage in the debate, and particularly the debate with regard to the philosophical issues surrounding games education. The Task Force aims to provide both student teachers and practicing teachers with the opportunity to access research and information, including collaborative research, regular TGfU conferences, conference proceedings, scholarly information, resource materials and a website (tgfu.org). Additionally, it is the aim of the task force to establish teaching programs, led by TGfU teaching squads within the countries represented. These will be organized by professional organizations within each country.

You are invited to visit our website at tgfu.org, and, of course, to submit papers that will continue to continue this exciting and radical dialogue. The word 'radical', derived from the Latin radix, pertains to the root, to original cause, or to fundamental principle. It is the hope of this author, and to those of us who are working to bring together advocates for a constructivist approach to games education, that this dialogue will continue to help our teachers promote research and good practice in games education, so that students throughout the world will strive together to become both thoughtful citizens and skilled athletes.

References

Bain, L. (2000). Research in sport pedagogy: Past, present and future. In Pieron, M., Valerio, M.A.G. (2000). *Ten years of Joese Maria Cagigal scholar lectures.* AIESEP. Universidade da Coruna. 25-55

Brozo, W. (1994). Literacy assessment in standardized and zero-failure context. *Reading and writing quarterly: Overcoming learning difficulties*, 10(3), 189-200.

Bunker, D. & Thorpe, R. (1982). A model for the teaching of games in the secondary school. *Bulletin of Physical Education*, 10, 9-16.

Butler, J. (1993). *Teacher Change in Sport Education.* Dissertation Abstracts International, 54 02A. (UMI No. 9318198).

Butler, J. (1995). Behind the smokescreen: do competitive activities have a place in humanistic teaching? Chapter in Lombardo, B.J., Mancini,V., and Wuest, D. *The humanistic sport experience: Visions and realities.* Times Mirror Higher Education Group Inc. Dubuque, Iowa.

Butler, J. (1996). Teacher responses to teaching games for understanding. *Journal of Physical Education, Recreation and Dance* (67), 9, 17-20

Cuban, L. (1986) Persistent Instruction: Another Look at Constancy in the Classroom. *Phi Delta Kappa*, (68), 1, 7-11.

Etchberger, M. & Shaw, K. (1992). Teacher change as a progression of transitional images: A chronology of a developing constructivist teacher. *School Science and Mathematics.* 92(8), 411-417.

Evans, R. (1989). The faculty in midcareer: implications for school improvement. Educational Leadership, 46(8), 10-15.

Festinger, L. (1957). *A theory of cognitive dissonance.* Evanston Ill. Row Peterson.

Griffin, L.L., Mitchell, S.A., & Oslin, J.L. (1997). *Teaching sport concepts and skills: A tactical games approach.* Champaign, Il: Human Kinetics

Kidman, L. (2001). Developing decision makers: An empowerment approach to coaching. Christchurch, New Zealand. Innovative Print Communications.

Kretchmar, S. (2004). Understanding and the Delights of Human Activity. In Griffin, L. and Butler, J. (2004) *Teaching games for understanding: Theory, Research and Practice.* Champaign, IL: Human Kinetics.

Launder, A.L. (2001). Play practice: *The games approach to teaching and coaching sports.* Champaign, IL: Human Kinetics.

Light, R. & Butler, J. (in print). A Snap Shot of Pre-service and Beginning Teachers' Experiences of Implementing TGfU. Physical Education and Sport Pedagogy.

Lortie, D. (1975). *The school teacher.* Chicago, University of Chicago Press.

Lueddeke, G. (1999). UK higher education at a crossroads: reflections, issues and practice in teaching and learning.

McCaughtry, N. & Rovegno, I. (2003). Development of pedagogical content knowledge: Moving from blaming students to predicting skillfulness, recognizing motor development and understanding emotion. *Journal of Teaching Physical Education* 22(4), 355-369.

McNeil, M.C., Fry, J.M., Wright, S.C., Tan, W.K.C., Tan, K.S.S., Schempp, P.G. (2004), In the local context: Singaporean challenges to teaching games on practicum. *Sport, Education & Society*, 9(1), 3-33.

NASPE, (2004). *Moving into the future: national standards for physical education* (2nd ed). Reston, VA

NASPE, (2001). Initial physical education program report manual: NASPE/NCATE 2001 Initial physical education standards, 5th edition, Reston, VA.

Pace, G. (1992). Stories of teacher-initiated change from traditional to whole language literacy instruction. *The Elementary School Journal*, 92(4), 461-476.

Prawat, R. (1992). Teachers' beliefs about teaching and learning: A constructivist perspective. *American Journal,* 100(3), 354-395.

Rusch, E., & Perry, E.A. (1993). Resistance to Change: Fact or stereotype. Paper presented at *American Educational Research Association* (Atlanta, GA).

Ryan, K. & Cooper, J. (1972). *Those who can, teach*. Boston. Houghton Mifflin.

Ryan, K. & Cooper, J. (1989). Reference in lecture at Boston University. Confirmed in email.

Tate, P. (2000). Excellence in teaching. Keynote presentation at the AIESEP conference, Rockhampton, Queensland, Australia.

U.S. Department of Education, National Center for Educational Statistics. (2000). *Schools and Staffing Survey (SASS)*, "Public Teacher Questionnaire, Charter Teacher Questionnaire, and Private Teacher Questionnaire" and "Public School Questionnaire, Charter School Questionnaire, and Private School Questionnaire. Retrieved October 25, 2004, from http://nces.ed.gov/prgrams/coe/2003/images/tables/t29_1.gif.

14

A Personal Journey: TGfU Teacher Development in Australia and the USA

Richard Light (University of Sydney)
& Joy Butler (University of British Columbia)

This work has been republished with kind permission from Taylor & Francis, taken from Physical Education and Sport Pedagogy, 10:3, 241-254,
DOI: 10.1080/17408980500340778

Introduction

Teaching Games for Understanding (TGfU) is constituted by sets of social relationships and interactions amongst learners and between teacher and learner(s) that are very different to those that characterise more traditional, technical approaches. The repositioning of the teacher required to adopt a TGfU approach from a director to a facilitator of learning and the changes in his/her role in the learning process challenge long-established conceptions of teaching and learning in games and can make the implementation of TGfU difficult for established, pre-service and early-career teachers (Butler, 1996; Kirk & Claxton, 1999; Light, 2002). Combined with the weight of responsibility experienced by beginning teachers and resistance to change in schools cultures beginning teachers typically abandon innovative practice such as TGfU and adopt the 'path of least resistance' in their attempts to survive their initiation to teaching (Bullough & Baughman,1996; Evans & Clarke, 1988; Macdonald & Glover, 1997). This, of course, has serious implications for physical education teacher education programs that strive to make a difference in the quality of children's and young people's experiences of physical education in schools through the promotion of understanding approaches to teaching.

A considerable number of studies on early career teachers devlopment of innovative practice in education have focused on the ways in which structures such as school systems and cultures restrain early career teachers' implemenation of innovation (Bullough & Baughman, 1995, 1996). This paper, instead, draws on teachers' stories to focus on the personal and social nature of teacher development and on teacher agency. These teacher stories provide a means of studying teacher change and development and their power to provide understanding of pedagogy and the development of teacher knowledge is now widely recognised within the general education literature (Bullough & Baughman, 1996; Jalongo & Isenberg, 1995). Such personal accounts of teacher development offer the chance to invite engagement and reflection and can identify patterns of thought characteristic of teachers' work within particular contexts (Bullough & Baughman, 1996). For many teachers, such as those in this study, their desire to become a teacher, and the pedagogy they adopt, is embedded in the story of their life.

The study reported on in this paper takes a cross-sectional 'snap shot' of teacher development in the two distinctly different cultural and institutional settings of an Australian and USA teacher education program in which it examines teacher development of TGfU across a sequence covering the final two years of a teacher education program in which TGfU is emphasised and the first two years of teaching after graduating from the same programs. It explores the interrelated nature of the participants' own experiences of PE and sport prior to entering the teacher education program, their prior dispositions toward PE teaching, their reasons for adopting TGfU and their experiences of TGfU teaching. Examing pre-service and early career teacher's experiences of learning to teach TGfU in two distinctly different cultural and insitutional settings provides a means through which we might explore the effect that different cultural and instututional settings might have on TGfU teacher development. While the situated nature of learning is well understood when using a TGfU approach to teaching there has, with one exception (Light & Tang, 2004), been no research conducted on TGfU teacher developement that has specifically focused on the situated nature of learning for teachers and the effect of culture.

Method
Participant Selection
The pre-service teachers at both sites were randomly selected from third and fouth year students who had volunteered to take part in the study. The Australian pre-service teachers were chosen from those taking the HPE (Health & Physical Education) option

in which TGfU is emphasised and the pre-service teachers in the USA were chosen from members of the Teaching for Understanding Majors' Club in the Health Physical Education and Recreation (HPER) department. The early career teachers were selected from those graduating students who had been enrolled in the 3rd and 4th year HPE option in Australia or had been members of the TFU club in the USA and had kept in contact with their former professors through their attempts to develop their TGfU teaching. The balance between male and female participants for both sites reflects the gender balance in their respective teacher education courses.

The Participants

All USA participants graduated from, or were studying in, a Physical Education Major and specialising in a K-12 teacher certification option. Their course comprised of a general education course, core physical education classes, teacher certification classes and a range of electives. Students who attend Majors' Clubs are usually more motivated and commited to teaching and professional development (Butler, 2003). All participants in the Australian study graduated from, or were enrolled in, a general primary teacher education program. Within the first two years of the program HPE is compulsory but is offered as an option in 3rd and 4th year.

At the time of the USA study in 2003 'Pat' was a third year pre-service teacher, 'Halle' was a 4th year pre-service teacher and 'Bob' was working as a specialist secondary physical education teacher in his first year of teaching at a state high school (grades 9-12). 'Phillip' was in his second year of full time teaching as a specialist physical education teacher in an elementary (grades K-2) state school. At the time of the Australian study in 2003 'Karen' was a third year pre-service teacher, 'David' was a 4th year pre-service teacher and 'Kathy' was working as a specialist physical education teacher in an independent all-girls primary school (K-6). Following graduation 'Monica' was in her second year of full-time teaching as a specialist physical education teacher in an independent all-girls primary school (K-6). The names of participants and their institutions used in this paper are pseudonyms used to protect their anonymity.

	US Teachers	Experience	Australian Teachers	Experience
3rd Yr Student	Pat	Pre-service	Karen	Pre-service
4th Yr Student	Halle	Pre-service	David	Pre-service
1st Yr Student	Bob	PE specialist in State High School (9-12)	Kathy	PE specialist in K-6 independent girls' school
2nd Yr Student	Phillip	PE specialist in State Elementary School (k-2)	Monica	PE specialist in K-6 independent girls' school

The Sites

Participants in the USA study all graduated from, or were enrolled in, a four-year Physical Education major and specialising in a K-12 teacher education option. The teacher certification option classes are based on behaviourist learning theory and incorporate technique-based activity classes. While second year students are exposed to both behaviourist and constructivist learning theory at an introductory level the only other time that students have any exposure to constructivist learning theory is in the TFU Major's club. The teaching experience program offers little opportunity for 'hands on' teaching in the first two years with most practice teaching taking place in the fourth year. All participants in the USA study made particular reference to contradictory messages they received from staff other than their TFU Majors' Club advisor and the ways in which what they learnt in the club was so often contradicted by other HPER faculty.

Participants in the Australian study were enrolled in, or had graduated from, a four-year general primary school education program within which Health and Physical Education (HPE) was one of eight KLA (Key Learning Areas) that constitute the state syllabus. HPE is a compulsory subject for the first two years of the course during which students are exposed to conceptual approaches to athletics teaching and the TGfU approach to games teaching in second year over a six week period. In the third year HPE is offered as a year-long option in which TGfU forms the core of the course. Students taking the 4th year HPE option do a little more with TGfU and are exposed to other student-centred approaches such as Sport Education (Siedentop, 1994). Generic teaching and learning subjects and all KLA method subjects are all underpinned by a student-centred, inquiry based approach. Pre-service teachers in the Australian University have three, three week teaching experiences each year from first year with their initial teaching experience being primarily observation. Fouth year students finish with a term-long internship in which they spend two days a week teaching at the same school over an entire school term. Students have regular classroom teaching experience but little, and sometimes no, physical education teaching.

Data Generation and Analysis

Data at both sites were generated through a series of extended, in-depth, interviews structured around sets of focus questions aimed at generating reflection and extended responses from the participants. The participants were encouraged to tell us their personal stories of teaching. Interviews were conducted at the Australian university over an eight-month period from April to November 2003 by the first author who was also the 3rd year HPE subject coordinator. Interviews at the USA university were conducted over a seven-month period from September 2003 to March 2004 by the second author who was their TFU Majors' Club advisor. The pre-service teachers in both studies volunteered to take part in the study on the understanding that the research would in no way affect their assessment at university. All participants enjoyed close relationships with the researchers who were also their respective professors. Adopting a reflexive approach to the research (Bourdieu & Wacquant, 1992) we considered these relationships in our analysis. Interviews with the early career teachers were all conducted in their schools, and interviews with the pre-service teachers were conducted on campus. The data were examined and compared to identify themes and emergent ideas over the period of the study. These were explored further in subsequent interviews. This study thus sought to situate both the participants' decisions to adopt a TGfU approach and their attempts to implement it within the context of their life histories and their social interactions. Interviews were, therefore, designed to explore the participants' reasons for becoming teachers, their own experiences of sport and physical education and how this shaped their decision to adopt a TGfU approach and their experiences of its implemetation.

Results
Personal Experiences of Sport and Physical Education
The USA Site

All participants in the USA study spoke about the benefits that they felt sport and physical education had afforded them. More often than not, they described the value of participating in sport in affective and social terms. These included growth in confidence, positive responses to personal challenges, the idea of 'character building' experiences, discipline that would transfer to academic studies, improved personal relationships and social interactions as well as health related physical benefits. They suggested that playing sport had positively affected their social life and their academic achievement, both at school and at university. At high school Bob said that he had initially struggled in class but suggested that the confidence he gained through playing sport helped him develop the confidence needed to succeed academically. While the others reported on mixed memories of PE and Sport at school Pat said that she had uniformly very positive experiences of PE and Sport at school and this motivated her to reproduce such experiences for her own students: "I would say all of my experiences in PE and Sport have contributed to me wanting to help kids have the same experiences that I have had."

Physical education and Sport had formed a central part of Halle's life. She is a two-sport varsity athlete at the college level and describes sport and physical activity as "her whole life." Halle's encouraging parents exposed her to a variety of sports, including skiing at the age of two yet, despite her long and positive association with sport, Halle said that she 'hated gym' at high school due to the boredom of drill and the way it excluded the less able in her classes, "it was so boring it made me mad". As with Kathy in the Australian study, Halle is athletically talented yet is concerned with the way in which traditional teaching tends to exclude the less able and less confident. Like Kathy, she also wants to teach in a way that will address this concern and feels that TGfU can provide her with a means of doing so. Phillip was not particularly talented in sport at school but enjoyed being part of the team. The stress on skill performance at high school led him to describe his experiences in physical education as a "bad experience because I wasn't good at anything, I just played to be with my friends."

As much as they expressed a firm belief in the propensity of Sport and Physical Education to engender positive affective, social and physical learning Bob. Halle and Phillip also described numerous negative experiences where they had been marginalised or had their self-esteem tested.

All four participants, including Pat, were also critical of the teaching and coaching approaches to which they had been exposed. They were uniformly committed to teaching in a better way.

They also expressed concern with coaching. In particular they were concerned with an over-emphasis on winning in sport at the expense of providing positive experiences of sport for as many children as possible and not just the talented. They indicated that, although getting children to play better was important they valued coaching that was more inclusive and fair:

> One coach, he was one of those guys, no matter how well we did, it was always bad. It just really turned me off. It shouldn't be as competitive as it is (in high school). It definitely shouldn't be a do or die, life or death. I mean you are still there to have fun. *(Phillip, September 12th, 2003, USA)*

The Australian Site
Like their USA counterparts the Australian participants all valued the lessons that they felt sport could teach young people and children and had experienced differing degrees of success in competitive sport. Like Pat, Kathy and Karen had very rewarding experiences of sport at school and in local clubs and had been well supported by their parents. While Monica had been good at individual events such as running she had not enjoyed team sports and had not enjoyed physical education at school. David describes himself as a 'sports nut' who is interested in all sport but was, at best only 'half decent' at sport while at school. He liked participating but not competing. Like Phillip in the USA study, he enjoyed friendships built through sport and the social interaction that it stimulated.

Despite their belief in the benefits of playing sport, the Australian participants were all critical of the ways in which physical education had been taught when they were at school and were committed to doing better as teachers. For participants in both studies this critical reflection seemed to have been largely stimulated by their engagement in TGfU and the consequent exposure to a way of thinking about coaching and teaching that was very different to what they had previously experienced. The ways in which we provided sympathetic ears for such critical reflection is also likely to have encouraged them. Although Kathy and Karen had been good at PE and Sport, Kathy had been very concerned with the ways in which the emphasis on skill performance and competition in PE had alienated her friends who were not 'sporty.' She felt frustrated because this alienation from sport deprived them of the benefits that she felt sport could provide and was determined to teach in a way that did not exclude anyone. Karen was a successful gymnast and had enjoyed PE at school but also felt that the way it had been taught excluded too many students and deprived them of benefits such as fitness, good health and 'feeling good about yourself' that she felt sport could provide.

Monica said that in general, "I was just turned off by the way I was taught (PE) at school". She didn't like the ways in which aggressive males dominated and excluded the girls and the boredom of standing in line doing 'skill drills' as has been noted elsewhere (for example see, Ennis, 1999). David enjoyed physical activity and the friendships and group interaction it fostered but did not enjoy serious competition. For all of the Australian participants social interaction was a highly valued aspect of their participation in sport and what they saw as being one of the strengths of PE as a subject:

> I like the social aspect of PE, getting together. Everything is all about being together. I think you need to focus on the social and get the best out of them. *(Karen, May 13, 2003, Australia).*

The Appeal of TGfU
Perceptions of TGfU's Strengths
The USA participants had made a considered decision to study TGfU by joining the TFU Majors' club and each of them spoke with conviction and passion about its merits. Their interviews indicated that they felt hey had discovered something professionally and personally meaningful for them and were prepared to advocate for it strongly. Indeed, within a faculty where teaching staff often did not agree with the TGfU approach they needed a degree of belief and commitment to sustain their development of TGfU teaching. As a beginning teacher Bob felt that TGfU was common sense, that there really was no other way to teach, "It just seems so blatantly obvious that's what you should be doing". More specifically Halle liked the student-centred nature of TGfU and the ways in which it empowered the learner:

> TGfU allows students to think for themselves, to figure it out for themselves. It's real learning that involves making choices and decisions and making better ones with experience. *(Halle, September 12th, 2003, USA)*

One of the strongest themes running through the interviews conducted at both sites in terms of TGfU's appeal for pre-service and early-career teachers is their view of its capacity to provide more equitable experiences of sport for all involved than traditional approaches:

> The TGfU approach gives children a higher level of responsibility and thus creates a higher level of enthusiasm. The TGfU approach gives everyone the opportunity to be involved equally. Most PE classes are dominated by the more athletic student, but using the TGfU approach gives those children that are intimidated a chance to affect the game or activity by using their intellect. Giving these children a sense of ownership helps build their confidence and the amount of effort displayed in class. *(Bob, September 21st, 2003, USA)*

Of her first exposure to TGfU at the Australian university Karen said, "It was fun, it was different actually thinking about how you're doing things". David and Monica both said that, while they liked the constructivist approaches taken in maths, science and literacy they had never thought that such approaches could be used in PE. Indeed, prior to working with TGfU they had seen PE as being outside the rest of the general primary school curriculum. Reflecting upon her first exposure to TGfU at university Monica said that the different role of the teacher in TGfU and the way it took the teacher 'off centre stage' really surprised her:

> We were always taught this inquiry approach and to question and discovery learning in every other subject and then all of a sudden I came to PE and I discovered this fantastic new approach and I thought 'Wow.' I'd never heard of TGfU, I'd never seen that sort of approach. PE teaching for me was always standing out the front, telling people what to do.
> *(Monica, May 1, 2003, Australia)*

Monica and Kathy were both excited by their first exposure to TGfU in a practical class at university. They both immediately recognised TGfU as a means through which they could realise the teaching that they had aspired to and address their concerns with physical education teaching. Kathy was excited about her introduction to TGfU. Her 'anti sport' friends also enjoyed the session and, knowing Kathy's love of sport and the way in which she wanted to teach, rushed to her after the lesson:

> When we finished the first tute so many of my friends obviously knew I wanted to be a PE teacher and they were like 'How good was that? That makes sense' and, 'I'm so anti PE but I really enjoyed that lesson.' It was like, if these adults think like this then it can only benefit the kids and definitely people wanted to know how I thought about it. *(Kathy, May 7, 2003, Australia).*

Monica and Kathy said that their exposure to TGfU had provided them with a way of realising their ideals of providing inclusive and enjoyable physical education for children. Monica talked of the excitement she had felt being part of change in PE while at university and was almost evangelistic in her enthusiasm for TGfU, " I want to get out there. I want to see this thing (TGfU) happening in schools. You need someone to get out there and do it. It's got to start somewhere" (Monica, may 7, 2003). Monica's enthusiasm has seen her enjoy outstanding success in the development of her own teaching and the promotion of TGfU across her school and the cluster of eight schools it is part of through taking a leadership role in the development of TGfU.

TGfU Teaching

Despite resistance from some physical education teachers for the pre-service teachers, and some teaching staff at the USA university, participants in both studies were motivated by the positive responses to TGfU from children. They spoke of the ways in which TGfU stimulates student interaction, and helps the formation of strong relationships between students and between students and their teacher. They also felt, through its emphasis on the intellectual dimensions of games (Howarth, 2000; Light 2002b) that TGfU could help address their concerns with the ways in which physical education typically suffers low status within schools due to its perception as a 'non academic' subject.

Pre-service Teachers

The two pre-service teachers, Pat and Halle, had both experienced teaching a constructivist approach in after school programs (educational gymnastics in the spring semesters and inventing games in the fall/autumn semesters). When it came to teaching in practicum experiences, however, both participants maintained that whether or not they would try out the TGfU approach would be dependent upon the cooperating teacher's attitude to TGfU. While on most occasions cooperating teachers were receptive to the participants wanting to 'try out' TGfU during teaching practica they were sceptical of its practical value in schools. Reflecting upon one teaching practicum Phillip said that his cooperating teacher was happy for him to experiment but told him that TGfU would be "impractical in PE." Despite these practical problems, Pat and Halle are optimistic about TGfU, and are even stimulated by some of its challenges:

> I would say the thing that encourages me the most is just that it's different - it's new and it helps me enjoy teaching more because I have to work a little bit harder at making lesson plans so that students really enjoy it and understand what they're learning. *(Pat, September 26th, 2003, USA)*

The Australian pre-service teachers' attempts to implement TGfU in schools had been frustrating and much of this was due to the restraints imposed by the structure of practice teaching. The structure of their teaching experience as a series of three-week episodes made the implementation of innovative teaching difficult for the two pre-service teachers. They were provided with opportunities to teach sports such as soccer and cricket using TGfU within local schools as part of their physical education course but these were typically single two-hour 'clinics' limited in the time they offered for the development of their teaching. Despite resistance from physical education specialist teachers they were motivated by the positive responses from children in terms of the way in which it stimulated student interaction, the relationships between students and the relationship it encouraged between teacher and students. They saw it as a means through which they could transfer what they saw as 'good teaching practice' from the classroom to physical education lessons. They also saw TGfU as offering a means through which physical education could be made more intellectual and brought into 'the thinking curriculum' which was a strong theme in their teacher education program. Pre-service teachers at both sites recognised the structural restraints placed on them during teaching practica but, encouraged by the responses of the children they taught, intended to persevere with TGfU.

Early-career teachers

Phillip described himself as being "lucky" on his practicum at a middle school because he was able to slip straight into volleyball and try out some ideas he had learned from the TFU club. Although both Phillip and Bob are the only physical educators in their respective school they said that some other teachers, and even a few parents, had shown interest in TGfU. They both received support for their implementation of TGfU from their administrators and in particular from their respective principals. Light and Fawns (2003) argue that PE is typically located outside the school academic curriculum where it is seen as a non-intellectual subject and placed at the lower end of a knowledge hierarchy (Goodson, 1993). This appeared to be a particular problem for the USA pre-service teachers. Phillip was disappointed with what he saw as the low expectations of learning in PE that other staff had: "So long as there is control and the children seem happy no one really minds (what happens in PE)." Phillip and Bob said that the emphasis that TGfU placed on thinking could help raise the status of PE in their schools. Bob felt that other teachers in his school see PE as something separate from the rest of the school curriculum and more a distraction than a subject in which meaningful learning took place. He did, however, have a crucial ally in his supervising teacher who was impressed with TGfU:

> My supervisor is the assistant principal and she loves the idea of TGfU. She loves the change from traditionalism to constructivism. She received a crash course in it when I explained my Inventing Games unit to her and she then observed the rule-making process of that unit. I really believe that my explanation of the approach and especially the inventing games unit was a huge reason I received the job. They really were impressed with it during my interview. *(Bob, September 21st, 2003 USA)*

Ironically, while the USA early career teachers had encountered considerable resistance from HPER staff in their teacher education program outside their TFU Majors' Club, they found more support in their schools. Importantly some other teachers in their schools were also interested in TGfU and supportive of Bob and Phillip's efforts to develop it as beginning teachers. Phillip recounted how he had been encouraged by a colleague's comments on one of her student's responses to his teaching, "A teacher came up to me and told me something that she overheard in class. 'A 4th grade girl said that she use to really hate PE class, but now she really loves it'" (Phillip, January 14th, 2004, USA). Teaching kindergarten to grade two limited Phillip's ability to fully explore the TGfU approach but he used its underpinning principles to teach. In particular, he used movement education as the core of his program. Despite a degree of support in their schools Bob and Phillip felt a little isolated and would have liked more active collegial support for their TGfU teaching.

The USA participants described the problems they encountered in TGfU teaching as 'challenges' rather than 'difficulties.' They all felt that the TGfU model required a lot of preparation and a lot of adaptability. Halle felt that a teacher using this approach needed to be knowledgeable about offensive and defensive strategies and also about connecting drills. Recognising the need for teacher flexibility and creativity she felt that teachers who needed to stick with a strict plan would find TGfU most difficult. Pat said she saw why pre-service teachers might prefer a technique-based approach due to its instrumental approach but felt that it lacked excitement for her and the students: "It was easier for me to plan using a skills based approach, but now I think 'wow this is really boring...it takes 2 or 3 lessons to get to the actual game". (Halle, USA) At the Australian site Monica enjoyed an extremely successful start to her career in Australia. In her second year of full time teaching Monica had been promoted to Coordinator of Sport and Physical Education and the school had adopted TGfU for its entire PE program from Prep (the first year of school in the state of Victoria) to Year six. She had also been asked to teach in the junior years of the senior school (grades seven and eight) where she was introducing a TGfU approach into the secondary school. In her first year of teaching Kathy had taken it upon herself to not only develop her own teaching but also to have it adopted in the school. Other staff were interested in TGfU, she had good support from her mentor and the principal and had organised a professional development seminar at the school on TGfU. Despite her feeling that she had not been as successful as she had hoped to be she had made a significant impact upon the school. This is evident in her appointment for 2004 to a leadership position in developing TGfU across the entire junior school.

Children's Responses
Participants in both studies found that children often had some initial reservations about 'doing something different' and were unused to being empowered by the use of questioning in TGfU. The students' positive reaction to TGfU, however, was the main reason for them continuing to use it. The USA participants described the students as always being active, thinking, working together to figure out the problems presented and enjoying the process. Reflecting the ways in which, as Light and Fawns (2003) suggest, TGfU pedagogy is consistent with Dewey's (1936/86) philosophy of education, Halle identified the way in which students learn through the social interaction stimulated by the environment that the teacher structures in TGfU more than through what the teacher 'teaches' directly to the students. She describes the teacher's role as being, "more of a guide instead of a teacher, and so the students are figuring it out themselves and I think that's the best way for them to learn, to remember it." (Halle, September, 18th, USA). As full time teachers Kathy and Monica, in Australia, and Bob and Phillip in the USA, had the opportunity to experience this more than the pre-service teachers. The range of learning and enjoyment that they felt seemed to emerge from the student interaction that TGfU stimulated encouraged them all:

> Student interaction is definitely important. As soon as I start explaining (a new game) their eyes gleam and they're already looking at each other and they're trying to suss out how we go about playing this game. I start teaching them a game and they're already thinking about how they can modify the game. There's a lot more discussion and problem solving together.
> *(Monica, June 26, 2003, Australia)*

Pat described in detail how elevated student interaction, motivation and the learning that emerges from it in TGfU gave her satisfaction as a teacher:

> It (TGfU) empowers the students to be creative and work together and it's always great to see the student running up and down the court trying to figure out the game and all of the sudden they stop and they're like, 'Wait! Wait! This doesn't work! We have to change a rule.' That's what's so great about the TGfU approach…it helps the students really understand what they're learning and gives them a, 'Why?' *(Pat, October 3rd, 2003, USA)*

Pat's description of the learning moment here recalls Bruner's (1974) suggestion that "…constructivist learning strengthens the individual's ability both to find novel connections and to harness peripheral connections". As Phillip also points out, when TGfU is employed, "It isn't just a game anymore. They actually have to think, which is an added challenge that seems to be really appreciated."

Discussion

While the nature of the two case studies reported on in this paper limits the extent to which we can generalise, the similarities in results between studies conducted in two distinctly different cultural and institutional settings are compelling. Learning to teach involves more than just selecting and acting upon particular pedagogical approaches, it is a more complex matter of enacting sensibilities that are deeply embodied (Davis, Sumara and Luce-Kapler, 2000). Much of the ways in which the teachers in this study are learning to teach using TGfUs arises, we argue, from an embodied and often unarticulated recognition of it as something more than just a good way to teach. There is a personal, affective dimension to their belief in TGfU and the meaning it seems to hold for them. Their stories reveal a personal attachment to TGfU that has been shaped by their own life experiences of sport and physical education and their beliefs about, and dispositions toward, teaching. Certain ways of knowing that are non-textual and embodied are basic to teaching and teacher development (Rorty,

1980; Garfinkel, 1985). It is these embodied understandings, operating below the level of consciousness that work to create, maintain, reproduce and transform particular modes of social relationships that are central to teaching (Garfinkel, 1985). Through our own experiences of TGfU as researchers, teachers and learners we suggest that one of the features of TGfU that most distinguishes it from traditional directive teaching is the different sets of relationships that it fosters between learners and between learners and the teacher (Light & Fawns, 2003). TGfU challenges traditional hierarchical relationships between teacher and learner(s) and positions the teacher as a co-learner or partner in learning (Davis and Sumara, 1997). In TGfU learners are not passive receivers of knowledge but are actively co-constructing it by making meaning of the learning experience. It is our contention that the particular social relationships and interaction that constitute TGfU teaching make it so appealing for the teachers in this study and give it so much meaning for them.

The learning environments that so often typify schools do not provide relevant, real-life situations and are limited in their capacity to extend young people's intellectual and social predispositions within a context of relevant 'cultural poverty' in schools where the knowledge students bring to lessons is typically undervalued (Abbott & Ryan, 1999; Light & Quay, 2003). The TGfU approach to teaching games and sport allows the body to be made active, brought into being and mobilised in the development of social relations, not just among students, but also between the teacher and students. While some recent studies have highlighted the affective dimensions of learning in TGfU for learners (Light, 2003; Pope, 2003) there has, with the exception of Light and Tan's (2004) cross-cultural examination of TGfU teacher development, been scant attention paid to exploring the affective and social dimensions of learning to teach using TGfU pedagogy. There has been no significant attempt to inquire into teachers' understandings of TGfU at an embodied level in the TGfU literature. In a similar vein, while Lave and Wenger's (1991) notion of situated learning has been applied to learning in and through TGfU (Kirk & Macdonald, 1998; Kirk & McPhail, 2002) there has been less consideration of the deeply situated nature of learning to teach TGfU. While there have been a number of studies on Physical Education teacher socialisation these have tended to take a more structuralist approach that pays less attention to agency and the subjective nature of these processes (for example see, Armour & Jones, 1998; Dewar, 1989). Rovegno (1998) examines teachers' knowledge development in learning to apply constructivist learning theory to physical education teaching but does not address the notion of embodied understandings and dispositions that teachers bring to teacher education programs.

TGfU encourages more equitable and mutually beneficial social relations and positive social learning (Light & Fawns, 2001, 2003). It conceptualises knowledge as a way of discourse through which pedagogical relations between teacher, learners and the game redefine the status quo of power relations in schools. In this way, we suggest that TGfU represents, not only a preferred way of teaching for the participants in this study, but also a way of living, a way of being, that holds deep personal and cultural meaning and is largely understood as a 'non-conscious level' (Davis, et al., 2000). Over the past decade an expanding interest in TGfU is beginning to produce a wide range of research approaches and directions that explore diverse aspects of the model. As part of this growing research base we welcome the beginning of interest in the affective dimensions of learning in and through TGfU. We suggest, however, that more attention needs to be paid to the social and affective dimensions of learning to teach using TGfU and of understandings that are non-conscious and embodied in teacher preparation programs that emphasise TGfU.

References

Abbott, J. & Ryan, T. (1999). Constructing knowledge, reconstructing schooling. *Educational Leadership, ASCD.* 57(3), 66-69

Armour, K. and Jones, R. (1998). *Physical education teachers lives and careers.* London: Falmer Press.

Bourdieu, P. & Wacquant, J.D. (1992). *An invitation to reflexive sociology.* Cambridge: Polity Press.

Bruner, J. (1974). *On knowing: Essays for the left hand.* New York: Belknap.

Bullough, B. & Baughman, K. (1996). Narrative reasoning and teacher development: A longitudinal study. *Curriculum Inquiry,* 26(4), 385-415.

Bullough, B. & Baughman, K. (1995). Continuity and change in teacher development: First year teacher after five years. *Journal of Teacher Education,* 44(2), 86-95.

Butler, J. (1996). Teacher responses to Teaching Games for Understanding. *Journal of Physical Education, Recreation and Dance* 67(1), 28-33.

Butler, J. (2003). Starting a Majors' Club. *Journal of Physical Education, Recreation and Dance,* 74, 3, 33-37

Davis, B. and Sumara, J. (1997). Cognition, complexity and teacher education. *Harvard Educational Review,* 67(1), 105-125.

Davis, B., Sumara, D. & Luce-Kapler, R. (2000). *Engaging minds: learning and teaching in a complex world*, New Jersey: Lawrence Erlbaum Associates, Publishers.

Dewar, A. (1989). Recruitment in physical education teaching: Toward a critical approach. In T. Templin & P. Schempp (Eds.), *Socialisation into physical education: Learning to teach* (pp. 39-58). Indianapolis: Benchmark Press.

Dewey, J. (1936/86). How we think: A restatement of the relation of reflective thinking to the educative process. In J. Boydson (Ed.) *John Dewey: The later works, 1925-1953*, vol 8 (pp. 105-352), Carbondale: Southern Illinois University Press.

Evans, J. & Clarke, G. (1988). Changing the face of physical education. In J Evans (Ed.) *Teachers, teaching and control in physical education & recreation*, London, Falmer.

Ennis, C. (1999). Creating a culturally relevant curriculum for disengaged girls. *Sport, Education and Society*, 4(1), 31-50.

Garfinkel, H. (1985). *Studies in ethnomethodology.* Englewood Cliffs: Prentice-Hall.

Howarth, K. (2000). Context as a factor in teachers' perceptions of the teaching of thinking skills in physical education. *Journal of Teaching in Physical Education*, 19, 270-286.

Jalongo, M. R. and Isenberg, J. P. (1995). *Teachers' stories: From personal narrative to professional insight.* San Francisco, Jossey-Bass.

Kirk, D. and Claxton, C. (1999). Learning, excellence and gender: Promoting girls' participation in physical education and sport. Paper presented at the BAALPE Annual Conference, University of Wales institute, Cardiff, July.

Kirk, D. and Macdonald, D. (1998). Situated learning in physical education. *Journal of Teaching in Physical Education*, 17, 376-387.

Kirk, D. & McPhail, A. (2002). Teaching games for understanding and situated learning: Rethinking the Bunker-Thorpe model. *Journal of Teaching in Physical Education*, 21, 117-192.

Light, R. (2002). The social nature of games: Pre-service primary teachers' first experiences of TGfU, *European Physical Education Review.* 8(3), 291-310

Light, R. (2002b). Engaging the body in learning: Promoting cognition in games through TGfU, *ACHPER Healthy Lifestyles Journal*, 49(2): pp. 23-26.

Light, R. (2003). The joy of learning: Emotion, cognition and learning in games through TGfU, *New Zealand Journal of Physical Education*, 36(1): 94-108.

Light, R. & Fawns, R. (2001). The thinking body: Constructivist approaches to games teaching in physical education. *Melbourne Studies in Education*, 42(2), 69-87.

Light, R., & Fawns, R. (2003). Knowing the game: Integrating speech and action in games through TGfU. *Quest*, 55, 161-177.

Light, R. & Quay, J. (2003). Identity, physical capital and the disjunction between young men's experiences of soccer in school and community-based clubs, *Melbourne Studies in Education*, 44(2): 89-106.

Light, R. & Tan, S. (2004). Early career teachers' experiences of implementing TGfU/GCA in Australia and Singapore. *Conference Proceedings of the II International Conference for Physical Educators* (ICPE2004), Hong Kong Institute of Education, Hong Kong, July 6-10, 2004.

Macdonald, D. & Glover, S. (1997). Subject matter boundaries and curriculum change in the Health and Physical Education Key Learning Area. *Curriculum Perspectives*, 17(1), 23-30.

Pope, C. (2003). Once more with feeling: Affect and TGfU. Paper presented at the Second International Conference: *Teaching Sport and Education for Understanding*, December 11-14 2003, Melbourne, Australia.

Rorty, P. (1980). *Philosophy and the mirror of knowledge*. Oxford: Blackwell.

Rovegno, I. (1998). The development of in-service teachers' knowledge of a constructivist approach to physical education: Teaching beyond activities. *Research Quarterly for Exercise and Sport* 69(2), 147-162.

15

Final Reflections

Linda L. Griffin & Steve Mitchell

Here we offer our final reflections as a tribute to Len and Joy. Our tribute is a sign of respect and admiration for their accomplishments. After careful and thoughtful review of their scholarly work and knowing Len and Joy personally, we offer three themes that connected them.

First, they both found their passion and became champions who advocated for a cause(s). Early in a scholar's career, we are encouraged to pursue an area of interest that gives you passion. Len's passion early in his career was reflected in his work with Rod Thorpe and David Bunker related to Teaching Games for Understanding (TGfU), which brought to the forefront an alternative games pedagogy. Len was also involved in the primary physical education movement and championed its usefulness in supporting the value of physical literacy. Joy's passion was centered on inclusiveness and fair play in games education through TGfU and games inventing. Through this passion she even took on the oppressiveness of the game of dodgeball.

Second, Len and Joy championed their passions through grass roots efforts. They used their collective action to affect change at the local, regional, national, and international levels. They believed that praxis mattered. Through TGfU, Len was involved with teachers' action research projects in the original TGfU workshops. He promoted the healthy school initiative, managed the Health Education Authority project at Loughborough, and was influential in the Jump Rope for Heart Fund development. Joy's grass roots efforts started with the formation of a TGfU Club at her first academic position at Plymouth State University in New Hampshire. Her undergraduate student members started spreading the TGfU word all over the New England in the local public schools. She worked tirelessly to spread the TGfU word through teacher workshops and practical presentations locally and beyond. Joy's inventing games work was developed with teachers and for teachers through grant support. These grass roots efforts remind us that they never forgot where they came from.

Third, Len and Joy engaged with the scholarly community through research, scholarly publications and presentations. They both produced a range of publications articulating their passion, sharing their ideas, and challenging the scholarly community through the debate of ideas. As you read the chapters in this edited book, you can hear them being the champion of their ideas and making the case for us to listen. Both were consummate and collaborative professionals, as evidenced by their many co-authored works, and both engaged with a wide range of professionals around the world.

Finally, Len and Joy left their marks as leaders. They were not afraid to stand up for their beliefs and neither was willing to just go along to get along. Through their actions, both saw leadership to the profession as a highly valued part of their work. Len and Joy were stewards. Len's work with Physical Literacy and the Early Years led to him becoming an initial member that helped establish the AIESEP Early Years Special Interest Group (SIG). Joy had a vision and enacted it on an international level. The organization and development of the AIESEP TGfU SIG was hers and began at the Conference Town Hall Meeting at the first International TGfU Conference. Although Joy had her vision and goals for that meeting, she listened and was inclusive in a process that helped create this TGfU community.

One final word: The AIESEP International Teaching Games for Understanding Special Interest Group (TGfU SIG) Executive Committee, both past and present officers, want to recognize Len for his leadership and service to the SIG and the TGfU movement ,and Joy for her distinguished service, leadership and determination to make the SIG an influential international community. We truly hope this international community will continue to thrive and we can learn from the past, live in the present, and build for the future.

www.ingramcontent.com/pod-product-compliance
Lightning Source LLC
Chambersburg PA
CBHW081147230426

43664CB00018B/2834